on \\ Peter Anderson \\ Ross Anderson \\ Amale Andraos \\ Marc Angelil \\ Sunil Bald \\ Benjamin Ball \\ Mojdeh Baratloo \\ Julie Bargmann \\ rg \\ Ronald Bentley \\ Thomas Bercy \\ Wayne Berg \\ Deborah Berke \\ rlon Blackwell \\ Darcy Bonner \\ Louise Braverman \\ Elena Brescia \\ Tom Buresh \\ Wendell Burnette \\ Andy Cao \\ Sara Caples \\ John J. lo Castro \\ Theodore M. Ceraldi \\ Walter Chatha____Calvin Chen \\ Shane Coen \\ Preston Scott Cohen \\ Stuart _____leman Coker \\ Lauren Crahan \\ Teddy Cruz \\ Gary Cur_____tler \\ James \\ Kathryn Dean \\ Jared Della Valle _____Neil Denari rchill Drake \\ Andres Duany \\ Winka D_____an Dunn \\ Julie \\ Karen Fairbanks \\ Homa Farjadi \\ _____lders \\ Martin Felsen Ted Flato \\ Peter Forbes \\ Stephanie Forsythe \\ John Frane \\ John ik \\ Leslie Gill \\ Ron Golan \\ Nicholas Goldsmith \\ Jeff Goldstein eth Gray \\ Ravi GuneWardena \\ Danelle Guthrie \\ Paul Haigh \\ Annie ise Harpman \\ Steven Harris \\ Laura Hartman \\ John Hartmann \\ Brian Chuck Hoberman \\ Kimberly Holden \\ Steven Holl \\ John Hong \\ Eric obert Hutchison \\ Wonne Ickx \\ Florian Idenburg \\ Jeffrey Inaba \\ cent James \\ Everardo Jefferson \\ Carlos Jimenez \\ Brian Johnsen \\ \\ Makram el Kadi \\ Eric A. Kahn \\ John Keenen \\ Diane Legge Kemp \\ an Koch \\ Fred Koetter \\ Sulan Kolatan \\ Hank Koning \\ Craig Konyk e \\ Susan Lanier \\ Salvatore LaRosa \\ William Leddy \\ Jennifer Lee Lerup \\ David Leven \\ David Lewis \\ Paul Lewis \\ Giuseppe Lignano ni \\ Brad Lynch \\ Peter Lynch \\ William Mac Donald \\ Todd MacAllen l Manfredi \\ Scott Marble \\ Christos Marcopoulos \\ I. Guyman Martin tum \\ Johnny McDonald \\ Patrick McDonald \\ Tim McDonald \\ William a Meyers \\ Daniel Mihalyo \\ B. Alex Miller \\ David Miller \\ Samuel Moss \\ Carol Moukheiber \\ Brian A. Murphy \\ Michael Murphy \\ Ralph \\ Lorcan O'Herlihy \\ Luke Ogrydziak \\ Richard Oliver \\ Kate Orff \\ ncisco Pardo \\ Jinhee Park \\ Gregg Pasquarelli \\ Anne Perl de Pal \\ w \\ Peter Pfau \\ Scott Phillips \\ Patrick Pinnell \\ David Piscuskas Prillinger \\ M. Ross Primmer \\ Bart Prince \\ Rob Wellington Quigley alli \\ Elizabeth Ranieri \\ Lisa Rapoport \\ Hani Rashid \\ William \\ Lyn Rice \\ James Richärd \\ Alan Ricks \\ Juergen Riehm \\ Terry hael Rotondi \\ Margie Ruddick \\ David Ruy \\ Michele Saee \\ Stanley muels \\ Joel Sanders \\ Mark Sanderson \\ Patricia Sapinsley \\ Gilles \\ Frederic Schwartz \\ Warren Schwartz \\ Mack Scogin \\ Craig Scott \\ Josh Shelton \\ Lola Sheppard \\ Brigitte Shim \\ Jennifer Siegal c \\ Henry Smith-Miller \\ Ken Smith \\ Ted Smith \\ Julie V. Snow \\ rcelo Spina \\ Saidee Springall \\ Richard Stacy \\ Howard Steinberg \\ Ali Tayar \\ Jeff Taylor \\ Harry Teague \\ Nader Tehrani \\ Georgeen rt H. Timme \\ Ada Tolla \\ Susana Torre \\ Victor F. "Trey" Trahan III n Valerio \\ Lauretta Vinciarelli \\ Frano Violich \\ Peter D. Waldman son \\ Charles Wolf \\ Dan Wood \\ Jenny Wu \\ Katsuhiro Yamazaki \\ Andrew Zago \\ Giuseppe Zambonini \\ Carlos Zapata \\ Todd Zwigard

30
YEARS
OF
EMERGING
VOICES

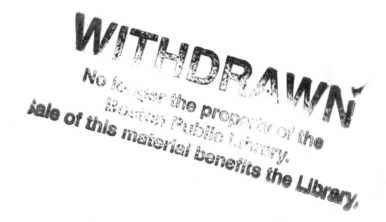

30 YEARS OF EMERGING VOICES

IDEA, FORM, RESONANCE

The Architectural League of New York

Princeton Architectural Press, New York

Published by
Princeton Architectural Press
37 East Seventh Street
New York, New York 10003

Visit our website at
www.papress.com.

This book has been supported,
in part, by public funds from
the National Endowment for the
Arts. Additional support has been
provided by the Graham Foundation
for Advanced Studies in the Fine
Arts, the LEF Foundation, and
the Next Generation Fund of The
Architectural League.

The Architectural League
of New York
Editor: Anne Rieselbach
Associate Editor: Ian Veidenheimer
Assistant Editors: Sophie Elias,
Jessica Liss, Melissa Russell
Consulting Editor: Abby Bussel

Princeton Architectural Press
Editor: Meredith Baber

Graphic Design: Michael Bierut and
Laitsz Ho, Pentagram

Special thanks to:
Nicola Bednarek Brower,
Janet Behning, Erin Cain,
Megan Carey, Carina Cha,
Andrea Chlad, Tom Cho,
Barbara Darko, Benjamin English,
Russell Fernandez, Jan Haux,
Mia Johnson, Diane Levinson,
Jennifer Lippert, Katharine Myers,
Jamie Nelson, Rob Shaeffer,
Sara Stemen, Marielle Suba,
Kaymar Thomas, Paul Wagner,
Joseph Weston, and Janet Wong
of Princeton Architectural Press
—Kevin C. Lippert, publisher

30 Years of Emerging Voices :
Idea, Form, Resonance / Foreword
by Billie Tsien ; Introduction
by Anne Rieselbach ; Afterword by
Rosalie Genevro.—First edition.
pages cm
ISBN 978-1-61689-197-8 (hardback)
1. Emerging Voices (Architectural
competition) (Architectural League
of New York) 2. Architecture—North
America—History—20th century.
3. Architecture—North America—
History—21st century. I. Tsien,
Billie, writer of foreword.
II. Rieselbach, Anne, writer
of introduction. III. Genevro,
Rosalie, writer of afterword. IV.
Title: Thirty Years of Emerging
Voices.
NA2335.A15 2014
724'.6—dc23

2014037600

CONTENTS

Foreword

Billie Tsien
President, The Architectural
League of New York

As I look at the names and work in this book, I see the passage of time. I write not only about the first thirty years of the Emerging Voices lecture series, but also about each page of this book; each person or studio reveals, as well, changes over time. Every page is a lens, and work comes slowly into focus. As architects we have the luxury of a lifetime of work. The possibility of learning something new endures. And when we learn, we change. We connect to our past and what we know, and we look forward to the future and what we do not know. This book evokes for me a long chain of architects and designers holding hands. As Wendell Berry wrote in *What Are People For?*,

> We clasp the hands of those
> who go before us, and the hands
> of those who come after us;
> we enter the little circle
> of each other's arms,...

In this book, I see each Emerging Voice lending a hand to the next.

Funding for this book comes from a number of generous sources. We thank the National Endowment for the Arts, the Graham Foundation for Advanced Studies in the Fine Arts, and the LEF Foundation.

We are grateful to the corporate supporters of the lecture series, from founding sponsor Krueger to the current sponsor, Maharam, with additional support through the years from USM and Miele.

We offer our appreciation to the Next Generation Fund of The Architectural League and League members and friends for supporting both the book and the series.

The wisdom, guidance, and design intelligence of the book's advisory committee has been invaluable, so thanks go to Michael Bierut, Henry N. Cobb, Reed Kroloff, and Karen Stein, as well as to the League's immediate past president, Annabelle Selldorf.

The essays by Ashley Schafer, Reed Kroloff, and Karen Stein illuminate the big picture. And the commentaries by Suzanne Stephens, Henry N. Cobb, Thomas de Monchaux, Paul Makovsky, Alexandra Lange, and Alan G. Brake are pointed and poignant.

The graphic identity of The Architectural League rests on the shoulders of Michael Bierut, who with his colleague Laitsz Ho of Pentagram brought clarity and organization to this huge trove of information and images.

Thank you for this labor of love to Anne Rieselbach (editor), Ian Veidenheimer (associate editor), Sophie Elias, Jessica Liss, and Melissa Russell (assistant editors), and Abby Bussel (consulting editor).

And we are grateful to Princeton Architectural Press: Meredith Baber (editor), Jennifer Lippert (editorial director), and Kevin Lippert (publisher).

Anne Rieselbach

INTRODUCTION

The Emerging Voices juried lecture series recognizes architects, landscape architects, and urban designers who have both significant work to show *and* significant ideas to share. From the inaugural presentations more than thirty years ago to the present, firms selected by The Architectural League as Emerging Voices have spoken compellingly about their work while framing its relationship to theory, practice, and place. In real time and, more recently, through the League's digital programs, the lectures amplify each firm's design voice within the context of contemporary discourse. In recording and reassessing their voices, individually and collectively, this publication offers an extraordinary opportunity, as Ashley Schafer notes in her essay, for "the reader to connect the dots across the years, or write a new narrative of this work from the perspective of recent history."

Close to 250 individuals and firms have presented their projects in the League's Emerging Voices program, which recognizes North American practitioners whose maturing voices and inventive work show the potential to influence architectural discourse and form. The sheer volume of their collective voices reverberates through this book's kaleidoscopic cover, which features one project designed by each individual or firm at (or close to) the time of their lecture. The cover also gives a sense of the extraordinary range of design vocabularies and modes of practice represented in this densely packed compendium, which documents every Emerging Voice through the 2013 cycle and critically considers the work and the program within the broader historical context of contemporary architectural design and theory.[1] Recurrent themes—tectonic, stylistic, and operational—speak to a dynamic interplay of tradition and invention, of design and place.

Exploring the diverse possibilities inherent in the relationship between idea and form, the interplay between the critical and documentary elements of this book reflects the underlying purpose and structure of the Emerging Voices program since its inception. Inaugurated in 1982 by Emilio Ambasz and Marita O'Hare, then the League's president and executive director, respectively, the lecture series was launched to provide an opportunity for promising younger practitioners to present exceptional and challenging work to their peers and the greater design community—the kind of recognition and intergenerational engagement that has been part of the League's mission since its founding in 1881.

Selecting each year's Emerging Voices is a multistep process that has remained consistent since Rosalie Genevro joined the League as executive director in 1985 and I began directing the program in 1986. We research potential candidates with the assistance of recommendations from curators, academics, journalists, and past Emerging Voices. In the predigital era, this involved tracking down print publications and delving into library holdings; today, we also sift through a wealth (if not surfeit) of online resources. From this research, we identify and invite approximately fifty firms and individuals annually to submit a small selection of work, biographical information, and a brief statement of their design philosophy. A jury composed of the League president and other board members, past Emerging Voices, curators, and journalists reviews the materials and creates a short list of firms invited to submit full portfolios. The jury meets a second time to select those whose curricula vitae and portfolios reveal an accomplished body of work that expresses a distinct philosophical point of view and exhibits evidence of a developing formal clarity. Each annual "class" is also chosen with an eye toward engagement with educational or community concerns, geographic distribution, and typological and formal diversity.

The diversity that characterizes the series annually, and as a whole, can also be found in the backgrounds and perspectives of the critical voices tasked with analyzing this extensive collection of work. Schafer traces the evolution and intersections of theory and practice, exploring the "backdrop of discourses that gave clarity and coherence to the designers' voices." Registering myriad stylistic paths architects have taken in the past three decades, Reed Kroloff finds order in shifting modes of practice and their relationship to tectonics and place. Stepping away from theoretical and stylistic debates, Karen Stein weighs the value of design awards in an increasingly metric-focused society, as well as the professional and personal impact of public recognition. Rosalie Genevro places the Emerging Voices program in the broader context of past and ongoing League activities designed to identify "ideas that are original, useful, challenging, and fertile." These essays are complemented by shorter commentaries in which journalists and architects—including some who were there then—connect the work to its time by focusing on contemporary issues that particularly impacted each five-year segment of this thirty-year survey.

The majority of these pages, however, are devoted to documenting the Emerging Voices and their work, opening with a list of the names used by the firms at the time of their selection for the program. Firm profile pages provide a concise picture of each practice to date. As with their lectures, we invited the Emerging Voices to outline the story of their practices, and they did so with great enthusiasm. Each firm or individual provided basic biographical information and submitted project images from the era of their selection as well as more recent designs, which may include work produced by successor firms, other partnerships, or reconfigured practices.[2] The profiles, grouped by year, include firm name and location at the time of selection as an Emerging Voice, office locations, and academic credentials for each principal. When applicable, firms provided "Practice Updates," identifying new partners and partnerships, locations, and successor firms.

Due to space limitations on the profile pages, we prioritized two biographical areas that speak to educational and professional influence and recognition, mindful that

further information can be accessed through firm websites, which are noted on almost every profile. Each
Emerging Voice was asked to provide up to five teaching
positions and academic leadership posts, which, unless
otherwise noted, are in design programs. We also tasked
them with identifying three notable honors from what are
in some cases scores of professional achievements, such
as project awards, grants, fellowships, publications,
and inclusion in museum collections and exhibitions.

In contrast to the immediacy of the work as it is
presented from lecture to lecture, this comprehensive
collection of biographies and project images, considered and contextualized by insightful essays and
commentaries, affords a remarkable opportunity to exam-
ine the work of each Emerging Voice in a broader context. Individually, from year to year, or across an
extended historical continuum, reviewing thirty classes
of Emerging Voices is an open-ended proposition with
any number of entry points. Whether reviewing the work
chronologically or thematically, the topics of inquiry
are boundless, from modes of practice and the impact of
contemporary theory and pedagogy to typological varia-
tions, approaches to material experimentation, and the
influence of region and place. What remains consistent
is the accomplishment and potential of these "voices."

IDEA:
CLAIMING
TERRITORIES

Since 1982 The Architectural League's Emerging Voices
program has captured a protean moment in the lives
of architects, landscape architects, and urban designers, when they are neither recent graduates nor fully
mature practitioners. During this fleeting but intense
career phase, conceptual rawness and clarity coexist;
work unpredictably oscillates between an innocent opti-
mism and an experienced confidence. Idealistic, experimental, and formally clumsy on occasion, some of their
projects could be dismissed as hypothetical, utopian,
or even naive. Steven Holl's (EV82) Bridge of Houses
proposal for the then-abandoned High Line on New York's
West Side may have seemed fantastical at the time and,
more than a decade later, Reiser + Umemoto's (EV96)
complex network structure for the Yokohama International
Port Terminal competition may have appeared structur-
ally impossible to calculate, let alone construct. Yet,
within three decades of the program's inception, a host
of newly completed buildings engage James Corner Field
Operations (EV01) and Diller Scofidio + Renfro's High
Line park, and Jesse Reiser and Nanako Umemoto's struc-
turally complex Taipei Pop Music Center is under construction. In another thirty years will we look back at
SCAPE / LANDSCAPE ARCHITECTURE's (EV12) Oyster-tecture,
which is being tested in a pilot project in Brooklyn's
Gowanus Bay, with the same knowing appreciation that we
now regard the prescience of those two earlier works?

If the League's record for predicting future design
leaders in North America holds, we will. While relatively
few past winners have yet reached "starchitect" status,
and only one, Thom Mayne of Morphosis (EV83), has been
awarded a Pritzker Architecture Prize, nearly sixty of
them have become deans, chairs, or heads of architecture
schools. The percentage of prominent academics begs
the question: What exactly does the program recognize?
While the Emerging Voices jury reviews "significant
bodies of realized work," this catalog reveals that the
award is focused on the testing of limits and the evidence of intentions rather than on the demonstration of
an established practice.[1] More pointedly, the program
seeks to identify immanent potential for intellectual
contribution to the field, and, although never explicitly stated, it has consistently honored practitioners
who actively question the disciplinary status quo.

In order to read this catalog as more than a compila-
tion of seductive images, we must take the term voices
quite literally. While the honorees' required public
lectures compose an oral history outside the scope of
this volume, the images, particularly the drawings and
renderings, stand as a graphic novel inviting the reader
to connect the dots across the years, or write a new
narrative of this work from the perspective of recent
history. At times the story reveals dramatic cracks and
warbles in the discourse, telegraphed through architectural representation techniques as the underlying para-
digms change. And the program's first thirty years have
encompassed many changes: from the end of high postmodernism and the emergence of critical architecture under

the influence of poststructuralist philosophy (primarily
via Gilles Deleuze and Jacques Derrida); to a fascination with systems theory—organic and biological forms and
structures—concurrent with early digital design practices (circa 1992); to the influence of Dutch program-
matically driven work (following the publication of Rem
Koolhaas's *S,M,L,XL* in 1995); to obsessions with surface, sensory and atmospheric "affects," infrastructure,
and landscape in the late 1990s and early 2000s; to the
ascendancy of ecological and social issues in the 2000s
that echo experimental practices of the late 1960s.[2]

In any given year the selected voices are sufficiently
diverse to elude discrete labeling, but the collection
in its entirety reveals the shifting preoccupations that
have defined the trajectories of both individual practices and the discipline, along with its concomitant discourse, over three decades: linguistics, fragmentation,
and disjunction in the 1980s; dynamic systems, flows, and
formal, digital experimentalism in the 1990s; and collaborative networks, parametricism, and a nascent socioenvi-
ronmentalism in the early 2000s. Each passes through its
own cycle of youth, adolescence, and maturity. Browsing
through this collection of images, it is easy to spot the
onset of significant disciplinary moments, such as the
rise and maturation of digital practices and the opening
of the field to extradisciplinary influences, particularly landscape and urban design. Less apparent in this
catalog is the backdrop of discourses that gave clarity
and coherence to the designers' voices. In this essay,
I will identify some of those underlying influences as
a means to shed light on their effects and implica-
tions for the Emerging Voices and the field at large.

High postmodernism and its discourse of semiotics and
symbols dominated the architectural landscape when the
League established the award in 1982 as a public platform for an ascending generation of designers. That same
year the League organized the *Precursors of Postmodernism*
exhibition and hosted a lecture by Michael Graves in
which he discussed his recently completed Portland
Building.[3] Yet cracks were beginning to appear in the
facade of the prevailing discourse, even as postmodernism's canonical projects were topping off. The year
1982 also held the Parc de la Villette competition, with
entries from Bernard Tschumi (the winner) and Koolhaas
presaging a shift from postmodernism's semiotics to
event-program and formal juxtaposition. The year also
saw the first English-language edition of Aldo Rossi's
The Architecture of the City, the founding of Storefront
for Art and Architecture, the prototype installation of
Falkestrasse by Coop Himmelb(l)au, and the last issue
of *Oppositions* to be published under the editorship of
Peter Eisenman, Kenneth Frampton, and Mario Gandelsonas.[4]

The 1980s and 1990s were fractious decades, when discourse was often forged through public debate—perhaps
none so infamous as Christopher Alexander and Eisenman's
"Contrasting Concepts of Harmony in Architecture" at
Harvard University's Graduate School of Design, which
also took place in 1982.[5] Notorious for Alexander's charge

that Eisenman was "fucking up the world," the event
was significant because the debate precipitated
an ideological turn in the discipline. While both
were interested in design as process, Alexander main-
tained the position that form be related to function
through an uncovering of natural order, or what he
termed "objective order," whereas Eisenman specifically
rejected function, meaning, and aesthetics, likening
order to something subjective or socially constructed.

Taken as a collection, these events portended a shift
from high postmodernism toward the tectonic expression and the fragmented or "disturbed" forms that would
inspire Philip Johnson and Mark Wigley's *Deconstructivist
Architecture* show at New York's Museum of Modern Art
(MoMA) in 1988. This disciplinary debate registers in the
juxtapositions of radically different representation and
design strategies during the early years of the Emerging
Voices program. Tod Williams (EV82) and Billie Tsien's
materially expressive and formally austere Feinberg
Hall and Morphosis's decentered space and articulated
steel structure for 72 Market Street restaurant seem
the product of a different era than the iconic bill-
board-flat, blue-tiled arches of Taft Architects' (EV82)
YWCA Masterson Branch and the Campidoglio-inspired,
historic-symbolic reference in Stuart Cohen and Anders
Nereim's (EV82) East Ruskin Street Beach Pavilion in
Seaside, Florida.[6] Indeed, it would only be a few more
years before quotation of classical references virtually
disappeared from the repertoire of the Emerging Voices.

By 1988 the reification of contemporary "anxiety" in
conflicting forms eclipsed historical reference in the
League's program, with Ralph Lerner's (EV88) Progressive
Architecture (P/A) Award-winning Indira Gandhi National
Centre for the Arts in New Delhi being possibly the last
neoclassical postmodern facade presented in an Emerging
Voices lecture. As the influence of history, allegory,
and symbolism waned, K. Michael Hays wrote "Critical
Architecture: Between Culture and Form," an influential
essay published in *Perspecta* that sought to disrupt the
dialectic opposition of "culture and form," establish-
ing the discourse of critical theory that would dominate
the 1990s.[7] At the time a significant number of architects and writers found inspiration in media, cultural
studies, and philosophy; as Hays noted, "Since 1968
'architecture theory' has all but subsumed 'architecture culture'" and "theory [has] displaced architectural
criticism."[8] Mappings, traces, and indices became the de
rigueur means by which designers embodied instability,
material expression, and juxtaposition in their projects. In turn, these forms and operations were deployed
for the sake of producing concepts to be registered as
effects in the broader social and cultural field. From
1988 onward, this shift could be found in projects such
as the arthropodan steel sidewalk canopy of Scogin Elam
and Bray Architects' (EV88) Buckhead Branch Library.

For the next several years the Emerging Voices' work
increasingly reflected the influence of deconstruction,
despite a tacit and uncomfortable acknowledgment among

01

02

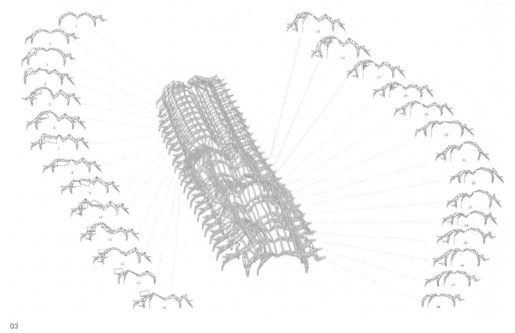

03

01 **Steven Holl Architects** Bridge
of Houses, New York, NY,
proposal, 1979. © Steven Holl
02 **SCAPE / LANDSCAPE ARCHITECTURE**
Oyster-tecture, New York
Harbor, 2010
03 **Reiser + Umemoto** Yokohama
International Port Terminal,
Yokohama, Japan, competition
entry, 1995
04 **Stuart Cohen and Anders Nereim
Architects** East Ruskin Street
Beach Pavilion, Seaside, FL,
1986. Photo Steven Brooke
05 **Tod Williams Billie Tsien
Architects** Feinberg Hall,
Princeton University,
Princeton, NJ, 1986.
© Michael Moran
06 **Scogin Elam and Bray Architects**
Buckhead Branch Library,
Atlanta, GA, 1989.
© Tim Hursley
07 **Taft Architects** YWCA Masterson
Branch, Houston, TX, 1982
08 **Morphosis** 72 Market Street,
Venice, CA, 1983.
Photo Tom Bonner
09 **Schwetye Luchini Maritz
Architects** Maritz Residence,
St. Louis, MO, 1988. Photo Sam
Fentress, Photography

04

07

05

08

06

09

academics and practitioners alike that the unstable
forms served as mere metaphor rather than as an oper-
ative condition. The stairs supported by skewed columns
in Adrian Luchini's (EV92) Maritz Residence would not
plunge into the pool nor would the listing chimney of
Coleman Coker and Samuel Mockbee's (EV90) Cook House
topple. Even in less formally expressive practices, an
interest in materially tectonic expression distanced
this work from the amateriality of the prior decade: the
flat, smooth, and often color-coded surfaces that were
the hallmark of high postmodernism. Thomas Hanrahan and
Victoria Meyers's (EV93) highly articulated models and
drawings of the Canal Street Waterline project and Joel
Sanders's (EV93) section drawing for the *House Rules*
exhibition at the Wexner Center for the Arts exemplified
a fascination with highly articulated assemblies—
typically of unfinished materials such as steel, sheet
metal, cables, and concrete. Their drawings reveal the
influence of Frampton's writings on tectonics. Although
his *Studies in Tectonic Culture* was not published until
1995, its central premise—that structure, materiality,
and construction are fundamental to architecture—
pervaded many of his essays (on Carlo Scarpa, Santiago
Calatrava, and Renzo Piano) in the early 1990s, and it
was most explicitly outlined in his 1990 "Rappel à l'ordre: The Case for the Tectonic." In it, he argues for
the joint as the primary "art" of architecture and for
"the structural unit as the irreducible essence of architectural form."[9] The resulting fascination with detail
coincided with the moment when computers found their way
into architecture offices. Early computer-aided-draw-
ing software facilitated the conceptualization of more
detailed and complex drawings, even before the computer
became the primary tool in design offices to produce
those drawings. While many practitioners were still
constructing presentation drawings by hand, in pencil
or ink, the protocols and attributes of computer drawing (layers, precision, and almost infinite scalability)
fundamentally transformed the way architects imagined
the construction of drawings and process of design.
Karen Bausman and Leslie Gill's (EV92) axonometric drawing of office interior partition systems for the Elektra
Entertainment Group headquarters, for example, contains a
complexity in form and detail that belies its hand-drawn
ink construction. The photocopy-toner texture in Keenen
Riley Architects' (EV90) 1989 Bronx School photomontage self-consciously references the use of technology
in its creation, foreshadowing the direct adoption of
digital processes that would come to define the 1990s.
  Concomitant with the adoption of digital technologies
and the rise of theory came extended ruminations about
the relation between theory and practice. These discussions played out primarily in architecture schools,
in the pages of architecture journals (particularly
Assemblage), and in several of critic, writer, and editor Cynthia Davidson's decade-long series of annual ANY
conferences that gathered practicing architects, his-
torians, critics, philosophers, and others—mostly East

Coast academics—to interrogate the state of the discipline.[10] Ironically, despite these heated debates, it was precisely the collision of theories of deconstruction with the emergence of digital technologies, and their use in practice, that spawned the discourses of non-linearity, systems theory, and biological logics that were subsequently adopted by a younger generation, among its ranks designers recognized by the Emerging Voices program in the mid-to-late 1990s. For this younger generation of mostly digital-savvy designers, the direct application of theory into form had reached an end-game. Although influenced by poststructuralist theories, they recognized that mere critical awareness would not serve to change the underlying political and social structures to which they were reacting. For these practitioners, the computer offered a potential link between design and theory that could genuinely produce new possibilities within the realm of architecture.

In this regard, the year 1992 was a watershed. It saw the death of James Stirling, the release of the World Wide Web to the public, the completion of Koolhaas's Kunsthal in Rotterdam, and the publication of Greg Lynn's "Multiplicitous and Inorganic Bodies" essay in *Assemblage* (his influential guest-edited edition of *AD*, entitled "Folding in Architecture," was published the following year).[11] In many ways, it was a pivotal time for the discipline, as the aesthetics of collision and disjunction met early spline-based geometries; the Emerging Voices program recognized one of its first firms of digital designers, Kolatan/Mac Donald Studio (EV92). Early adopters of the computer as a design tool, Sulan Kolatan and William Mac Donald embraced digital technologies as both a conceptual process and a means to produce designs. The partners' Yokohama International Port Terminal competition entry, produced a few years later, directly appropriated the technique of horseshoe mapping from the mathematics of chaos theory to mix program elements through a series of geometric squeezing, stretching, and folding operations; this process generated a series of sections that were "skinned" with a continuous surface.

The transformation of the architect from composer of form to designer of process marked a significant shift from the classical design process. Kolatan/Mac Donald Studio's competition entry contained nascent strategies of topology, network thinking, and parametric design that saw wide proliferation among Emerging Voices in the latter half of the decade. Stan Allen (EV93) was also prescient in exploring theories of continuity and process-based design, although he focused on emergent fields of self-similar elements rather than a topological surface. The notion of "field conditions" (published in 1997 in his essay "From Object to Field") challenged the classical—and modern—duality of figure and field in favor of localized and distributed relationships between a finer grained set of parts and played out in his competition entry for the National Diet Library in Kansai, Japan, and the treatment of the ground at the Museo del Prado in Madrid.[12] Allen explicitly stated that

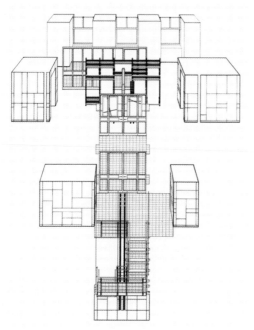

10

11

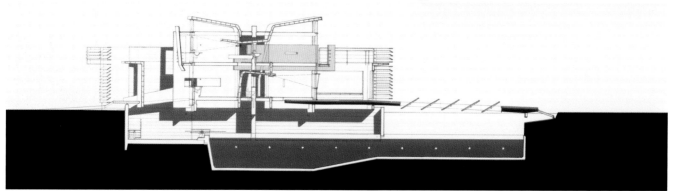

12

10 **Bausman Gill Associates** Elektra
   Entertainment Group, New York,
   NY, hand-drawn ink on Mylar,
   1991
11 **hanrahan Meyers architects**
   Canal Street Waterline, New
   York, NY, 1993
12 **Joel Sanders Architect** Sight
   Specific, *House Rules*, Wexner
   Center for the Arts, Columbus,
   OH, 1994
13 **Keenen Riley Architects** Bronx
   School design study, *New
   Schools for New York*, The
   Architectural League of New
   York and Public Education
   Association, Bronx, NY, 1989
14 **Kolatan/Mac Donald Studio**
   Yokohama International Port
   Terminal, Yokohama, Japan,
   competition entry, 1993
15 **Office dA** Installation for
   Fabrications, Museum of Modern
   Art, New York, NY, 1998
16 **Stan Allen Architect** National
   Diet Library, Kansai, Japan,
   competition model, 1994
17 **nARCHITECTS** *Canopy*, MoMA PS1
   Young Architects Program,
   Queens, NY, winning proposal,
   2004

13

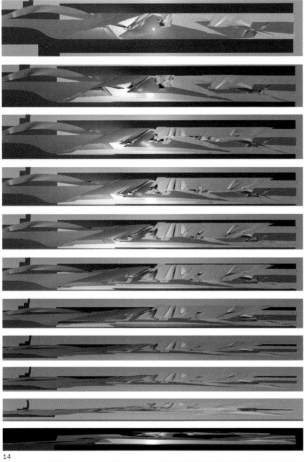

14

15

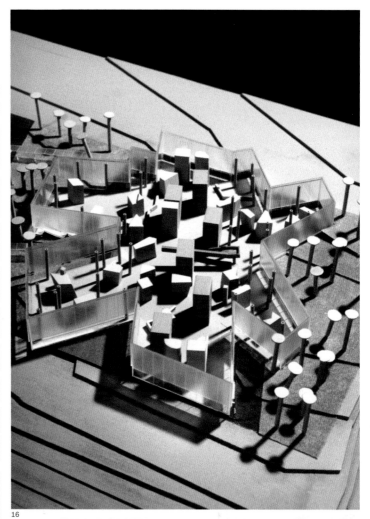

16

17

he was attempting to provide "a bridge between building and form-making" (i.e., between Frampton's tectonics
and Wigley and Johnson's deconstructivism) by proposing
that "form matters, but not so much the forms of things
as the forms between things."[13] And while Allen's work
of this time might not seem born out of a digital mind-
set, it was deeply influenced by the discourse of network thinking and computational logics that dominated
Columbia University, where he directed the Advanced
Architectural Design Program from 1990 to 2002.

Still, the adoption of computational logics articulated as a design thesis was slow to take hold, and
four years passed before the Emerging Voices program recognized another practice using the computer
as a generative design tool. Like Kolatan/Mac Donald
Studio's Yokohama proposal, the infrastructural ten-
drils of Reiser and Umemoto's Bucharest 2000 urban
design proposal and the topological manipulations of
their water garden for Jeffrey Kipnis were designed
through dynamic computational processes rather than by
the composition of static elements. The large, topological, continually varied surfaces served to create a
vast variety of open-ended spaces. The relatively slow
pace with which these techniques and ideas prolifer-
ated in design practices resulted in part from limitations within the technologies themselves. At the time,
the software with the greatest computational design
power came with a large price tag and a steep learning
curve, so it remained within the domain of architecture
schools, primarily Columbia University, until the end
of the decade, when software with similar real-time,
three-dimensional interfaces made the technology more
accessible. A critical mass of projects that experimented with the computer as a design tool appears in
the Emerging Voices class of 1999, in the work of Evan
Douglis Studio, Asymptote Architecture, and Loom Studio.

Just as the computer had fully arrived on the scene
with the new millennium, the euphoric discourses sur-
rounding the potentials for indeterminacy, self-organiza-
tion, and nonlinear systems waned. Although the American
architectural scene has long supported and thrived on
vigorous discussions between camps, in the late 1990s
design and discourse shattered into multiple factions
that adopted (or entirely rejected) new technologies in
such different ways that it made exchange difficult.
Two of the most prominent camps were Dutch-influenced
programism and digital-material experimentalism.[14] The
programists were alumni of or influenced by the offices
of Koolhaas and MVRDV who exploited computational technologies to visualize data into diagrams and diagrams
into building form, while the experimentalists used
computation to generate complex geometries and material
effects. More often than not, the early projects of
the latter camp were realized in installations and
interior projects exploring the interaction between digital design and material resistance: Office dA's (EVO3)
scored and folded metal plates for MoMA's *Fabrications*
show and nARCHITECTS's (EVO6) "canopy" of bamboo arches,

installed in the MoMA PS1 courtyard as the 2004 winner of the museum's Young Architects Program (YAP) competition. The projected, truncated forms of Preston Scott Cohen's (EV04) Eyebeam Atelier Museum of Art and Technology competition entry relied on three-dimensional modeling software to describe a geometric complexity that foreshadowed the Lightfall atrium in his Herta and Paul Amir Building for the Tel Aviv Museum of Art almost a decade later. SHoP Architects (EV01) spanned the data and geometry camps by using computer-numerically controlled (CNC) technologies to produce designs that required large numbers of nonstandard parts, such as the wood planks for its YAP-winning *Dunescape* (2000), the glass-and-steel frame in the Greenport Carousel House, and a custom-fabricated zinc panel system for the Porter House.

The complexity of geometry, fabrication, and production (the process of realization itself) required extraordinary expertise that often obscured discourse about issues beyond the making of the work. Against this backdrop, Robert Somol and Sarah Whiting published their canonical critique of the project of criticality, "Notes Around the Doppler Effect and Other Moods of Modernism," in 2002. In this essay, they sought to slacken the relation of theory and practice by freeing practice from indexicality in order to enable "alternative...arrangements or scenarios."[15] Their manifesto for projective practice offered a "plan" to circumvent or undermine the perceived stranglehold the critical paradigm had held on practice, limiting the potential for producing new solutions and possibilities.[16] In actuality, many designers embracing the projective seemed to simply displace angst from issues outside the discipline to those directly related to design expertise. Somol and Whiting's "relaxed, easy" and "cool" remained largely elusive for many firms as the intricacies of technologically challenging production replaced the production of meaning.

The very title of Ball-Nogues Studio's (EV11) Emerging Voices lecture, "Fast, Cheap & in Control," delivered by Benjamin Ball, exemplified this paradox of conflicting desires: the burden and anxiety shifts from the conceptualization of the work to its execution (a direct inversion of Eisenman's houses of the 1970s, for example).[17] Ball and Gaston Nogues argued against a belabored design intention, transferring the intensity of effort into the exquisitely detailed fabrications of atypical materials (computer-machine-cut-and-painted string, for example) created by a hybridizing process of computer design, CNC fabrication, and handcraft. Claiming fabrication as territory for the designer marked a change from the previous generation of Emerging Voices, shifting the focus from the design of process to the design of production. The exhaustion of the critical project fomented the disciplinary turn from theory, and it was aided and abetted by both a preoccupation with increasingly complex technologies and a newfound concern for the exigencies of pressing economic, social, and ecological problems.

The latest Emerging Voices are largely digital natives whose process and practice fully and unconsciously

18

20

19

21

18 **SHoP Architects** The Porter
House, New York, NY, 2003.
Photo Seong Kwon

19 **Lateral Office** Water Economies/
Ecologies, Salton Sea, CA, 2009

20 **Preston Scott Cohen Studio**
Eyebeam Atelier Museum of Art
and Technology, New York, NY,
2001

21 **WORKac** *Public Farm 1*, MoMA
PS1 Young Architects Program,
Queens, NY, winning proposal,
2008. Photo Ray Adams

22 **Ball-Nogues Studio** *Feathered
Edge*, Museum of Contemporary
Art, Los Angeles, CA, 2009.
Photo Benny Chan

23 **MOS Architects** *The Zombies Are
Late*, film still, 2008

24 **MASS Design Group** Butaro
Hospital, Butaro, Rwanda, 2011.
Photo Iwan Baan

25 **arquitectura911sc** Integrara
Iztacalco, Mexico City, Mexico,
2011. Photo Rafael Gamo

22

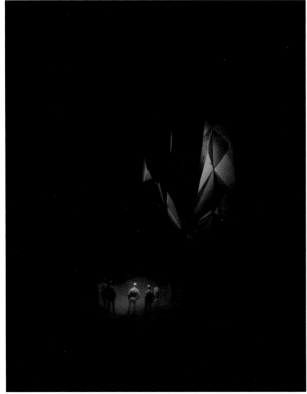

23

24

25

integrate the computer. The delirious promises of formal indeterminacy (and its attendant smooth topological
surfaces), as a means to produce socially sensitive or
democratic design that accompanied the early days of the
digital revolution, gave way to a fascination with the
power and impact of a newer form of digital technology—
social media—and its ability to transform design culture
through participation and collaboration. To date, there
is no identifiable formal trope associated with Web 2.0.
Instead, its impact seems more structural: a call to
change the protocols for how architecture is produced
and information is managed, facilitating new forms of
practice and changing conventional relations between
clients, builders, and designers. It has expanded the
very subject of design, as what constitutes architectural information becomes more social and environmental.
Arguably, WORKac (EV08) was the first of the Emerging
Voices to directly incorporate these practices. The
firm's *Public Farm 1*, which won the YAP in 2008, intro-
duced the potentials of hybridizing systems (in this
case, a network of farmers) with social structures and
plants. In a few short years, designing with collaborative networks of people and nonconventional architectural material became the dominant modus operandi among
Emerging Voices. Lateral Office's (EV11) proposal for
buoyant pools in the Salton Sea directly addressed eco-
systems, economies, hydrology, agriculture, and tourism.
And Interboro Partners (EV11) mined extensive community
input to design its YAP-winning entry, *Holding Pattern*,
with items that fit the needs of neighboring institutions, such as Ping-Pong tables, trees, and mirrors.
  Open-source design protocols that change the role
of the architect from master designer to collaborator
or orchestrator have the potential to replace the sin-
gularity of artistic authorship that has defined the
profession since the Renaissance. So far, the effect
is less a new design paradigm and more an interest in
the collective and communal as a program and politic.
Teddy Cruz's (EV06) Casa Familiar deploys a flexible
urban infrastructure that embraces the cultural norms of
informal housing developments. Designed as a multistage
project in San Ysidro, California, the Casa Familiar
intrinsically accommodates evolving community needs and
financial opportunities by subverting the constraints
of zoning codes with normative social structures—tacitly
acknowledging that unprogrammed spaces will be appropriated for informal uses. A number of projects by the
most recent Emerging Voices directly engage the public realm, such as arquitectura911sc's (EV12) Integrara
Iztacalco housing in Mexico City and urban regeneration
master plan for the northwest sector of Ciudad Juarez,
Mexico. The firm's efforts are motivated less by form and
more by the design of social or political interactions.
This concern with the social vis-à-vis the public realm
echoes the preoccupations of experimental practices in
the 1960s and 1970s, including those of Archigram and
Superstudio. Not content with utopian visions, today's
Emerging Voices are dedicated to the feasibility of their

proposals, even if their political agendas and design propositions are less radical than those of their predecessors. To construct MASS Design Group's (EV13) schools and hospitals in Haiti, Liberia, and Rwanda required an effort and expertise outside of the conventional realm of the architect: to negotiate cultural, social, and economic landscapes, the firm collaborated with governments and NGOs, as well as facilities experts. Almost a counterpoint to its contemporaries' design of production, MASS is focused on the design of practice.

Questioning the structures of production and practice requires a deeply self-reflective stance about the discipline itself. In the 1990s the critical project reacted to the autonomy of the 1980s by opening the field to broader cultural issues. Today, however, it seems we are on the verge of a return to the building of knowledge within the discipline (those concerned with a kind of digital material formalism) and about it (those concerned with changing the protocols of practice in order to address social and cultural problems). Given the relatively direct and prosaic nature of these pursuits, the claim that we are "after-theory" seems a logical conclusion. However, several recent Emerging Voices are grappling with a new paradigm that escapes easy classification into a formal or social practice. The art and architecture collaborative Lead Pencil Studio (EV06) explicitly seeks to create what its partners have described as "everything about architecture with none of its function." The studio's work spans sculptural gallery installations and environmental art, such as the *Non-Sign II*, and architecture with a focus on materiality. MOS Architects' (EV08) hybrid production, including short films (such as *The Zombies Are Late*), furniture installations, houses, and even software development, entirely eludes categorization. However, it is the disjunction between modes of making that enables the firm's work to escape an instrumentalization of its voice into form.

The League founded the Emerging Voices program at a time when few media venues existed for designers to broadcast their work. Since then, numerous institutions and publications, from MoMA PS1 (YAP) to *Architectural Record* (Design Vanguard), have followed the League's example in granting awards to amplify design's independent voices. Furthermore, a multitude of design websites enables even the smallest firms to reach an international audience. Sites such as ArchDaily, Architizer, and Dezeen provide a steady flow of news and information, as well as countless images.[18] In this culture of saturation, when access to architectural images and information has never been greater, what purpose does the Emerging Voices program serve? Perhaps rather than a platform, the award, in its support of concept over form and operation over representation, now acts as a filter—like noise-canceling headphones—that allows us to hear the slightly unsure, idealistic, precocious voices of a new generation just beginning to be audible.

FORM:
PROCESS,
PLACE,
PRODUCTION

How does one characterize the output of more than two hundred visionary North American architects and designers recorded over the past thirty years? During an earlier period, say, between 1945 and 1975, a certain level of consistency would have made the answer relatively clear. This survey, however, picks up after the monolith of modernism had cracked, or at least the version of it cataloged by Henry-Russell Hitchcock and Reyner Banham. The Architectural League's Emerging Voices program began in 1982, sixteen years after Robert Venturi published *Complexity and Contradiction in Architecture* and the same year that Michael Graves's Portland Building left locals—and much of the architectural rank and file—scratching their heads. Since then, architects have taken various paths through postmodernism, deconstructivism, minimalism, neotraditionalism, neorationalism, and even neomodernism. It's been a busy time.

This list might suggest that architectural investigation during the first three decades of the Emerging Voices program lacked seriousness, and compared to the clinical sobriety of modernism, one might be forgiven for reaching that conclusion. But it would be hasty. Despite a propensity for rhetorical excess, architects during this period undertook earnest research, and architecture underwent profound change, particularly relative to the computer as a design and visualization tool. Not since the arrival of the steel frame and the mechanical elevator has the profession gone through a more fundamental reordering.

What does that reordering look like? Well, a lot like this book. As its name implies, the Emerging Voices program recognizes maturing, often polemical designers, thereby creating a catalog of contemporary architectural design and discourse. In a post-9/11 world, for example, it may seem surprising, even quaint, that people once argued passionately over which classical flourishes were appropriate for postwar architecture. But, in the first few years of Emerging Voices, Stuart Cohen and Anders Nereim (EV82), Taft Architects (EV82), Susana Torre (EV82), Andres Duany and Elizabeth Plater-Zyberk (EV83), Fred Koetter and Susie Kim (EV86), Mark Simon (EV86), and Ralph Lerner (EV88), all serious types, did exactly that. Architecture was in thrall to art history. By 1992, however, all of that was gone. Karen Bausman and Leslie Gill, Sulan Kolatan and William Mac Donald, Adrian Luchini, Toshiko Mori, and Central Office of Architecture, all among that year's awardees, lost little sleep over which of the Orders stacked up—literally or figuratively—against the others in composing a facade. The conversation had shifted to issues of materiality, structure, and form, and, for the most part, it stayed there for another decade.

By the turn of the millennium, somewhat remarkably given its loudly proclaimed demise less than twenty years earlier, modernism reappeared—and in seeming good health. Whether it was LOT-EK's (EV99) shipping-container reboot of industrial precedent, the sculptural romanticism of Saucier + Perrotte architectes (EV01), or a reimagining of the Chicago school by Brininstool + Lynch (EV03), architects reembraced many of modernism's structural and formal arguments, if not its original social agenda. But even that reemerged a few years later, first in the borderland work of Teddy Cruz (EV06) and later in the focus on technology and urban issues by firms like Interboro Partners (EV11) and A-I-R [Architecture-Infrastructure-Research] (EV09), as well as in the countless offices that have embraced sustainability as a social, rather than merely technical, agenda.

Modernism's resurrection, however, and, even more so, the airless, internalized debates of postmodernism, were mere surface disturbances compared to the seismic shifts the digital revolution had already unleashed. Frank Gehry's pioneering work with digital fabrication software originally developed for the aviation and automobile industries sparked the process in the profession in the early 1990s, but a wave of university-led research and experimentation—most notably at the schools of architecture at Columbia University, Massachusetts Institute of Technology, and the University of California, Los Angeles, starting in the late 1980s—was already producing a generation of young designers whose ideas would remake architectural form and practice.

These "Digitati" began filtering through the Emerging Voices program in the 1990s, led by firms such as Kolatan/Mac Donald Studio (EV92). They appeared in more significant numbers at the turn of the millennium; Asymptote Architecture's (EV99) proposals for a virtual Guggenheim and a sinuous trading floor at the New York Stock Exchange, for example, were otherworldly in their seeming disregard for orthogonal form and the laws of physics. In 2001 Winka Dubbeldam, Douglas Garofalo, and SHoP Architects debuted—most of them educated at Columbia's Graduate School of Architecture, Planning and Preservation, and all of them early adopters of digital technology. Many more followed, including Thom Faulders (EV02), Preston Scott Cohen (EV04), nARCHITECTS (EV06), Ammar Eloueini Digit-all Studio (EV07), Lisa Iwamoto and Craig Scott (EV07), MOS Architects (EV08), L.E.FT (EV10), Ball-Nogues Studio (EV11), and P-A-T-T-E-R-N-S (EV11). And a number of Emerging Voices, including Thomas Leeser (EV93), Joel Sanders (EV93), Neil Denari (EV95), Mark Rakatansky (EV95), Craig Konyk (EV96), Michael Maltzan (EV98), Raveevarn Choksombatchai and Ralph Nelson (EV99), and Evan Douglis (EV99) who had been selected for other reasons, went on to embrace the digital as their primary mode of research and expression.

Formal experimentation was certainly the most obvious manifestation of the profession's digital revolution, but it was hardly the only one. After architects spent the second half of the twentieth century in a liability-driven, professionally vitiating flight from responsibility for the building process, some of the Digitati argued that powerful, affordable computing offered designers access to analytical tools for real estate analysis, cost controls, and product supply chains that previously had been the province of other professions.

   With these tools, architects could extend their role
to include services that had long ago slipped from their
grasp. SHoP used this logic to convince a New York real
estate developer that the firm could build the Porter
House condominium, completed in 2003, and save the
client time and money; never mind that the architects
had never built high-rise housing and had only been
in business since 1996. Their success suggested that
architects could, with proper research (and the
reassumption of a certain amount of risk), reinsert
themselves into positions of greater authority and
greater professional satisfaction. SHoP is now a
hybrid practice offering architectural design,
construction management, and sustainable technologies consulting. Brothers and partners Mark Anderson
and Peter Anderson (EV07) had been building their
own work for years by the time they became Emerging
Voices. El dorado (EV08) began by making furniture
for other architects' projects and now, in addition
to an active architectural practice, has a design-
build arm. Ted Smith (EV86) and Onion Flats (EV08)
opened their doors as offices that design, develop, and
build their own work, and that's still their model.
   Underlying the new-modes-of-practice argument is a
battle for architectural identity. If the theory-based
caterwauling of the 1980s painted the profession as the
province of ivory-tower aesthetes, architects in the
digital age are recasting themselves as more closely
aligned with the rational, productive worlds of research
and science. Hence, there are firms with names like
UrbanLab (EV10), which could have been Dunn and Felsen
Architects; Lateral Office (EV11), which could have
been Sheppard and White Architects and describes its
practice as being committed "to design as a research
vehicle"; and SsD (EV12), which believes architecture is "equal parts research and production." One
of the most successful practices of the past twenty
years went so far as to make research a part of their
name: ARO, or Architecture Research Office (EV01), was
founded with an explicit message to potential clients
about what the firm intended to bring to the table.
   The nature of the research varies from firm to firm,
but its heralding as a mode of practice suggests to
colleagues and clients that architects are prioritiz-
ing issues related to making buildings, rather than
simply talking about them. Had molo (EV10) been practicing during the downturn of the 1980s, the firm
might have busied itself with the timeless question
of how to incorporate poché into contemporary design;
instead, following the recession of 2008, the office
is reconsidering the nature of materials. Ball-Nogues
Studio, reflecting its SCI-Arc training, slips easily
between studies of large-scale structural innovation
and small-scale product design. In short, the shift
to digital has created a generation of designers whose
work has helped edge architects back into the conversation about how buildings are made, not simply how
to make them look like something that came before.

There are other lines of inquiry in architecture, of course, and the Emerging Voices program has acknowledged many of them, from architecture as installation art to the revival of socially engaged practice. Among the most fascinating of these, because it seems to defy both time and fashion, is regionalism. In the 1980s architectural theorists Alexander Tzonis, Liane Lefaivre, and Kenneth Frampton argued that modern architecture can and should heed its geographical and cultural context, despite modernist dogma to the contrary. In his seminal essay "Towards a Critical Regionalism: Six Points for an Architecture of Resistance," Frampton offered a taxonomy of identifying characteristics. It is surprising to note just how many Emerging Voices laureates seem to be regionalists; if an architect is not located in New York, Chicago, or Los Angeles, odds are better than even that the practice is a regionalist one of some stripe.

The trend among winners began with Arquitectonica's (EV82) Miami-ready interpretations of Rem Koolhaas's inflected modern towers. The firm's attention to light, color, tectonics, and climate fulfill most of the checklist Frampton developed. University of Texas at Austin School of Architecture professors Robert James Coote (EV84) and Lawrence W. Speck (EV85) were influenced by postmodern historicism, but they clearly contributed to a long conversation about whether there is an architectural language that is distinctly Texan. (Indeed, Speck would go on to edit the scholarly journal *Center*, which addressed this subject in some detail, beginning with an expanded essay on regionalism by Frampton). Speck and Coote share Emerging Voices status with fellow University of Texas at Austin professor David Heymann (EV00) and San Antonio-based Ted Flato and David Lake (EV92). Farther west, the League found itself entranced for a time with a group of designers whose work even more clearly hews to Frampton's criteria. Wendell Burnette (EV99), Rick Joy (EV00), Kelly Bauer and James Richärd (EV01), and Marwan Al-Sayed (EV02) practice in Arizona's spectacular Sonoran desert, a landscape and climate of such distinctive character that any architectural response not cognizant of its particularities looks just plain wrong.

There is an even larger group of Emerging Voices that one can understand as kindred, if not as closely aligned intellectually or geographically as the members of the Arizona school or the latter-day Texas Rangers. For lack of a better term, they could be called the "rural school"—and yes, Coleman Coker and Samuel Mockbee (EV90) would have been among them when they were tapped by the program. The work does not propose a language specific to one region so much as to the buildings and landscapes of the hinterlands: architecture that looks to agrarian precedent for inspiration yet retains a clear modern agenda and form. Find it in the work of architects as diverse as Turner Brooks (EV86), Harry Teague (EV88), Steven Harris (EV89), William Rawn (EV89), James Cutler (EV94), Charles Rose and Maryann Thompson (EV97), Marlon Blackwell (EV98), Brian MacKay-Lyons (EV00),

Robert Hull and David Miller (EV00), Frank Harmon (EV03),
Rand Elliott (EV04), Tom Kundig (EV04), and Roberto de
Leon Jr. and M. Ross Primmer (EV11).

At the end of the day, though, the Emerging Voices
program is remarkable not only for its record of trend
spotting, but also for its prescience with designers. Go
back and look at just the first years of the program and
you will find the names of some of the most influential
architects practicing today: Steven Holl (EV82), Tod
Williams (EV82), Thom Mayne and Michael Rotondi (EV83),
Andres Duany and Elizabeth Plater-Zyberk (EV83), and
Eric Owen Moss (EV84). Many other marquee offices are
sprinkled across the subsequent years of the program—
familiar now, but hardly household names when they were
first invited to lecture. If architecture had a stock
market, the Emerging Voices program would certainly be
one of the most sought-after pickers in the business.

Of course, the wealth created by the program is
indexical rather than financial. Its primary value rests
in ordering an era that otherwise might easily look
unfocused. Viewed through the prism of Emerging Voices,
however, the past thirty years of architecture can be
seen as a time of steady and important progress; one
that lifts the profession's gaze toward a horizon
of new technologies and new modes of practice that,
diligently pursued, could prepare it for a period
of renewed leadership.

Emerging Voices
1982-2013

■

Firms and partnerships
at the time of selection
as Emerging Voices

1982

Susana Torre
The Architectural Studio

Laurinda Spear
Arquitectonica

Jon Michael Schwarting
The Design Collaborative

Franklin D. Israel
Franklin D. Israel Design
Associates

David Slovic
Friday Architects

George Ranalli
George Ranalli, Architect

Lauretta Vinciarelli
Lauretta Vinciarelli

Giuseppe Zambonini
Open Atelier of Design

Paul Segal
Paul Segal Associates
Architects

Roger C. Ferri
Roger C. Ferri and Associates

Steven Holl
Steven Holl Architects

Stuart Cohen, Anders Nereim
Stuart Cohen and Anders
Nereim Architects

John J. Casbarian, Danny M.
Samuels, Robert H. Timme
Taft Architects

Tod Williams
Tod Williams Associates

1983

Anthony Ames
Anthony Ames Architect

Andres Duany,
Elizabeth Plater-Zyberk
Duany Plater-Zyberk & Company

Ronald Adrian Krueck
Krueck & Olsen Architects

David T. Jones,
I. Guyman Martin
Martin & Jones Architects

Thom Mayne, Michael Rotondi
Morphosis

Peter D. Waldman
Peter D. Waldman Architect

Richard Oliver
Richard Oliver Architect

Peter Wilson
Wilson Associates

1984

Ronald Bentley, Salvatore
LaRosa, Franklin Salasky
Bentley LaRosa Salasky

Joseph Valerio
Chrysalis Corporation
Architects

Eric Owen Moss
Eric Owen Moss Architects

Frederick Fisher
Frederick Fisher, Architect

Henry Smith-Miller
Henry Smith-Miller, Architect

Robert James Coote
Robert James Coote, Architect

Stanley Saitowitz
Stanley Saitowitz Office

Theodore M. Ceraldi
Theodore Ceraldi, Architect

1985

Heather Willson Cass,
Patrick Pinnell
Cass & Pinnell Architects

Richard Fernau, Laura Hartman
Fernau + Hartman Architects

Darcy Bonner, Scott Himmel
Himmel/Bonner Architects

Lawrence W. Speck
Lawrence W. Speck Associates

William McDonough,
J. Woodson Rainey Jr.
McDonough, Rainey Architects

Rob Wellington Quigley
Rob Wellington Quigley

Diane Legge Kemp
Skidmore, Owings & Merrill

Wayne Berg
Wayne Berg, Architect

1986

Bart Prince
Bart Prince, Architect

Peter de Bretteville
de Bretteville/Polyzoides

Mark Simon
Centerbrook Architects and
Planners

Paul Haigh
Haigh Space

Susie Kim, Fred Koetter
Koetter, Kim & Associates

Peter C. Papademetriou
Peter C. Papademetriou

Ted Smith
Smith and Others Architects

Turner Brooks
Turner Brooks, Architect

1988

Ross Anderson,
Frederic Schwartz
Anderson/Schwartz Architects

Brian A. Murphy
BAM Construction/Design

W.G. Clark
Clark and Menefee

Harry Teague
Harry Teague Architects

Peter Forbes
Peter Forbes & Associates

Ralph Lerner
Ralph Lerner Architect

Patricia Sapinsley
Sapinsley Architecture

Merrill Elam, Mack Scogin
Scogin Elam and
Bray Architects

1989

Lars Lerup
Lars Lerup

Mark Mack
Mack Architect(s)

Warren Schwartz,
Robert Silver
Schwartz/Silver Architects

Steven Harris
Steven Harris Architects

Zack McKown, Calvin Tsao
TsAO & McKOWN Architects

William L. Rawn
William Rawn Associates

1990

Wes Jones, Peter Pfau
Holt Hinshaw Pfau Jones

John Keenen, Terry Riley
Keenen Riley Architects

Julie Eizenberg, Hank Koning
Koning Eizenberg Architecture

Coleman Coker, Samuel Mockbee
Mockbee/Coker Architects

Ralph Johnson
Perkins+Will

Walter Chatham
Walter Chatham Architect

1992

Karen Bausman, Leslie Gill
Bausman Gill Associates

**Ron Golan, Eric A. Kahn,
Russell N. Thomsen**
Central Office
of Architecture

**Sulan Kolatan, William
Mac Donald**
Kolatan/Mac Donald Studio

Ted Flato, David Lake
Lake|Flato Architects

Adrian Luchini
Schwetye Luchini Maritz
Architects

Toshiko Mori
Toshiko Mori Architect

1993

**David Piscuskas,
Juergen Riehm**
1100 Architect

Peggy Deamer, Scott Phillips
Deamer + Phillips,
Architecture

Deborah Berke
Deborah Berke Architect

**Thomas Hanrahan,
Victoria Meyers**
hanrahan Meyers architects

Joel Sanders
Joel Sanders Architect

Laszlo Kiss, Todd Zwigard
Kiss + Zwigard

Thomas Leeser
Leeser Architecture

Stan Allen
Stan Allen Architect

1994

Marc Angélil, Sarah Graham
Angélil/Graham Architecture

Carlos Jimenez
Carlos Jimenez Studio

Gary Cunningham
Cunningham Architects

Nicholas Goldsmith
FTL Happold

James Cutler
James Cutler Architects

Sheila Kennedy, Frano Violich
Kennedy & Violich
Architecture (KVA)

**William Leddy, Marsha
Maytum, Richard Stacy,
James L. Tanner**
Tanner Leddy Maytum Stacy
Architects

Enrique Norten
TEN Arquitectos

1995

Neil Denari
Cor-Tex Architecture

Homa Farjadi
Farjadi/Mostafavi Associates

Gisue Hariri, Mojgan Hariri
Hariri & Hariri

Chuck Hoberman
Hoberman Associates

Susan Lanier, Paul Lubowicki
Lubowicki Lanier Architecture

Mark Rakatansky
Mark Rakatansky Studio

**Brigitte Shim,
Howard Sutcliffe**
Shim-Sutcliffe Architects

Wellington Reiter
Urban Instruments

1996

Brad Cloepfil
Allied Works

Audrey Matlock
Audrey Matlock Architect

**Clifton Balch,
Mojdeh Baratloo**
Baratloo-Balch Architects

Carlos Zapata
Carlos Zapata Design
Studio (CZDS)

Craig Konyk
Konyk Architecture

Linda Lindroth, Craig Newick
Lindroth + Newick \\
Newick Architects

Louise Braverman
Louise Braverman, Architect

Jesse Reiser, Nanako Umemoto
Reiser + Umemoto

1997

Kathryn Dean, Charles Wolf
Dean/Wolf Architects

Tom Buresh, Danelle Guthrie
Guthrie+Buresh Architects

Anne Perl de Pal
Perl de Pal Architects

Michele Saee
SAEE Studio

**Charles Rose,
Maryann Thompson**
Thompson and Rose Architects

**Michael Manfredi,
Marion Weiss**
WEISS/MANFREDI Architecture/
Landscape/Urbanism

1998

**Sara Caples,
Everardo Jefferson**
Caples Jefferson Architects

François de Menil
François de Menil Architect

Michael Gabellini
Gabellini Associates

Julie V. Snow
Julie Snow Architects

Karen Fairbanks, Scott Marble
Marble Fairbanks

Marlon Blackwell
Marlon Blackwell Architect

Michael Maltzan
Michael Maltzan Architecture

Vincent James
Vincent James Associates

1999

**Lise Anne Couture,
Hani Rashid**
Asymptote Architecture

Brian Healy
Brian Healy Architects

Kevin Daly, Chris Genik
Daly Genik

Evan Douglis
Evan Douglis Studio

**Raveevarn Choksombatchai,
Ralph Nelson**
Loom Studio

Giuseppe Lignano, Ada Tolla
LOT-EK

Michael Bell
Michael Bell Architecture

Wendell Burnette
Wendell Burnette Architects

2000

Brian MacKay-Lyons
Brian MacKay-Lyons
Architecture Urban Design

David Heymann
David Heymann, Architect \\
Michael Underhill, David
Heymann, and Laura J. Miller,
Architects

Julie Bargmann
D.I.R.T. studio

Robert Hull, David Miller
The Miller Hull Partnership

Lisa Rapoport
PLANT Architect

Rick Joy
Rick Joy Architects

2001

Winka Dubbeldam
ARCHI-TECTONICS

**Stephen Cassell,
Adam Yarinsky**
Architecture Research
Office (ARO)

Douglas Garofalo
Garofalo Architects

Mario Gooden, Ray Huff
Huff + Gooden Architects

James Corner
James Corner Field Operations

Kelly Bauer, James Richärd
richärd + bauer

**Jonathan Marvel,
Robert Rogers**
Rogers Marvel Architects

**André Perrotte,
Gilles Saucier**
Saucier + Perrotte
architectes

**Kimberly Holden, Gregg
Pasquarelli, Christopher
Sharples, Coren Sharples,
William Sharples**
SHoP Architects

Mehrdad Yazdani
Yazdani Studio of Cannon
Design

2002

Thom Faulders
Beige Design

Byron Kuth, Elizabeth Ranieri
Kuth|Ranieri Architects

**David Lewis, Paul Lewis,
Marc Tsurumaki**
Lewis Tsurumaki Lewis
Architects (LTL Architects)

Marwan Al-Sayed
Marwan Al-Sayed Architects
(MASA)

**Alan Koch, Lyn Rice, Galia
Solomonoff, Linda Taalman**
OpenOffice

Ali Tayar
Parallel Design Partnership

Louise Harpman, Scott Specht
Specht Harpman

Andrew Zago
Zago Architecture

2003

David Brininstool, Brad Lynch
Brininstool + Lynch

Frank Harmon
Frank Harmon Architect

Margie Ruddick
Margie Ruddick Landscape

**Monica Ponce de Leon,
Nader Tehrani**
Office dA

Jennifer Siegal
Office of Mobile Design

Peter Lynch
Peter Lynch Architect

2004

Pierre Thibault
Atelier Pierre Thibault

Rand Elliott
Elliott + Associates
Architects

John Friedman, Alice Kimm
John Friedman Alice Kimm
Architects

Lorcan O'Herlihy
Lorcan O'Herlihy Architects

Tom Kundig
Olson Kundig Architects

Preston Scott Cohen
Preston Scott Cohen Studio

Lawrence Scarpa
Pugh + Scarpa

Ken Smith
WORKSHOP: Ken Smith Landscape
Architect

2005

Taryn Christoff, Martin Finio
Christoff:Finio

Claude Cormier
Claude Cormier architectes
paysagistes

Lauren Crahan, John Hartmann
Freecell

John Ronan
John Ronan Architects

Pablo Castro, Jennifer Lee
OBRA Architects

John Frane, Hadrian Predock
Predock_Frane Architects

**Gary Hilderbrand,
Douglas Reed**
Reed Hilderbrand Landscape
Architecture

Zoltan Pali
Studio Pali Fekete architects
(SPF:a)

2006

Thomas Bercy, Calvin Chen
Bercy Chen Studio

Mark Goulthorpe
dECOi Architects

**Frank Escher,
Ravi GuneWardena**
Escher GuneWardena

Teddy Cruz
Estudio Teddy Cruz

George Yu
George Yu Architects

Annie Han, Daniel Mihalyo
Lead Pencil Studio

Eric Bunge, Mimi Hoang
nARCHITECTS

Jeanne Gang
Studio Gang Architects

2007

Ammar Eloueini
Ammar Eloueini Digit-all
Studio

An Te Liu
An Te Liu

Mark Anderson, Peter Anderson
Anderson Anderson
Architecture

**Andrew Bernheimer,
Jared Della Valle**
Della Valle Bernheimer

Eric Höweler, Meejin Yoon
Höweler + Yoon Architecture/
MY Studio

Lisa Iwamoto, Craig Scott
IwamotoScott Architecture

Sharon Johnston, Mark Lee
Johnston Marklee

Victor F. "Trey" Trahan III
Trahan Architects

2008

Hagy Belzberg
Belzberg Architects

Jamie Darnell, David Dowell, Dan Maginn, Josh Shelton, Douglas Stockman
el dorado

Brian Johnsen, Sebastian Schmaling
Johnsen Schmaling Architects

Granger Moorhead, Robert Moorhead
Moorhead & Moorhead

Michael Meredith, Hilary Sample
MOS Architects

Johnny McDonald, Patrick McDonald, Tim McDonald, Howard Steinberg
Onion Flats

Chris Reed
Stoss Landscape Urbanism

Amale Andraos, Dan Wood
WORKac

2009

Darren Petrucci
A-I-R [Architecture-Infrastructure-Research]

Andrew D. Berman
Andrew Berman Architect

Julio Amezcua, Francisco Pardo
AT103

Shane Coen
Coen + Partners

Derek Dellekamp
Dellekamp Arquitectos

Elizabeth Gray, Alan Organschi
Gray Organschi Architecture

Robert Hutchison, Tom Maul
Hutchison & Maul

Stella Betts, David Leven
LEVENBETTS

2010

James Dallman, Grace La
LA DALLMAN

Ziad Jamaleddine, Makram el Kadi
L.E.FT

Stephanie Forsythe, Todd MacAllen
molo

Michel Rojkind
rojkind arquitectos

Hayes Slade, James Slade
Slade Architecture

Sunil Bald, Yolande Daniels
studioSUMO

Tatiana Bilbao
Tatiana Bilbao

Sarah Dunn, Martin Felsen
UrbanLab

2011

Benjamin Ball, Gaston Nogues
Ball-Nogues Studio

Tobias Armborst, Dan D'Oca, Georgeen Theodore
Interboro Partners

Lola Sheppard, Mason White
Lateral Office

Roberto de Leon Jr., M. Ross Primmer
de Leon & Primmer Architecture Workshop

Georgina Huljich, Marcelo Spina
P-A-T-T-E-R-N-S

Karel Klein, David Ruy
Ruy Klein

B. Alex Miller, Jeff Taylor
Taylor and Miller Architecture and Design

Layng Pew, Claire Weisz, Mark Yoes
WYX Architecture + Urban Design

2012

Johanna Hurme, Sasa Radulovic
5468796 Architecture

Jose Castillo, Saidee Springall
arquitectura911sc

Manon Asselin, Katsuhiro Yamazaki
Atelier TAG

Jeffrey Inaba
INABA

Dwayne Oyler, Jenny Wu
Oyler Wu Collaborative

Elena Brescia, Kate Orff
SCAPE / LANDSCAPE ARCHITECTURE

John Hong, Jinhee Park
SsD

Christos Marcopoulos, Carol Moukheiber
Studio (n-1)

2013

Andy Cao, Xavier Perrot
cao|perrot

Jules Dingle, Jeff Goldstein, Mark Sanderson, Jamie Unkefer
DIGSAU

Susannah Churchill Drake
Dlandstudio architecture and landscape architecture

Jorge Gracia
graciastudio

Sierra Bainbridge, Michael Murphy, Alan Ricks, David Saladik
MASS Design Group

Luke Ogrydziak, Zoë Prillinger
Ogrydziak Prillinger

Carlos Bedoya, Wonne Ickx, Victor Jaime, Abel Perles
PRODUCTORA

Florian Idenburg, Jing Liu
SO - IL

1982-1986
1988-1993
1994-1998
1999-2003
2004-2008
2009-2013

The architects selected during the first five years of the Emerging Voices program varied dramatically in their orientations. At least that is how it seemed at the time. Looking back across the decades, however, unifying tendencies appear in greater relief. For example, a serious emphasis on drawing prevailed in those precomputer days. And architects knew and revered history, whether it was recent or centuries old. They looked at architecture as a formal language: it could be abstract or figurative, but it had its own semantics and syntax.

This was the heyday of postmodernism, although many architects, including those presenting their work at The Architectural League, severely questioned its stylistic indulgences. When the Emerging Voices program debuted in 1982, the first monument to postmodern architecture—Michael Graves's Portland Building in Oregon—was about to open, generating heated debate. Two years later Philip Johnson and John Burgee's controversial AT&T (now Sony) Building in New York City stirred up more debate. Yet other works, such as James Stirling's Neue Staatsgalerie, in Stuttgart, Germany, completed the same year, were lauded.

The postmodern path was hardly the only one to take. Early Emerging Voices, including Steven Holl (EV82), Laurinda Spear (EV82), Tod Williams (EV82), and Henry Smith-Miller (EV84), didn't buy into the prevailing mind-set.[1] They opted to investigate modernist vocabulary for its formal richness, especially as found in the legacies of Le Corbusier and Louis Kahn. These practitioners and others in their coterie had been guided by the previous generation of architects, such as Peter Eisenman, Charles Gwathmey, and Richard Meier, with whom they had studied or worked. Yet another cluster of Emerging Voices—based on the West Coast and counting East Coast-transplant Franklin D. Israel (EV82), Thom Mayne and Michael Rotondi (EV83), Frederick Fisher (EV84), and Eric Owen Moss (EV84) among its ranks—was inspired by Frank Gehry's ad hoc design of the 1970s. They proved that modernism had many sides.

No matter the path they chose, many of the Emerging Voices felt overshadowed by the attention the media showered on the older crowd, which included the architects dubbed the "Whites" (Eisenman, Gwathmey, Meier, and others) and the "Grays" (including Robert A.M. Stern, Charles Moore, and Jaquelin T. Robertson).[2] "We're the lost generation," Smith-Miller lamented at the time about his cohort, whose members were born after 1940. Since many of them had yet to design a work of architecture that would define their careers, they had reason to feel "the anxiety of influence," to borrow from Harold Bloom. Others felt overshadowed for a different reason. Women selected for the Emerging Voices program—Susana Torre (EV82), Lauretta Vinciarelli (EV82), Elizabeth Plater-Zyberk (EV83), Diane Legge Kemp (EV85), and Spear—had to contend with issues of identity in a male-dominated profession.[3] It was a topic addressed by Torre when she organized *Women in American Architecture: A Historic and Contemporary Perspective*, a game-changing exhibition sponsored by the League in 1977.

It is to the credit of Emilio Ambasz, the League's president at the time, that the younger generation of both women and men were heard. (He, too, was born after 1940.) With the help of executive director Marita O'Hare, he canvassed the names of up-and-comers to select the early Emerging Voices. Immediately, the program drew comment: Richard Oliver (EV83) wrote about the first group presenting in 1982 in *Skyline*, the tabloid newspaper of the Institute for Architecture and Urban Studies.[4] Later that year architecture critic Paul Goldberger would report on what he viewed as the quiet generation, including a number of current and future Emerging Voices, in the *New York Times*. It was a fraught time, but those voices became louder. And a "lost" generation found itself.

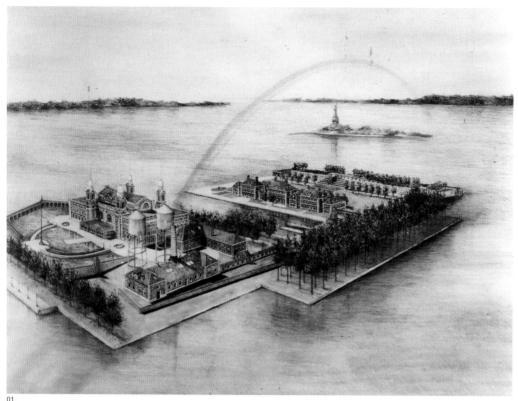

01

02

03

04

05

Susana Torre

The Architectural Studio, New York City (est. 1978)

Education Universidad de Buenos Aires, Architecture Dipl., Instituto Superior de Planeamiento Urbano, 1967; Universidad de Buenos Aires, fellowship at Columbia University, computer applications for urban planning, 1968-1969

Practice Update Susana Torre and Associates, Carboneras, Spain (est. 1990)
Teaching Positions Barnard College and Columbia University (director, Department of Architecture, 1982-1985); Cranbrook Academy of Art (director, architecture department, 1994-1995); Parsons The New School for Design
Notable Honors National Endowment for the Arts, grant recipient, 1990; National Gallery of Art, Center for Advanced Studies in the Visual Arts, Ailsa Mellon Bruce Visiting Senior Fellow, 2003; National Endowment for the Humanities, grant recipient, 2005
Website susanatorre.net

01 Ellis Island Park and Museum Master Plan, New York, NY, proposal, pencil on vellum, 1980. Drawing Susana Torre and Kevin Gordon
02 Roncaores Street Community, Carboneras, Spain, 2008; in collaboration with Estudio DA-3. Photo Daniel Bachman
03 Fire Station Five, Columbus, IN, 1987; in association with WASA Architects and Engineers. Photo Tim Hursley
04 Clark House, Southampton, NY, 1981. Photo Tim Hursley
05 The House of Meanings, architectural matrix (with projects in Dominican Republic, Puerto Rico, and Spain), mixed media on Mylar, 1972

Laurinda Spear

01

02

03

Arquitectonica, Miami (est. 1977); Bernardo Fort-Brescia, Laurinda Spear (principals)

Education Brown University, BFA, 1972; Columbia University, MArch, 1975; Florida International University, MLA, 2006

Practice Update Arquitectonica \\ ArquitectonicaGEO (est. 2005); Laurinda Spear (principal) \\ Dubai, Hong Kong, Lima, Los Angeles, Manila, Miami, New York City, Paris, São Paulo, Shanghai
Teaching Positions Harvard University; University of Hawai'i at Mānoa; University of Miami
Notable Honors AIA, Fellow, 1992; *Interior Design*, Hall of Fame, 1999; National Academy, National Academician, 2002
Websites arquitectonica.com \\ arquitectonica.com/geo

04

01 The Pink House, Miami Shores, FL, 1978. © Robert Lautman
02 Bronx Museum of the Arts, Bronx, NY, 2004. © Norman McGrath
03 Westin Hotel Times Square, New York, NY, 2002. © Norman McGrath
04 The Atlantis Condominium, Miami, FL, 1982

01

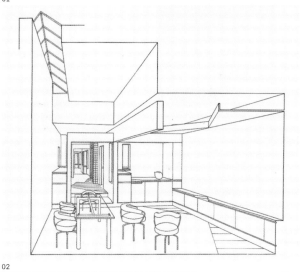

02

03

04

05

Jon Michael Schwarting

The Design Collaborative, New York City (est. 1978)

Education Cornell University, BArch, 1966; Institute for Architecture and Urban Studies, 1967-1968; Cornell University, MAUD, 1968

Practice Update Karahan/ Schwarting Architecture Company, New York City (est. 1984); Beyhan Karahan, Jon Michael Schwarting (principals) \\ Jon Michael Schwarting Architect, New York City (est. 1996) \\ Campani and Schwarting Architects (CASA), Port Jefferson, NY (est. 2000); Frances Campani, Jon Michael Schwarting (principals)
Teaching Positions Columbia University; Cooper Union; New York Institute of Technology; University of Pennsylvania; Yale University
Notable Honors American Academy in Rome, Rome Prize, 1968-1970; *Progressive Architecture*, P/A Award, 1985; AIA Long Island, Archi Award, 2002
Website casarchitects.net

01 **The Design Collaborative** The Italian Trade Center, New York, NY, 1981. © Norman McGrath
02 **Karahan/Schwarting Architecture Company** Hammer Residence, New York, NY, 1988
03 **The Design Collaborative** Homeless Shelter, New York, NY, proposal, 1983
04 **Campani and Schwarting Architects (CASA)** Ludlow and Broome Residences, New York, NY, 2011. © Paul Warchol
05 **Campani and Schwarting Architects (CASA)** Aluminaire House, Queens, NY, in progress

01

02

03

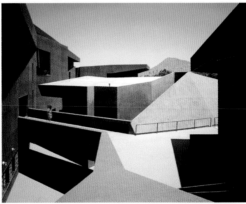

04

05

Franklin D. Israel

Franklin D. Israel Design Associates, Los Angeles (est. 1977)

Education University of Pennsylvania, BArch, 1967; Yale University, 1967-1968; Columbia University, MArch, 1971

Practice Update Israel Callas Chu, Los Angeles (est. 1993); Barbara Callas, Annie Chu, Franklin D. Israel (principals) \\ Israel Callas Chu Shortridge, Los Angeles (1994-1996); Barbara Callas, Annie Chu, Franklin D. Israel, Steven S. Shortridge (principals)
Teaching Positions Harvard University; University of California, Los Angeles
Notable Honors American Academy in Rome, Rome Prize, 1973-1975; *Progressive Architecture*, P/A Award, 1977; National AIA, Honor Award for Interior Architecture, 1994

Franklin D. Israel died in 1996.

01 **Franklin D. Israel Design Associates** Goldberg-Bean House, Hollywood, CA, 1991.
© Tom Bonner
02 **Franklin D. Israel Design Associates** Gillette Studio, New York, NY, 1985.
Photo Tim Hursley
03 **Franklin D. Israel Design Associates** Raznick House, Hollywood Hills, CA, 1991.
© Tom Bonner
04 **Israel Callas Chu Shortridge** Fine Arts Building, University of California, Riverside, 1994.
© Tom Bonner
05 **Franklin D. Israel Design Associates** Propaganda Films, Hollywood, CA, 1988.
© Tom Bonner

David Slovic

01

02

03

04

Friday Architects, Philadelphia (est. 1970)

Education Cornell University, BA philosophy, 1963; University of Pennsylvania, MArch, 1966

Practice Update Friday Architects (David Slovic, 1970-1983) \\ David Slovic Associates, Philadelphia (1983-2000); Ligia Rave, David Slovic (principals) \\ independent artist
Teaching Positions City College of New York; University of the Arts; Temple University; Tulane University; University of Pennsylvania
Notable Honors Harvard University, Loeb Fellowship, 1981
Website davidslovic.com

01 **Friday Architects** Grays Ferry Community Center, Philadelphia, PA, 1979. Photo Jon Naar
02 **David Slovic Associates** Latimer House, Philadelphia, PA, 1993. Photo Catherine Bogart
03 **Friday Architects** Old Pine Community Center, Philadelphia, PA, 1978. Photo Robert Harris
04 **Friday Architects** Temple University Student Center, Philadelphia, PA, 1980. Photo Robert Harris

01

George Ranalli

George Ranalli, Architect, New York City (est. 1977)

Education Pratt Institute, BArch, 1972; Harvard University, MArch, 1974

Teaching Positions City College of New York (dean, Bernard and Anne Spitzer School of Architecture, 1999-present); Cooper Union; Rhode Island School of Design; University of Illinois at Chicago; Yale University
Notable Honors City College of New York, Renaissance Award, 2005; AIA Brooklyn, Award of Excellence, 2010; Institute of Classical Architecture & Art, Stanford White Award, 2012
Website georgeranalli.com

02

03

04

05

01 Saratoga Avenue Community Center, Brooklyn, NY, 2009. Photo Paul Warchol
02 First of August Shop, New York, NY, 1977. Photo George Cserna
03 Callender School Renovation, Newport, RI, 1981. Photo Nick Wheeler © *Architectural Digest*
04 Chatham House, Chatham, NY, 2009. Rendering Arch Partners
05 Indoor Lap Pool, Kent, CT, photomontage, 1994

01

02

03

04

05

Lauretta Vinciarelli

Lauretta Vinciarelli,
New York City

Education Università di Roma,
Dottore di architettura e
pianificazione urbanistica,
1971

Teaching Positions City
University of New York;
Columbia University; Pratt
Institute
Notable Honors National
Gallery of Art, Museum of
Modern Art (New York City),
and San Francisco Museum
of Modern Art, permanent
collections; Brooklyn
Museum, *Women in American
Architecture*, exhibitor, 1977

*Lauretta Vinciarelli died
in 2011.*

01 *Courtyard in Southwest Texas*,
colored pencil on vellum, 1983
02 *Red Room* (series, 3 of 3),
watercolor on paper, 1990
03 *Una Piazza per Scicli:
Undulated Façade, Study No. 3*,
colored pencil on vellum, 1985
04 *Marfa I*, colored pencil on
vellum, 1981
05 *Per Peter*, watercolor on paper,
1993

All images courtesy The Estate of
Lauretta Vinciarelli.

01

02

03

Giuseppe Zambonini

Open Atelier of Design, New York City (est. 1977)

Education Università degli Studi di Firenze, Biennio di architettura, 1965; Istituto Universitario di Architettura, Dottore di architettura, 1971

Teaching Positions Columbia University; Georgia Institute of Technology; New York School of Interior Design (dean, 1973-1977); Open Atelier of Design (founder, president, 1977-1989); Yale University

Notable Honors Roman Theatre, Verona, Best Director, 1971; *Interiors Magazine*, Interiors Award, cowinner with Michael Kalil, 1979

Giuseppe Zambonini died in 1990.

04

01 12 West 29th Street, Apartment #2, New York, NY, 1987. Photo Jim D'Addio
02 Greenwich Village Loft, New York, NY, 1980. Photo George Cserna
03 Tribeca Loft, New York, NY, 1980. Photo George Cserna
04 Open Atelier of Design Studio, New York, NY, 1987. Photo Jim D'Addio

All photos © Zambonini Estate and courtesy Kellen Design Archives at The New School.

Paul Segal

Paul Segal Associates Architects, New York City (est. 1971); Michael Pribyl, Paul Segal (principals)

Education Princeton University, AB architecture, 1966; Princeton University, MFA architecture, 1969

Practice Update Paul Segal FAIA, Architect, New York City (est. 2010)
Teaching Positions Columbia University; Pratt Institute
Notable Honors AIA New York Chapter, Design Award; AIA, Fellow, 1986; AIA New York State, Fellows Award for Mentorship, 2012
Website paulsegalfaia.com

01

02

03

04

01 North Company House, Sagaponack, NY, 1980. Photo Norman McGrath
02 John and Yoko Bag One Art Gallery, New York, NY, 1988. Photo Len Jenschel
03 Rolling Stone Office, New York, NY, 1976. Photo Darwin Davidson
04 Columbia Law School, 9th Floor, New York, NY, 2006. Photo Norman McGrath

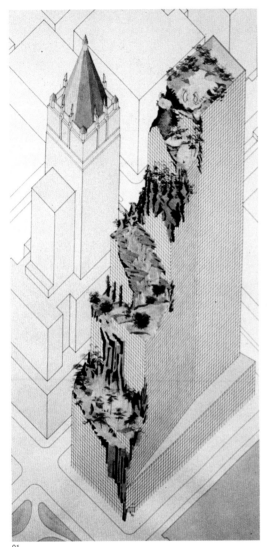

01

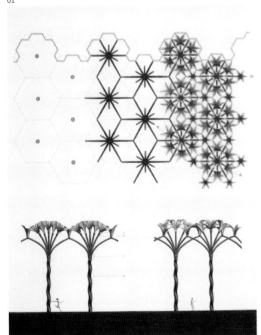

03

02

04

05

Roger C. Ferri

Roger C. Ferri and Associates, New York City (1975-1984)

Education Pratt Institute, BArch, 1972; Art Students League of New York, classical figure painting, 1978-1982

Practice Update Welton Becket Associates, New York City (principal, 1984-1987) \\ Roger Ferri Architect, New York City (1987-1991)
Notable Honor *Architectural Record*, Record Houses, 1982

Roger C. Ferri died in 1991.

01 Madison Square Skyscraper Project, 1978. Courtesy Van Alen Institute
02 Madison Square Skyscraper Project, 1978. Courtesy Van Alen Institute
03 Pedestrian City, Hypostyle Courtyard, ink and pastel on paper, 1979. Roger C. Ferri (1949-1991) © Copyright. Pedestrian City, Hypostyle Courtyard, project, Developed plan and section elevations. 1979. Ink and pastel on paper, 55 3/4 x 43 5/8" (141.6 x 110.8 cm). National Endowment for the Arts Project Funds. The Museum of Modern Art, New York, NY, U.S.A. Photo Credit: Digital Image © The Museum of Modern Art/Licensed by SCALA / Art Resource, NY
04 Odessa Pavilion, Seaside, FL, 1990. Photo Steven Brooke
05 Odessa Pavilion, Seaside, FL, 1990. Photo Steven Brooke

01

Steven Holl

Steven Holl Architects,
New York City (est. 1976)

Education University of
Washington, BArch, 1970;
Architectural Association,
MArch, 1976

Practice Update Steven Holl
(principal); Chris McVoy,
Noah Yaffe (partners);
Beijing, New York City
Teaching Positions Columbia
University; Parsons The New
School for Design; Syracuse
University
Notable Honors Royal
Institute of British
Architects, Jencks Award,
2010; National AIA, Gold
Medal, 2013; Japan Art
Association, Praemium
Imperiale, 2014
Website stevenholl.com

02

03

01 Bridge of Houses, New York, NY,
proposal, 1979
02 Vanke Center (Horizontal
Skyscraper), Shenzhen, China,
2009. Photo Iwan Baan
03 Daeyang Gallery and House,
Seoul, South Korea, 2012. Photo
Iwan Baan
04 Cité de l'Océan et du Surf,
Biarritz, France, 2011. Photo
Iwan Baan

04

01

02

03

04

05

Stuart Cohen, Anders Nereim

Stuart Cohen and Anders Nereim Architects, Chicago (est. 1981)

Education Cohen: Cornell University, BArch, 1965; Cornell University, MArch, 1967 \\ Nereim: University of Chicago, BA psychology, 1976; University of Illinois at Chicago, BArch, 1976

Practice Update Anders Nereim Architects, Chicago (est. 1987) \\ Stuart Cohen & Julie Hacker Architects, Evanston, IL (est. 1988)
Teaching Positions Cohen: University of Illinois \\ Nereim: School of the Art Institute of Chicago; University of Illinois at Chicago
Notable Honors Cohen: Venice Architecture Biennale, exhibitor, 1980; AIA, Fellow, 1985; *Residential Architect*, Hall of Fame Leadership Award, 2007 \\ Nereim: AIA Chicago, Young Architect Award, 1987; State of Illinois, Art-in-Architecture Program, competition winner, 2007; Lower Austrian Department of Arts and Culture, Artist in Residence, 2010
Websites cohen-hacker.com \\ saic.edu/profiles/faculty/andersnereim

01 **Stuart Cohen and Anders Nereim Architects** Carrigan Townhouse, Chicago, IL, 1985. Photo Nick Merrick/Hedrich Blessing
02 **Stuart Cohen & Julie Hacker Architects** Corner House, Glencoe, IL, 2004. Photo Jon Miller/Hedrich Blessing
03 **Stuart Cohen & Julie Hacker Architects** Stucco House, Glencoe, IL, 1991. Photo Jon Miller/Hedrich Blessing
04 **Anders Nereim Architects** Self-Actuating Intelligent Motorized Translucent Insulating Interior Screen, Van Pelt Summer House, Eagle Harbor, MI, 2005
05 **Stuart Cohen and Anders Nereim Architects** Cook's Spoon, Fox Valley, IL, 1979. Photo Barbara Karant/Karant + Associates

01

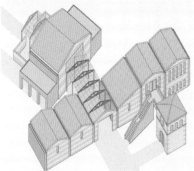

02

03

04

05   06

John J. Casbarian, Danny M. Samuels, Robert H. Timme

Taft Architects, Houston
(est. 1972)

Education Casbarian: Rice
University, BA architecture,
1969, BArch, 1972; California
Institute of the Arts,
MFA, 1971 \\ Samuels: Rice
University, BA architecture,
1969, BArch, 1971 \\
Timme: Rice University, BA
architecture, 1969, BArch,
1971, MArch, 1977

Teaching Positions Casbarian:
Rice University (associate
dean, School of Architecture,
1997-2010; dean, 2010;
director of external
programs, 2011-present);
University of Houston;
University of Illinois;
University of Pennsylvania;
Yale University \\ Samuels:
Rice University (director,
Rice Building Workshop,
School of Architecture,
1995-present); University
of Houston; University
of Illinois; University
of Pennsylvania; Yale
University \\ Timme:
University of Houston (dean,
Gerald D. Hines College of
Architecture, 1992-1995);
University of Illinois;
University of Pennsylvania;
University of Southern
California (dean, School of
Architecture, 1995-2005);
Yale University
Notable Honors *Progressive
Architecture*, P/A Award,
1980; National AIA, Honor
Award, 1983; American Academy
in Rome, Advanced Fellowship,
1985
Website taftarchitects.com

Robert H. Timme died in 2005.

01 Talbot House, Saint Kitts and
   Nevis, 1982
02 Winery in Pomerol, Pomerol,
   France, 2014
03 YWCA Masterson Branch, Houston,
   TX, 1982
04 River Crest Country Club, Fort
   Worth, TX, 1984. © Paul Warchol
05 TvL House, Houston, TX, 2012.
   © Paul Hester
06 Rice Children's Campus,
   Houston, TX, 2009.
   © Chad Loucks

01

02

03

05

04

06

Tod Williams

Tod Williams Associates,
New York City (est. 1976)

Education Princeton
University, AB fine arts,
1965; University of
Cambridge, fine arts, 1966;
Princeton University, MFA
architecture, 1967

Practice Update Tod Williams
Billie Tsien Architects, New
York City (est. 1986)
Teaching Positions Cooper
Union; University of
Michigan; University of Texas
at Austin; University of
Virginia; Yale University
Notable Honors University
of Virginia and Thomas
Jefferson Foundation, Thomas
Jefferson Foundation Medal in
Architecture, 2003; American
Academy of Arts and Letters,
Academician, 2007 (Tsien),
2009 (Williams); National
Endowment for the Arts,
National Medal of Arts, 2013
Website twbta.com

01 **Tod Williams Associates** Tarlo
   House, Sagaponack, NY, 1979.
   © Norman McGrath
02 **Tod Williams Billie Tsien
   Architects** Natatorium,
   Cranbrook Schools, Bloomfield
   Hills, MI, 1999.
   © Michael Moran
03 **Tod Williams Billie Tsien
   Architects** The Barnes
   Foundation, Philadelphia, PA,
   2012. © Michael Moran
04 **Tod Williams Billie Tsien
   Architects** American Folk Art
   Museum, New York, NY, 2001.
   © Michael Moran
05 **Tod Williams Billie Tsien
   Architects** Neurosciences
   Institute, The Scripps Research
   Institute, La Jolla, CA, 1995.
   © Michael Moran
06 **Tod Williams Billie Tsien
   Architects** Phoenix Art Museum,
   Phoenix, AZ, 2006.
   © Bill Timmerman

01

02

03

04   05

Anthony Ames

Anthony Ames Architect,
Atlanta (est. 1976)

Education Georgia Institute
of Technology, BArch, 1968;
Harvard University, MArch,
1978

Teaching Positions Columbia
University; Harvard
University; Princeton
University
Notable Honors American
Academy in Rome, Rome Prize,
1984; AIA Atlanta, Award of
Excellence Silver Medal,
1986; AIA Georgia, Design
Award, 2000
Website anthonyamesarchitect
.com

01 Hulse Residence, Atlanta, GA,
1985
02 Son of Chang, Augusta, GA, 1982
03 Martinelli Residence, Roxbury,
CT, 1988. Photo Wayne N. T.
Fujii
04 Garden Pavilion, Atlanta, GA,
1985. Photo Wayne N. T. Fujii
05 House in Delray Beach, Delray
Beach, FL, 2000. Photo Scott
Frances

01

02

03

Andres Duany, Elizabeth Plater-Zyberk

Duany Plater-Zyberk & Company, Miami (est. 1980)

Education Duany: Princeton University, BArch, 1971; Ecole des Beaux-Arts, architecture, 1972; Yale University, MArch, 1974 \\ Plater-Zyberk: Princeton University, BArch, 1972; Yale University, MArch, 1974

Practice Update Charlotte, NC, Miami, and Washington DC
Teaching Positions Duany: University of Miami \\ Plater-Zyberk: University of Miami (dean, School of Architecture, 1995-2013)
Notable Honors University of Virginia and Thomas Jefferson Foundation, Thomas Jefferson Foundation Medal in Architecture, 1993; National Building Museum, Vincent Scully Prize, 2001; University of Notre Dame, Richard H. Driehaus Prize, 2008
Website dpz.com

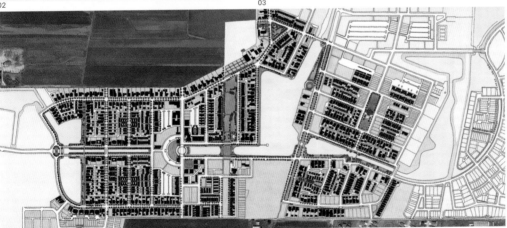

04

05

06

01 Town of Seaside, Walton County, FL, 1980 (photographed 2008). Photo Alex MacLean/Landslides
02 Town of Seaside, Walton County, FL, 1980 (photographed 2005)
03 Aqua, Miami Beach, FL, 2007. Photo Steven Brooke
04 New Town St. Charles Master Plan, St. Charles, MO, 2002
05 Vilanova House, Key Biscayne, FL, 1983. Photo Steven Brooke
06 Village of Rosemary Beach, Walton County, FL, 2007. Photo Richard Sexton

01

02

03

04

Ronald Adrian Krueck

Krueck & Olsen Architects, Chicago (est. 1979); Ronald Adrian Krueck, Keith Olsen (principals)

Education Illinois Institute of Technology, BArch, 1970; School of the Art Institute of Chicago, painting studies, 1976-1979

Practice Update Krueck + Sexton Architects, Chicago (est. 1991); Thomas Jacobs, Ronald Adrian Krueck, Mark P. Sexton (principals)
Teaching Positions Harvard University; Illinois Institute of Technology
Notable Honors *Interior Design*, Hall of Fame, 1993; *Businessweek/Architectural Record* Awards, finalist and winner, 2001; National AIA, Design Award, 2001
Website ksarch.com

01 Krueck + Sexton Architects
Spertus Institute of Jewish Studies, Chicago, IL, 2007. Photo William Zbaren
02 Krueck + Sexton Architects
The Crown Fountain, Chicago, IL, 2004; in collaboration with Juame Plensa. Photo Hedrich Blessing
03 Krueck & Olsen Architects
A Steel & Glass House, Chicago, IL, 1981. Photo Hedrich Blessing
04 Krueck & Olsen Architects
A Painted Apartment, Chicago, IL, 1983. Photo Hedrich Blessing

David T. Jones, I. Guyman Martin

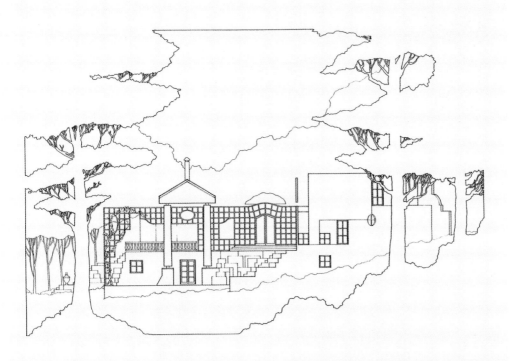

01

02

03

04

05

Martin & Jones Architects, Washington DC (est. 1977)

Education Jones: Princeton University, BA architecture, 1965; Princeton University, MFA architecture, 1967 \\ Martin: Princeton University, BA architecture, 1970; Princeton University, MFA architecture, 1972

Practice Update CORE Architecture and Design, Washington DC (est. 1990); I. Guyman Martin, Dale A. Stewart (principals) \\ David Jones Architects, Washington DC (1990-2014) \\ Jones & Boer Architects, Washington DC (est. 2014); Wouter Boer, David T. Jones (principals) \\ STUDIOS, Los Angeles, Mumbai, New York City, Paris, San Francisco, and Washington DC (est. 1985); I. Guyman Martin (principal, 1999-2007) **Websites** coredc.com \\ jonesboer.com

01 **Martin & Jones Architects** Sigal Residence, Washington DC, 1982
02 **Martin & Jones Architects** Barclay House Condominiums, Washington DC, 1982
03 **STUDIOS** Nysmith School, Herndon, VA, 2005. Photo Maxwell MacKenzie
04 **David Jones Architects** Cottage, Truro, MA, 2012. Photo Peter Vanderwarker
05 **CORE Architecture and Design** 600 Massachusetts Avenue, Washington DC, in progress

Thom Mayne, Michael Rotondi

Morphosis, Los Angeles (est. 1972)

Education Mayne: University of Southern California, BArch, 1968; Harvard University, MArch, 1978 \\ Rotondi: California Polytechnic State University, San Luis Obispo, 1968-1969; California State Polytechnic University, Pomona, 1970-1972; SCI-Arc, BArch, 1974

Practice Update Morphosis, Los Angeles, New York City, Shanghai; Thom Mayne (principal) \\ RoTo, Los Angeles (est. 1992); Michael Rotondi (principal), Clark Stevens (principal, 1992-2005)
Teaching Positions Mayne: Columbia University; Harvard University; SCI-Arc (founding board member); University of California, Los Angeles; Yale University \\ Rotondi: Columbia University; Moscow State University; SCI-Arc; University of Kentucky; University of Texas at Austin
Notable Honors Mayne: The Pritzker Architecture Prize, 2005; Cooper-Hewitt, National Design Museum, National Design Award, 2006; National AIA, Gold Medal, 2013 \\ Rotondi: American Academy of Arts and Letters, Arts and Letters Award in Architecture, 1992; AIA Los Angeles, Gold Medal, 2010; *DesignIntelligence*, 30 Most Admired Educators, 2013
Websites morphosis.com \\ rotoark.com

01 **Morphosis** 72 Market Street, Venice, CA, 1983
02 **Morphosis** Sixth Street Residence, Santa Monica, CA, 1992. Photo Tom Bonner
03 **Morphosis** 41 Cooper Square, Cooper Union, New York, NY, 2009. Photo Iwan Baan
04 **Morphosis** Perot Museum of Nature and Science, Dallas, TX, 2013. Photo Iwan Baan
05 **RoTo** Teiger House, Bernardsville, NJ, 1994
06 **RoTo** Prairie View A&M University Art + Architecture Building, Prairie View, TX, 2006; in collaboration with HKS Dallas

01

02

03

04

05

06

01

02

03

Peter D. Waldman

Peter D. Waldman Architect, Houston (est. 1974)

Education Princeton University, AB architecture, 1965; Princeton University, MFA architecture, 1967

Practice Update Peter D. Waldman, Architect, Houston (1987-1992), Charlottesville, VA (est. 1992) \\ Waldman-Genik Studio, Houston (est. 1985); Christopher Genik, Peter D. Waldman (principals)
Teaching Positions Princeton University; Rice University; University of Cincinnati; University of Virginia
Notable Honors Association of Collegiate Schools of Architecture, Distinguished Professor, 1996; American Academy in Rome, Fellow, 2000; Association of Collegiate Schools of Architecture, Creative Achievement Award, 2012
Website arch.virginia.edu/people/directory/peter-waldman

01 Alley Theatre, Houston, TX, proposal, 1982; design consultant for Morris/Aubry Architects. Photo Paul Hester
02 The Eric Goodwin Memorial Passage, University of Virginia, Charlottesville, 2004; in collaboration with Samuel Beall and Justin Walton. Photo Kirk Martini
03 Contemporary Arts Museum Houston, Houston, TX, competition entry, 1981; in collaboration with Tom Lonnecker, Peter Papademetriou, Douglas Rixey, and Victoria Rixey. Photo Paul Hester
04 Fein Residence (House for a Surveyor, Nomad, and Lunatic), Princeton, NJ, 1993; in collaboration with Philippe Baumann and Scott Bernhard. Photo Jeff Goldberg/Esto, GA Houses/Yukio Futagawa and Wayne N. T. Fujii
05 Wetcher Residence: An Oasis for the Stegosaurus and the Trojan Horse, Galveston, TX, 1992; in collaboration with Philippe Baumann and Martin Feiersinger. Photo GA Houses 44/Yukio Futagawa

04

05

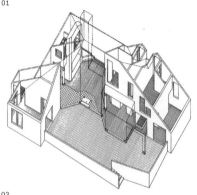

01

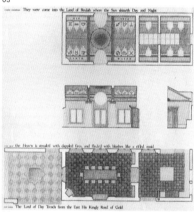

03

02

04

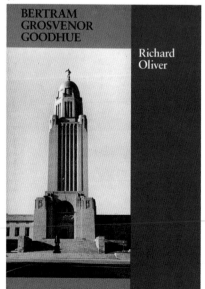

BERTRAM
GROSVENOR
GOODHUE

Richard
Oliver

05

06

Richard Oliver

Richard Oliver Architect,
New York City (est. 1980)
\\ Cooper-Hewitt, National
Design Museum, curator of
contemporary architecture and
design (1977-1980)

Education University of
California, Berkeley,
BArch, 1965; University
of Cambridge, 1965-1966;
University of Pennsylvania,
MArch, 1967

Teaching Positions Columbia
University; University of
California, Los Angeles;
University of Texas at Austin
Notable Honors University
of Cambridge, Fulbright
Scholarship, 1965-1966; AIA
New York Chapter, Arnold W.
Brunner Grant, 1977; AIA New
York State, Distinguished
Architecture Award, 1984

Richard Oliver died in 1985.

01 STEVE, A Soho Shop, New York,
NY, 1978; in collaboration
with Henry Meltzer and Stephen
Solomon. Drawing courtesy Henry
Meltzer
02 Robert Moses Information Desk
and Shop, New York, NY, 1982
03 Novoa House, Fire Island, NY,
1975
04 Project for the Dewey House,
Santa Fe, NM, circa 1980;
in collaboration with Henry
Meltzer
05 *American Monograph Series:
Bertram Grosvenor Goodhue*,
author, 1983
06 STEVE, A Soho Shop, New York,
NY, 1978; in collaboration
with Henry Meltzer and Stephen
Solomon. Photo courtesy Henry
Meltzer

01

02

03

Peter Wilson

Wilson Associates, New York City (est. 1977)

Education University of California, Los Angeles, BA political science, 1963; University of California, Berkeley, MArch, 1969

Practice Update Wilson Associates, Oakland, CA; Anthony Wilson, Peter Wilson (principals)
Teaching Position Pratt Institute
Notable Honors *Architectural Record*, Record Houses, 1982; Ecole des Beaux-Arts, Exposition, 1982; *GA Houses* #10, 1983
Website wilson-associates.net

04

01 Market Hall, Oakland, CA, 1985. Photo Jeff Milstein
02 Esprit Showroom, Chicago, IL, 1979. Photo Norman McGrath
03 Peitzke Fire Island House, Fire Island, NY, 1981. Photo Norman McGrath
04 Peitzke Fire Island House, Fire Island, NY, 1981. Photo Norman McGrath

01

02

03

04

Ronald Bentley, Salvatore LaRosa, Franklin Salasky

Bentley LaRosa Salasky, New York City (est. 1981)

Education Bentley: Bowdoin College, AB sociology, government, and legal studies, 1974; Columbia University, MArch, 1979 \\ LaRosa: Indiana University, business, 1969-1971; Pratt Institute, BFA, 1976; Columbia University, MArch, 1980 \\ Salasky: Rhode Island School of Design, BFA, 1974; Rhode Island School of Design, B.Int.Arch, 1975

Practice Update B Five Studio, New York, Philadelphia (est. 1995); Ronald Bentley, Victoria Borus, Charles Capaldi, Salvatore LaRosa, Franklin Salasky (principals)
Teaching Positions LaRosa: Parsons The New School for Design; Pratt Institute
Notable Honors *Architectural Record*, Record Houses, 1983; *Architectural Record*, Record Interiors, 1991 \\ La Rosa: AIA Interfaith Forum on Religion, Art and Architecture, Religious Art and Architecture Design Awards, Honor, 2012
Website bfivestudio.com

01 **Bentley LaRosa Salasky** Hog Hill House, Central Maine, 1982. Photo Tim Hursley
02 **Bentley LaRosa Salasky** Park Avenue Entry, New York, NY, 1992. Photo Michael Mundy
03 **B Five Studio** Hamptons House, Long Island, NY, 1998. Photo Scott Frances
04 **B Five Studio** Hamptons House, Long Island, NY, 2013. Photo Scott Frances

01

02

03

04

05

Joseph Valerio

Chrysalis Corporation Architects, Milwaukee (est. 1970)

Education University of Michigan, BArch, 1970; University of California, Los Angeles, MArch, 1973

Practice Update Epstein and Sons, Chicago (Valerio: vice president of architecture, 1985-1987) \\ Valerio Associates, Chicago (est. 1987) \\ Valerio Dewalt Train Associates, Chicago and Palo Alto, CA (est. 1994); Mark Dewalt, David Jennerjahn, Randy Mattheis, David Rasche, Louis Ray, Joseph Valerio (principals)
Teaching Position University of Wisconsin-Milwaukee
Notable Honors National AIA, Honor Award, 1993; National AIA, Honor Award for Interiors, 2003; Society for College and University Planning, Excellence in Architecture, 2011
Website buildordie.com

01 **Chrysalis Corporation Architects** Energy House, Los Angeles, CA, 1971
02 **Valerio Dewalt Train Associates** Rita Atkinson Residences, University of California, San Diego, 2010. Photo Nic Lehoux
03 **Chrysalis Corporation Architects** Arbor Park, Phoenix, AZ, 1984. Photo Barbara Karant
04 **Valerio Dewalt Train Associates** Garmin Flagship Store, Chicago, IL, 2007. Photo Steve Hall and Scott McDonald/Hedrich Blessing
05 **Valerio Dewalt Train Associates** Barry Center, Walsh College, Troy, MI, 2008. Photo Steve Hall/Hedrich Blessing

01

02

03

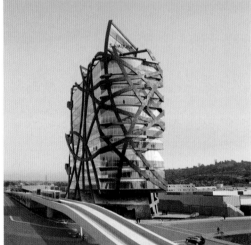

04

05

Eric Owen Moss

Eric Owen Moss Architects, Culver City, CA (est. 1973)

Education University of California, Los Angeles, BA English literature and mathematics, 1965; University of California, Berkeley, MArch, 1968; Harvard University, MArch, 1972

Teaching Positions Columbia University; Harvard University; SCI-Arc (director, 2003-present); University of Applied Arts Vienna; Yale University
Notable Honors American Academy of Arts and Letters, Arts and Letters Award in Architecture, 1999; AIA Los Angeles, Gold Medal, 2001; Royal Institute of British Architects, Jencks Award, 2011
Website ericowenmoss.com

01 Petal House, Los Angeles, CA, 1984. Photo Tim Street-Porter
02 Playa del Rey Apartments, Playa del Rey, CA, 1979
03 Samitaur Tower, Culver City, CA, 2012. Photo Tom Bonner
04 (W)rapper, Los Angeles, CA, in progress
05 Pterodactyl, Culver City, CA, 2014

01

02

03

04

05

Frederick Fisher

Frederick Fisher, Architect, Los Angeles (est. 1980)

Education Miami University, 1967-1968; Great Lakes College Association Arts Program, 1971; Oberlin College, BA art and art history, 1971; University of California, Los Angeles, MArch, 1975

Practice Update Frederick Fisher and Partners Architects; Frederick Fisher (principal); Joseph Coriaty, David Ross (partners)
Teaching Positions Harvard University; Otis College of Art and Design (trustee, 2003-present; chair, Board of Trustees, 2011-present); SCI-Arc; University of California, Los Angeles; University of Southern California (board of councilors, School of Architecture, 2011-present)
Notable Honors Municipal Art Society of New York, Brendan Gill Prize, 1998; American Academy in Rome, Franklin D. Israel Rome Prize, 2007; AIA Los Angeles, Gold Medal, 2013
Website fisherpartners.net

01 Vena-Mondt Loft, Los Angeles, CA, 1983. Photo Tim Hursley
02 The Walter and Leonore Annenberg Center for Information Science and Technology, California Institute of Technology, Pasadena, 2009. Photo Benny Chan
03 P.S. 1 Contemporary Art Center, Terra Gallery, Queens, NY, 2012. Photo Michael Moran/OTTO
04 Caplin Residence, Venice, CA, 1978. Photo Tim Street-Porter
05 Annenberg Community Beach House, Santa Monica, CA, 2009. Photo Grant Mudford

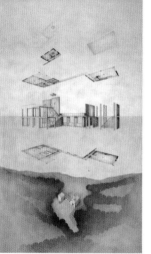

01

02

03

Henry Smith-Miller

Henry Smith-Miller, Architect, New York City (est. 1982)

Education Princeton University, BArch, 1964; Yale University, 1964-1965; University of Pennsylvania, MArch, 1966

Practice Update Smith-Miller + Hawkinson Architects, New York City (est. 1984); Laurie Hawkinson, Henry Smith-Miller (principals) \\ SMH+U, New York City (est. 2013); Laurie Hawkinson, Henry Smith-Miller, Christian Uhl (principals)

Teaching Positions Parsons The New School for Design (interim director, Graduate Architecture Program, 2008); Pratt Institute; SCI-Arc; University of Virginia; Yale University

Notable Honors American Academy of Arts and Letters, Arnold W. Brunner Memorial Prize, 2001; AIA New York Chapter, Medal of Honor, 2002; The National Academy, Canon Prize, 2002

Website smharch.com

04

05

01 Henry Smith-Miller, Architect Institute for Contemporary Art, Philadelphia, PA, 1980
02 Henry Smith-Miller, Architect Vultee House for Three Generations, Stratford, CT, watercolor, 1979. Drawing Yoshiko Sato
03 Smith-Miller + Hawkinson Architects 405-9 West 53rd Street, New York, NY, 2011. Photo Michael Moran/Michael Moran Photography
04 Smith-Miller + Hawkinson Architects U.S. Land Port of Entry at Champlain, Champlain, NY, 2009. Photo Michael Moran/Michael Moran Photography
05 SMH+U Zerega Avenue EMS Station, Bronx, NY, 2014. Photo Michael Moran

Robert James Coote

01

**Robert James Coote,
Architect**, Austin, TX
(1965-1985)

Education Haverford College,
BA political science, 1953;
Harvard University, MArch,
1960

Teaching Position University
of Texas at Austin, 1965-1998
Notable Honor The Fulbright
Program, Rome, 1960

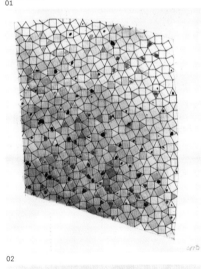

02

03

04

01 Browder Residence, Austin, TX,
   1982
02 *Islamic Veil*, ink and watercolor pencil on paper, 1989
03 *Cairo Women Dancing*, watercolor
   and pencil on paper, 2001
04 James David and Gary Peese
   Residence, Austin, TX, ink and
   colored pencil on paper, 1979

Stanley Saitowitz

Stanley Saitowitz Office, San Francisco (est. 1978)

Education University of the Witwatersrand, BArch, 1974; University of California, Berkeley, MArch, 1977

Practice Update Stanley Saitowitz/Natoma Architects; Neil Kaye, Ulysses Lim, Michael Luke, Stanley Saitowitz (principals)
Teaching Positions Cornell University; Harvard University; Syracuse University; University of California, Berkeley; University of the Witwatersrand
Notable Honors National Monuments Council, South Africa, National Monument, Transvaal House, 1997; AIA New York State, Henry Bacon Award for Memorial Architecture, 1998; Cooper-Hewitt, National Design Museum, National Design Award Finalist, 2006
Website saitowitz.com

01 Uptown Cleveland, Cleveland, OH, 2012. Photo Rien van Rijthoven
02 Yerba Buena Lofts, San Francisco, CA, 2002. Photo Tim Griffith
03 1022 Natoma Street, San Francisco, CA, 1987. Photo Richard Barnes
04 Beth Shalom Synagogue, San Francisco, CA, 2008. Photo Rein van Rijthoven
05 Transvaal House, Transvaal, South Africa, 1978

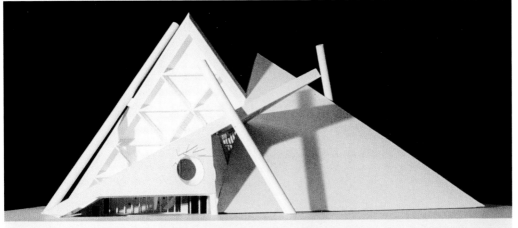

01

02

03

04

Theodore M. Ceraldi

Theodore Ceraldi, Architect,
Nyack, NY (est. 1974)

Education Farmingdale State
College, AAS construction
technology, 1965; Cooper
Union, BArch, 1970

Practice Update TMC
Architects & Planners,
Craftsbury, VT (est. 1984);
Theodore M. Ceraldi, Thomas
Hofmann (principals) \\
independent artist
Teaching Positions State
University of New York
College of Environmental
Science and Forestry;
State University of New
York Rockland Community
College; Syracuse University;
University at Buffalo, The
State University of New York
Notable Honors National AIA,
Honor Award, 1984; AIA New
York Chapter, Excellence in
Design, 1989; *Architectural
Record*, Record Houses, 1989
Website ceraldi.net

01 **TMC Architects & Planners**
St. Elizabeth Ann Seton
Catholic Church, Lexington, KY,
proposal, 1985. Photo Brad Hess
02 **TMC Architects & Planners**
Gainesway Farm, Lexington, KY,
1984; in collaboration with
A.E. Bye Landscape Architects.
Photo A.E. Bye
03 **TMC Architects & Planners**
Hudson River House, Nyack, NY,
1989. Photo Brad Hess
04 **Theodore M. Ceraldi** *First
Light*, painted steel, 2013.
Photo Carol Ceraldi

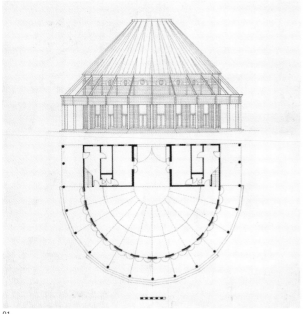

01

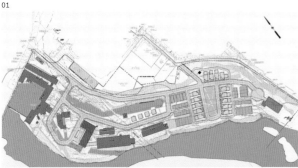

03

02

05

Heather Willson Cass, Patrick Pinnell

Cass & Pinnell Architects, Washington DC (est. 1978)

Education Cass: Mount Holyoke College, BA history of art, 1969; Yale University, MArch, 1972 \\ Pinnell: Yale University, BA English literature, 1971; Yale University, MArch, 1974

Practice Update Cass & Associates Architects, Washington DC (est. 1989) \\ Patrick L. Pinnell, AIA/ Architecture & Town Planning, Haddam, CT (est. 1989)
Teaching Positions Cass: Ohio State University; University of California, Berkeley; University of Illinois at Chicago; University of Maryland; University of Miami \\ Pinnell: Institute for Architecture and Urban Studies; University of Illinois at Chicago; University of Maryland; University of Miami; Yale University
Notable Honors Cass: Henry Luce Foundation, Luce Scholar, 1974; AIA, Fellow, 1997 \\ Pinnell: *Yale University: The Campus Guide*, author, 1999, 2013
Website patrickpinnellaia.com

01 Cass & Pinnell Architects
Seaside Pantheon, Seaside, FL, ink on Mylar, 1986
02 Cass & Associates Architects
Miller-Schiller House, Washington DC, 1995. Photo Robert Lautman
03 Patrick L. Pinnell, AIA/ Architecture & Town Planning
Collinsville Axe Factory, Collinsville, CT, 2010; in collaboration with Fuss & O'Neill
04 Cass & Associates Architects
Gage House, Fort Washington, MD, 1993. Photo Robert Lautman
05 Cass & Pinnell Architects Lynn and Joe Montedonico House, Washington DC, 1984

01

02

03

04

05

Richard Fernau, Laura Hartman

Fernau + Hartman Architects, Berkeley, CA (est. 1981)

Education Fernau: University of California, Santa Cruz, BA philosophy, 1969; University of California, Berkeley, MArch, 1974 \\ Hartman: Smith College, BA art, 1974; University of California, Berkeley, MArch, 1978

Practice Update Berkeley, CA, and Clyde Park, MT
Teaching Positions Fernau: University of California, Berkeley \\ Hartman: University of California, Berkeley; University of Oregon; University of Utah
Notable Honors American Wood Council, Honor Award, 1989; The Architectural League of New York, *Ten Shades of Green*, exhibitor, 2000; National AIA, Housing Award, 2005
Website fernauhartman.com

01 Collective Housing for the Cheesecake Consortium, Philo, CA, 1993. © Richard Barnes
02 Fernau/Cunniff House, Berkeley, CA, 1992. © Christopher Irion
03 Avis Ranch and Granary Retreat, Clyde Park, MT, 2012. © Tim Hursley
04 Berggruen House, Napa County, CA, 1988. © Christopher Irion
05 Performing Arts Center, Eastside College Preparatory School, East Palo Alto, CA, 2006. © Sharon Risedorph

01

03

Darcy Bonner, Scott Himmel

Himmel/Bonner Architects, Chicago (est. 1979)

Education Bonner: Tulane University, BArch, 1976; University of Illinois at Chicago, MArch, 1981 \\ Himmel: Tulane University, MArch, 1977

Practice Update Darcy Bonner and Associates, Chicago (est. 1994); Darcy Bonner, John Forehand (principals) \\ Mattaliano, Chicago (est. 1994); Darcy Bonner, Cassandra Flandermeyer (principals) \\ Scott Himmel, Architect, Chicago (est. 1994)
Teaching Position Bonner: School of the Art Institute of Chicago
Notable Honors National AIA, Distinguished Building Award, 1986; AIA Chicago, Interior Architecture Award, 1993, 1994
Websites darcybonner.com; mattaliano.com \\ scotthimmel.com

01 **Darcy Bonner and Associates** Private Residence, Chicago, IL, 2007. Photo Tom Rossiter
02 **Himmel/Bonner Architects** Playboy Headquarters, New York, NY, 1990. Photo Hedrich Blessing
03 **Scott Himmel, Architect** Urban Townhome, Chicago, IL, 2009. Photo Tony Soluri
04 **Darcy Bonner and Associates** Private Residence, Chicago, IL, 2007. Photo Tom Rossiter
05 **Himmel/Bonner Architects** Atrium at Stanley Korshak, Chicago, IL, 1983. Photo Sadin/Karant Photography

04

05

01

02

03

04

Lawrence W. Speck

Lawrence W. Speck Associates, Austin, TX (est. 1975)

Education Massachusetts Institute of Technology, BS art and design, BS management, 1971; Massachusetts Institute of Technology, MArch, 1972

Practice Update Page Southerland Page (Page), Austin, Dallas, Denver, Houston, and Washington DC (est. 1999); Robert Burke, Arturo Chavez, John Cryer III, Mattia Flabiano III, Matthew Kreisle III, Michael Mace, Thomas McCarthy, Lawrence W. Speck, James Wright (principals)
Teaching Positions Massachusetts Institute of Technology; University of Texas at Austin (dean, School of Architecture, 1992-2001)
Notable Honors Texas Society of Architects, Firm Award, 2009; AIA and Association of Collegiate Schools of Architecture, Topaz Medallion, 2011; *World Architecture News*, Buro Happold Effectiveness Award, 2011
Websites larryspeck.com \\ pagethink.com

01 **Lawrence W. Speck Associates** Wimberley Ranch House, Wimberley, TX, 1988
02 **Lawrence W. Speck Associates** Barbara Jordan Passenger Terminal at ABIA, Austin, TX, 1988. © John Edward Linden Photography
03 **Lawrence W. Speck Associates** Concrete House, Austin, TX, 1996
04 **Page Southerland Page (Page)** Austin Convention Center Expansion, Austin, TX, 2002. Photo Tim Griffith

01

02

03

04

05

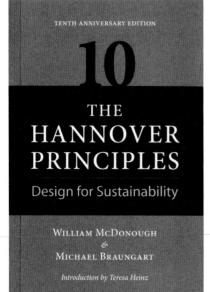

06

07

William McDonough, J. Woodson Rainey Jr.

McDonough, Rainey Architects, New York City (est. 1981)

Education McDonough: Dartmouth College, BA, 1973; Yale University, MArch, 1976 \\ Rainey: University of Utah, BFA architecture, 1963; University of Utah, BArch, 1965

Practice Update William McDonough + Partners, Charlottesville, VA, and San Francisco (est. 1994); David Johnson, William McDonough (principals) \\ Architect J. Woodson Rainey Jr., New York City (est. 2008)

Teaching Positions McDonough: Cornell University; Stanford University; Tongji University; University of Virginia (dean, School of Architecture, 1994-1999; professor, Darden School of Business) \\ Rainey: Columbia University; Pratt Institute; University of Utah

Notable Honors See page 296

Websites 2onyx.com \\ mcdonoughpartners.com

01 **J. Woodson Rainey Jr. at McDonough, Rainey Architects** Vail House, Vail, CO, 1986. Photo Jennifer Ladler

02 **William McDonough at McDonough, Rainey Architects** Environmental Defense Fund, New York, NY, 1985

03 **J. Woodson Rainey Jr.** Steelcase Work Life Center, New York, NY, 1998. Photo Peter Aaron/Esto

04 **William McDonough + Partners** Park 20|20 Master Plan and Architecture, Beukenhorst Zuid, Hoofddorp, the Netherlands, 2011

05 **J. Woodson Rainey Jr.** Polygram Corporate Headquarters, New York, NY, 1994. Photo Nick Wheeler

06 **William McDonough** The Hannover Principles: Design for Sustainability, Expo 2000, Hannover, Germany, 1992. William McDonough + Partners and McDonough Braungart Design Chemistry

07 **William McDonough + Partners** Sustainability Base, NASA Ames Research Center, Moffett Field, CA, 2012. © Cesar Rubio

Rob Wellington Quigley

Rob Wellington Quigley, San Diego (est. 1978)

Education University of Utah, BArch, 1969

Practice Update Palo Alto, CA, and San Diego
Teaching Positions Stanford University; University of California, Berkeley; University of California, San Diego
Notable Honors AIA, Fellow, 1991; AIA California, Firm Award, 1995; AIA California, Maybeck Award, 2005
Website robquigley.com

01 Jaeger Residence, Del Mar, CA, 1985. Photo Brighton Noing
02 Torr Kaelan, San Diego, CA, 2013
03 Asche Residence, Coronado, CA, 1985. Photo Brighton Noing
04 Seven Trees Community Center and Branch Library, San Jose, CA, 2010
05 New Central Library, San Diego, CA, 2013
06 Oxley Residence, La Jolla, CA, 1985. Photo Kim Brun

01

02

03

04

Diane Legge Kemp

Skidmore, Owings & Merrill, Chicago (est. 1936; Legge Kemp, 1977-1989)

Education Wellesley College, science and mathematics, 1967-1969; Stanford University, BA architecture, 1972; Princeton University, MArch, 1975

Practice Update DLK Civic Design, Chicago (est. 1989) \\ RTKL Associates, Chicago, Shanghai (est. 1946); Legge Kemp (2010-present)
Notable Honors AIA Chicago, Honor Award, 1985; National AIA, Honor Award, 1996; AIA Chicago, Honor Award, 2007
Website rtkl.com/people/dkemp

01 Skidmore, Owings & Merrill Boston Globe Printing Plant, Billerica, MA, 1984. Photo SOM © Nick Wheeler
02 Skidmore, Owings & Merrill McCormick Place, Phase 2, Chicago, IL, 1986. Photo SOM © Wayne Cable
03 RTKL Associates Sanya Train Station, Sanya, China, 2012
04 RTKL Associates Qingpu New Town, Shanghai, China, 2012

01

02

Wayne Berg

Wayne Berg, Architect,
New York City (est. 1978)

Education University of
Montana, BArch, 1969

Practice Update Pasanella
+ Klein, Stolzman + Berg
Architects, New York City
(est. 1964); Wayne Berg
(principal, 1986-1999), Arvid
Klein, Giovanni Pasanella,
Henry Stolzman (principals)
Teaching Positions Columbia
University; Montana State
University
Notable Honors AIA New York
Chapter, Distinguished
Architecture Award, 1984;
Architecture, P/A Award, 1999
Website pksb.com

Wayne Berg died in 1999.

03

04

05

01 **Pasanella + Klein, Stolzman +
Berg Architects** Vagliano Loft,
New York, NY, 1990. Photo Paul
Warchol
02 **Pasanella + Klein, Stolzman +
Berg Architects** The Root House,
Ormond Beach, FL, 1995. Photo
Paul Warchol
03 **Wayne Berg, Architect** Gallatin
County Detention Center,
Bozeman, MT, 1983. Photo Paul
Warchol
04 **Pasanella + Klein, Stolzman +
Berg Architects** Education and
Development Center, University
of Virginia's College at Wise,
1998. Photo Esto
05 **Pasanella + Klein, Stolzman +
Berg Architects** Reed Library,
State University of New York
at Fredonia, 1994. Photo Paul
Warchol

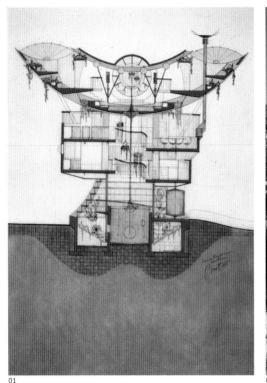

Bart Prince

Bart Prince, Architect,
Albuquerque, NM (est. 1972)

Education Arizona State
University, BArch, 1970

Teaching Positions Miami
University of Ohio;
University of New Mexico;
University of Oklahoma
Notable Honors *Architectural
Record*, Record Houses, 1987,
1991; AIA New Mexico,
Lifetime Achievement Award,
2005
Website bartprince.com

01

03

01 Hanna Residence, Albuquerque,
   NM, pencil on Mylar, 1974
02 Bart Prince Studio/Residence,
   Albuquerque, NM, 1984
03 Joe and Etsuko Price Residence,
   Corona del Mar, CA, 1988. Photo
   Nikolas Koenig
04 Steve Skilken Residence,
   Columbus, OH, 1998
05 Jane Whitmore Residence,
   Glorieta, NM, 2004. Photo
   Robert Reck

04

05

01

02

Peter
de Bretteville

de Bretteville/Polyzoides,
Los Angeles (est. 1982);
Peter de Bretteville,
Stefanos Polyzoides
(principals)

Education Yale University,
BA, 1963; Yale University,
MArch, 1968

Practice Update Peter de
Bretteville, Architect,
Hamden, CT (est. 1990)
Teaching Positions
California Institute of
the Arts; University of
California, Los Angeles;
University of Southern
California; Yale University
Notable Honors Graham
Foundation for Advanced
Studies in the Fine Arts,
grant recipient, 1965;
Progressive Architecture,
Design First Award, 1971
Website pdebarc.com

03

04

05

01 **de Bretteville/Polyzoides**
   Willow Glen Houses,
   Los Angeles, CA, 1984
02 **de Bretteville/Polyzoides**
   Sunset Guest House, Los
   Angeles, CA, 1980; in collabo-
   ration with Charles Calvo
03 **Peter de Bretteville, Architect**
   Gould House, Mountain Lake,
   FL, 1996; in collaboration with
   John Eberhart. Photo Robert
   Benson Photographer
04 **Peter de Bretteville, Architect**
   Amaz Condominiums, Beverly
   Hills, CA, 1993
05 **Peter de Bretteville, Architect**
   Blair House, Chicago, IL, 1994;
   in collaboration with Neal
   Deputy. Photo Robert Benson
   Photographer

02

03

01

04

Mark Simon

Centerbrook Architects and Planners, Centerbrook, CT (est. 1982); Glenn Arbonies, Chad Floyd, William Grover, Robert Harper, Jefferson Riley, Mark Simon (partners)

Education Brandeis University, BA sculpture, 1968; Yale University, MArch, 1972

Practice Update James Childress, Chad Floyd, Jefferson Riley, Mark Simon (principals)
Teaching Positions Carnegie Mellon University; North Carolina State University; Rhode Island School of Design; University of Maryland; Yale University
Notable Honors National AIA, Firm Award, 1998; National AIA, Honor Award for Interiors, 1998; Industrial Designers Society of America, Silver Award, 2008
Website centerbrook.com

05

01 Crowell Studio, Quogue, NY, 1984. © Tim Hursley
02 East Hampton Library, East Hampton, CT, 1986. © Steve Rosenthal
03 Private Library, New York, NY, 1985. © Tim Hursley
04 Lancaster Campus of History, Lancaster, PA, 2013. © Peter Aaron
05 Lakewood House, New England, 2009. © Peter Aaron

01

02

03

04

05

06

Paul Haigh

Haigh Space, New York City (est. 1981)

Education Leeds Polytechnic, BA 3-D design, 1972; Royal College of Art, MDes, 1975

Practice Update
HAIGHArchitects, Greenwich, CT (est. 1986); Barbara H. Haigh, Paul Haigh (principals)
Teaching Positions Arizona State University; New Jersey Institute of Technology; Parsons The New School for Design
Notable Honors National AIA, Honor Award, 1992; National AIA, Honor Award for Interiors, 1995; Royal Institute of British Architects, Finalist Award, 2002
Website haigharchitects.com

01 **Haigh Space** =mc2, New York, NY, 1985. Photo Elliott Kaufman
02 **Haigh Space** Modern Mode Showroom, New York, NY, 1983. Photo Langdon Clay
03 **HAIGHArchitects** Brooks Brothers, New York, NY, 1999. Photo Elliott Kaufman
04 **HAIGHArchitects** VitraUSA, Fogelsville, PA, 1990. Photo Elliott Kaufman
05 **HAIGHArchitects** Hedgehog Vase, 2008; in collaboration with GlassLab. Photo Frank Borkowski
06 **HAIGHArchitects** IFDA Springboard Chair, International Furniture Design Fair Asahikawa, Asahikawa, Japan, competition finalist, 2011. © IFDA2011

01

02

04

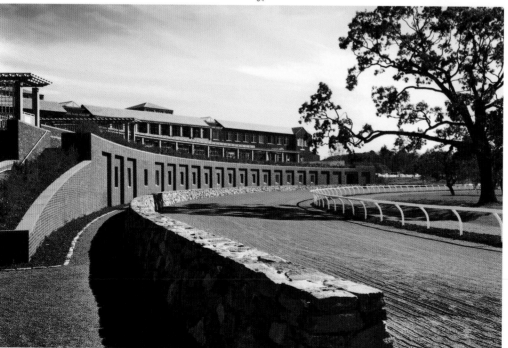

05

Susie Kim,
Fred Koetter

Koetter, Kim & Associates, Boston (est. 1979)

Education Kim: Cornell University, BArch, 1972; Harvard University, MAUD, 1977 \\ Koetter: University of Oregon, BArch, 1962; Cornell University, MArch, 1966

Practice Update Mark deShong, Susie Kim, Fred Koetter (principals)
Teaching Positions Kim: Carnegie Mellon University; Harvard University; Massachusetts Institute of Technology; Rhode Island School of Design \\ Koetter: Cornell University; Harvard University; University of Kentucky; Yale University (dean, School of Architecture, 1993-1998)
Notable Honors National AIA, Honor Award, 1989; AIA and American Library Association, Library Building Awards, Grand Prize, 1993; Congress for the New Urbanism, Charter Award, 2005
Website koetterkim.com

01 Dorothea I. Shaffer Arts Building, Syracuse University, Syracuse, NY, 1990. Photo Jeff Goldberg/Esto
02 United States Courthouse, Rockford, IL, 2012. Photo Mark Ballogg/Ballogg Photography
03 Social Sciences Building, Yale University, New Haven, CT, 2009. Photo Eduard Hueber/Arch Photo
04 Physical Sciences Building, Cornell University, Ithaca, NY, 2010. © Jeff Goldberg/Esto
05 Meditech Headquarters, Canton, MA, 1986. © Steve Rosenthal

01

02

03

04

05

Peter C. Papademetriou

Peter C. Papademetriou, Houston (est. 1979)

Education Princeton University, BA architecture, 1965; Yale University, MArch, 1968

Practice Update New York City
Teaching Positions New Jersey Institute of Technology; Rice University
Notable Honors AIA New York Chapter, Arnold W. Brunner Grant, 1981; Graham Foundation for Advanced Studies in the Fine Arts, grant recipient, 1984; John Simon Guggenheim Memorial Foundation, Fellow, 1986

01 Strauss House, Lake Charles, LA, 1983
02 Davis House, Houston, TX, 1981. Photo Paul Hester
03 Private Residence, New York, NY, 1990-2012. Photo David Brodherson
04 Davis House, Houston, TX, 1981. Photo Paul Hester
05 Strauss House, Lake Charles, LA, 1983. Photo Peter Aaron/ Esto

01

02

03

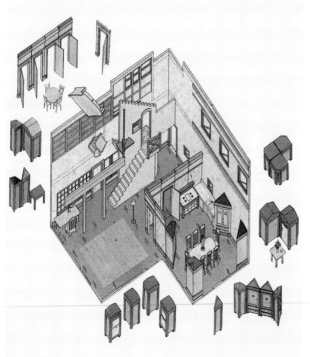

05

06

04

Ted Smith

Smith and Others Architects, San Diego (est. 1974)

Education University of Virginia, BArch, 1971

Practice Update McCormick, Smith and Others, San Diego (est. 1981); Kathleen McCormick, Ted Smith (principals)
Teaching Position Woodbury University (chair, Real Estate and Development, School of Architecture, 2005-present)
Notable Honors Museum of Contemporary Art San Diego La Jolla, *The California Condition*, exhibitor, 1982; Venice Architecture Biennale, exhibitor, 2008; Museum of the City of New York, *Making Room: New Models for Housing New Yorkers*, exhibitor, 2013

01 Transit Node Housing, Long Beach, CA, 2007
02 Richman-Poorman Building, San Diego, CA, mixed-income housing, 1990
03 Essex Lofts, San Diego, CA, 2002; in collaboration with Lloyd Russell
04 The Upas Street Houses, San Diego, CA, pastel ink and cut paper, 1983
05 Groove House, Vista, CA, 1983. Photo Steve Simpson
06 Competing Proforma Battle Rendering, San Diego, CA, pastel and ink, 1996

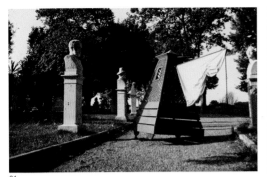

01

02

03

04

05

06

07

Turner Brooks

Turner Brooks, Architect,
Starksboro, VT (est. 1972)

Education Yale University,
BA history and history of
art, 1966; Yale University,
MArch, 1970

Practice Update New Haven, CT
Teaching Position Yale
University
Notable Honors American
Academy in Rome, Rome Prize,
1984; Housing Vermont,
Most Dedicated Housing
Architectural Firm, 1990;
AIA New York Chapter, Design
Award, 2010
Website turnerbrooksarchitect
.com

01 *The Adventures of Il
Risorgimento: Seeking Advice
for Garibaldini*, Rome, Italy,
1984
02 *The Adventures of Il
Risorgimento: Bathing in the
Fountain Acqua Paola*, Rome,
Italy, 1984
03 Peek House, Monkton, VT, 1988.
Photo Scott Frances/Esto
04 House for 2 Geologists,
East Branch, NY, 2013
05 *Coal Hopper*, charcoal on paper,
2009
06 Center for Discovery, Harris,
NY, 2009. Photo Albert Večerka/
Esto
07 Gilder Boathouse, Yale
University, Derby, CT, 2000.
Photo Michael Marsland

1982-1986

1988-1993

1994-1998

1999-2003

2004-2008

2009-2013

"I didn't have a discernible voice." "Voice is shaped by the zeitgeist." "A body of work makes a voice." "Voice is part of body language." "My voice has changed." "Before you perfect voice, the most important thing is to have character." "To have a voice is to be active, engaged, out there." These were among the comments offered at a 2012 roundtable of honorees from the second half-decade of the Emerging Voices program. The diversity of opinion as to the meaning of "voice" is notable for the absence of an assertion by any of those present that he or she was at the time of the award giving "voice" to a specific theoretical construct or ideological position in architecture. Nonetheless, the work for which the honorees were selected gives ample evidence of having been at least marginally and, in some cases, deeply informed by a wide-ranging theoretical discourse—a discourse in which the dying embers of postmodern historicism coexisted with an unrepentant modernism, an ascendant regionalism, and the destabilizing propositions of poststructuralism.

Indeed, traces of these contending strands can be found in the work of honorees throughout this period, thus bearing eloquent witness to two key features of the Emerging Voices program: the catholicity of its embrace, on the one hand, and the consistency of its search for a discernible intention beyond mere instrumentality, on the other. The loyalty of successive juries to these quite distinct but complementary goals was perhaps never more significant than during the program's early years, as exemplified in 1988 by the selection of, among others, W.G. Clark, Ralph Lerner, Merrill Elam and Mack Scogin, and Harry Teague—architects whose work embodied an exceptionally wide range of formal tendencies, from the modern to the postmodern and from the deconstructivist to the regional.

During this period the Emerging Voices program continued to recognize work from all regions of the country, although there is a curious anomaly in 1993, when (due to budgetary constraints) all eight honorees were New Yorkers, albeit with widely divergent bodies of work. Another interesting and provocative anomaly occurred in 1990 with the selection of Ralph Johnson of Perkins+Will, who remains one of only two winners—along with Diane Legge Kemp (EV85), then of Skidmore, Owings & Merrill—in the history of the program to have come from large, well-established practices. It appears to be virtually impossible for individuals working within such practices to establish sufficient evidence of "authorship" unless and until they reach the status of principals, by which time they are no longer deemed to be "emerging voices."

Today, inasmuch as the period 1988 to 1993 is now a generation behind us, the honorees from those years find themselves immersed in their midcareer. Although some of the original Emerging Voices partnerships have dissolved, many have survived and continue to produce significant built work. Almost without exception, the recipients from this period have made substantial contributions to architecture through teaching. Among them, Lerner, Lars Lerup (EV89), Stan Allen (EV93), and Thomas Hanrahan (EV93) have served as deans of architecture schools; and Scogin, William Mac Donald (EV92), Toshiko Mori (EV92), and Joel Sanders (EV93) have served as department chairs or program directors. Walter Chatham (EV90) became active in the League and served as its president from 1994 to 1998, as did Calvin Tsao (EV89), who held the post from 2006 to 2010.

Three winners have died at the height of their powers: Ralph Lerner, a gifted architect who became a leading educator; Samuel Mockbee (EV90), a cofounder of Auburn University's Rural Studio whose vigorous and profoundly influential reaffirmation of architecture as a social art was recognized by a MacArthur Foundation Fellowship in 2000 and, posthumously, by the AIA Gold Medal in 2004; and Frederic Schwartz (EV88), who made significant contributions to architecture and urban design in New York City, including the THINK Design team's second-place entry in the World Trade Center competition.

01

03

05

02

04

07

Ross Anderson, Frederic Schwartz

Anderson/Schwartz Architects, New York City (est. 1984)

Education Anderson: Stanford University, BA human biology, 1973; Harvard University, MArch, 1977 \\ Schwartz: University of California, Berkeley, BArch, 1973; Harvard University, MArch, 1978

Practice Update anderson architects, New York City (est. 1996) \\ Frederic Schwartz Architects, New York City (est. 1996)
Teaching Positions Anderson: Carnegie Mellon University; Columbia University; Parsons The New School for Design; The Thacher School; Yale University \\ Schwartz: Columbia University; Harvard University; Princeton University; University of California, Berkeley; Yale University
Notable Honors See page 296
Websites andersonarch.com \\ schwartzarch.com

Frederic Schwartz died in 2014.

01 **Frederic Schwartz at Anderson/ Schwartz Architects** City Lights, Statue of Liberty 100th Anniversary Design Competition, New York, NY, mixed-media collage, 1983
02 **Ross Anderson at Anderson/ Schwartz Architects** Napa House, Napa, CA, 1989. © Michael Moran
03 **Frederic Schwartz Architects** Staten Island Ferry Terminal and Plaza, New York, NY, 2006. Photo Jody Kivort
04 **Frederic Schwartz Architects** Chennai International Airport, Chennai, India, 2012
05 **anderson architects** Abercrombie & Fitch Headquarters, Columbus, OH, 2001. © Michael Moran
06 **anderson architects** Levi Strauss & Co. Headquarters, San Francisco, CA, 2010. © BAR architects
07 **Frederic Schwartz Architects** Empty Sky, New Jersey 9/11 Memorial, Jersey City, NJ, 2011. © David Sundberg/Esto

01

02

03

04

05

06

Brian A. Murphy

BAM Construction/Design,
Santa Monica, CA (est. 1982)

Education University of
California, Los Angeles, BA,
1970

Teaching Position University
of California, Los Angeles
Website bamcdi.com

01 Dixon Residence, Venice, CA,
   1982. Photo Tim Street-Porter
02 Hopper Residence, Venice, CA,
   1989. Photo Tim Street-Porter
03 Salinger Residence, Pacific
   Palisades, CA, 1992
04 Oyler Residence, Pacific
   Palisades, CA, 1988
05 Ramis Residence, Santa
   Monica, CA, 1984. Photo Tim
   Street-Porter
06 Topanga Residence, Topanga, CA,
   1995. Photo Tim Street-Porter

W.G. Clark

Clark and Menefee,
Charleston, SC (est. 1974);
W.G. Clark, Charles Menefee
III (principals)

Education University of
Virginia, BArch, 1965

Practice Update W.G. Clark
Architects, Charlottesville,
VA (2001-2012)
Teaching Positions Harvard
University; University of
Virginia (chairman, School of
Architecture, 1989)
Notable Honors National AIA,
Design Award, 1987, 1989,
1992
Website wgclark-architects
.com

01

02

03

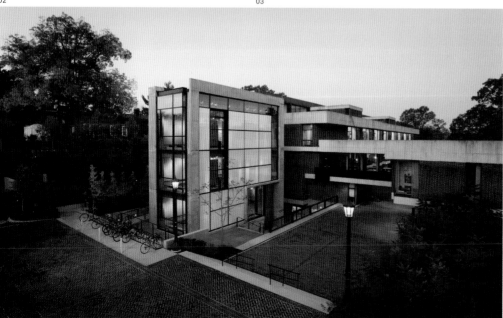

04

01 **Clark and Menefee** Middleton
Inn, Charleston, SC, 1985.
Photo Tom Crane
02 **W.G. Clark Architects**
Cameron Lane House Addition,
Charlottesville, VA, 2007.
Photo Scott Smith
03 **Clark and Menefee** Croffead
House, Charleston, SC, 1989.
Photo Tim Hursley
04 **W.G. Clark Architects** School
of Architecture East Addition,
University of Virginia,
Charlottesville, 2008. Photo
Scott Smith

Harry Teague

01

02

04

05

03

06

Harry Teague Architects,
Aspen, CO (est. 1975)

Education Dartmouth College,
BA art history, 1966; Yale
University, MArch, 1972

Practice Update Basalt, CO
Notable Honors AIA Western
Mountain Region, Firm of the
Year, 1993; AIA Colorado,
Architect of the Year, 2000;
Residential Architect,
Leadership Awards, Hall of
Fame, 2010
Website harryteaguearchitects
.com

01 Benedict Music Tent, Aspen, CO,
2000. Photo Tim Hursley
02 Hotel Lenado, Aspen, CO, 1985.
Photo Tim Hursley
03 Boyles Residence, Aspen, CO,
1982
04 Pond Cluster, Bucksbaum Campus,
Aspen, CO, 2013. Photo Alex
Irwin
05 Basalt River Lofts, Basalt,
CO, 2007
06 Shiny Metal House, Carbondale,
CO, 1984. Photo Tim Hursley

01

02

03

04

05

Peter Forbes

Peter Forbes & Associates, Boston (est. 1980)

Education University of Michigan, BArch, 1966; Yale University, MArch, 1967

Practice Update Peter Forbes, FAIA, Architects, Florence, Italy (est. 2000)
Teaching Positions Catholic University of America; Florence Institute of Design International; Harvard University; Technical University of Nova Scotia; University of Michigan
Notable Honors National AIA, Honor Award, 1986; Wentworth Institute of Technology, Honorary D.Eng, 1991; *New England Home*, New England Design Hall of Fame, 2009

01 Wenglowski House, Deer Isle, ME, 1986. Photo Paul Warchol
02 Wenglowski House, Deer Isle, ME, 1986. Photo Paul Warchol
03 Miller House, Mount Desert, ME, 1991. Photo Paul Warchol
04 Chiesa di San Lorenzo, Florence, Italy, 2012. Photo Alejandro Amador
05 Maniatis House, Seal Harbor, ME, 2004. Photo Wayne N. T. Fujii

01

Ralph Lerner

Ralph Lerner Architect, Princeton, NJ (est. 1984)

Education Cooper Union, BArch, 1974; Harvard University, MArch, 1975

Practice Update Lisa D. Fischetti, Ralph Lerner (principals)
Teaching Positions Harvard University; Polytechnic of Central London; Princeton University (dean, School of Architecture, 1989-2002); University of Hong Kong (dean, Department of Architecture, 2006-2010); University of Virginia
Notable Honors AIA New Jersey, Design Award, 2004; Public Design Commission of the City of New York, Award for Excellence in Design, 2005; Cooper Union, John Q. Hejduk Award for Architecture, 2012

Ralph Lerner died in 2011.

02

03

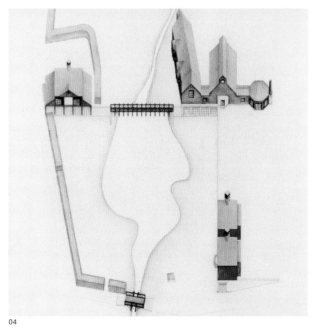

04

01 Indira Gandhi National Centre for the Arts, New Delhi, India, 1987-2003
02 Indira Gandhi National Centre for the Arts, New Delhi, India, 1987-2003
03 Princeton Charter School, Princeton, NJ, 2005
04 Skowhegan School, Skowhegan, ME, competition entry, 1982. Rendering Lisa D. Fischetti

Patricia Sapinsley

01

02

03

04

05

Sapinsley Architecture, New York City (est. 1982)

Education Hampshire College, BA, 1975; Institute for Architecture and Urban Studies, 1976; Harvard University, MArch, 1980

Practice Update Build Efficiently, New York City (est. 2012) \\ Watt Not, New York City (est. 2012)
Teaching Positions Columbia University; Harvard University, Wyss Institute for Biologically Inspired Engineering; Institute for Architecture and Urban Studies; Parsons The New School for Design
Websites build-efficiently .com \\ watt-not.com

01 Water Tank House, pencil on vellum, 1989
02 Penthouse Addition, New York, NY, 1989. © Durston Saylor
03 Townhouse, New York, NY, 1984. © Paul Warchol
04 SPORTS Restaurant, New York, NY, 1985. © Durston Saylor
05 Townhouse, New York, NY, 1984. © Paul Warchol

01

02

03

04

05

Merrill Elam, Mack Scogin

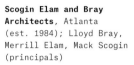

Scogin Elam and Bray Architects, Atlanta (est. 1984); Lloyd Bray, Merrill Elam, Mack Scogin (principals)

Education Elam: Georgia Institute of Technology, BArch, 1971; Georgia State University, MBA, 1982 \\ Scogin: Georgia Institute of Technology, BArch, 1966

Practice Update Mack Scogin Merrill Elam Architects, Atlanta (est. 2000)
Teaching Positions Elam: Harvard University; Ohio State University; University of Texas at Austin; University of Toronto; Yale University \\ Scogin: Harvard University (chair, Department of Architecture, Graduate School of Design, 1990-1995)
Notable Honors Chrysler Group, Chrysler Design Award, 1996; American Academy of Arts and Letters, Arnold W. Brunner Memorial Prize, 2011; Cooper-Hewitt, National Design Museum, National Design Award, 2012
Website msmearch.com

01 **Scogin Elam and Bray Architects** House Chmar, Atlanta, GA, 1989
02 **Mack Scogin Merrill Elam Architects** Lulu Chow Wang Campus Center and Davis Garage, Wellesley College, Wellesley, MA, 2005
03 **Mack Scogin Merrill Elam Architects** The Gates Center for Computer Science and Hillman Center for Future Generation Technologies, Carnegie Mellon University, Pittsburgh, PA, 2009
04 **Mack Scogin Merrill Elam Architects** United States Courthouse, Austin, TX, 2013
05 **Scogin Elam and Bray Architects** Clayton County Headquarters Library, Jonesboro, GA, 1986

All images © Tim Hursley.

01

02

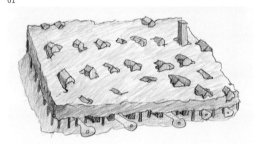

03

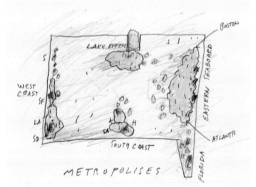

05

06

07

Lars Lerup

Lars Lerup, Berkeley, CA

Education University of California, Berkeley, BA civil engineering, 1960; Harvard University, MAUD, 1970

Practice Update Houston
Teaching Positions Rice University (dean, School of Architecture, 1993-2009); University of California, Berkeley
Notable Honors Menil Collection, *room*, exhibitor, 1999; LTH Lund Royal Institute of Technology, Teknologie Doktor Honoris Causa, 2002; American Academy of Arts and Letters, Arnold W. Brunner Memorial Prize, 2010

01 *House of Flats*, San Francisco Museum of Modern Art, San Francisco, CA, 1985; in collaboration with Richard Rodriguez
02 *House of Flats*, San Francisco Museum of Modern Art, San Francisco, CA, 1985; in collaboration with Richard Rodriguez
03 *One Million Acres and No Zoning*, author and illustrator, Architectural Association Publications, 2011
04 *Maus*, installation for *room*, Menil Collection, Houston, TX, 1999
05 *One Million Acres and No Zoning*, author and illustrator, Architectural Association Publications, 2011
06 *One Million Acres and No Zoning*, author and illustrator, Architectural Association Publications, 2011
07 *Life and Death of Objects*, author and illustrator, in progress

01

02

03

04

05

Mark Mack

Mack Architect(s),
San Francisco (est. 1985)

Education Höhere Technische
Lehranstalt, engineering,
1969; Academy of Fine Arts
Vienna, Mag.Arch, 1974

Practice Update Venice, CA
Teaching Positions University
of California, Berkeley;
University of California,
Los Angeles
Notable Honors *Progressive
Architecture*, P/A Award,
1990; *Architectural Record*,
Record Houses, 1996; ASLA,
Merit Award, 1996
Website markmack.com

01 Knipschild Residence,
Glen Ellen, CA, 1984.
Photo Rainer Blunk
02 Frauengasse Housing, Judenberg,
Austria, 1998. Photo Manfred
Seidl
03 Gerhardt Residence, Sausalito,
CA, 1986. Photo Richard Barnes
04 Nexus Housing, Fukuoka, Japan,
1991. Photo Richard Barnes
05 Zooom Offices, Fuschl am See,
Austria, 2003, 2010. Photo
Ulrich Grill

01

02

03

04

05

Warren Schwartz,
Robert Silver

Schwartz/Silver Architects,
Boston (est. 1980)

Education Schwartz: Cornell University, BArch, 1966; Harvard University, MAUD, 1967 \\ Silver: Queens College, BA physics, 1966; University of Cambridge, MArch, 1969; Harvard University, MArch, 1970

Practice Update Angela Hyatt, Mark Schatz, Warren Schwartz, Robert Silver, Jonathan Traficonte (principals)
Teaching Positions Schwartz: Harvard University; Rhode Island School of Design \\ Silver: Harvard University
Notable Honors National AIA, Honor Award, 1994, 2000, 2008
Website schwartzsilver.com

01 Shaw Center for the Arts, Baton Rouge, LA, 2005. Photo Tim Hursley
02 Tanglewood House I, West Stockbridge, MA, 1988. Photo Chris Little
03 New England Aquarium, West Wing Expansion, Boston, MA, 1999. Photo Matt Wargo
04 Tanglewood House II, West Stockbridge, MA, 2009. Photo Alan Karchmer
05 360 Newbury Street, Boston, MA, 1989; in collaboration with Gehry Partners. Photo David Hewitt

01

02

03

05

04

06

Steven Harris

Steven Harris Architects,
New York City (est. 1985)

Education New College of
Florida, BA philosophy,
1972; Rhode Island School of
Design, BFA, 1975; Princeton
University, MArch, 1977

Teaching Positions Harvard
University; Institute
for Architecture and
Urban Studies; Princeton
University; Yale University
Notable Honors AIA New York
Chapter, Honor Award, 2007;
Interior Design, Hall of
Fame, 2008; *Architectural
Digest*, AD100, 2011
Website
stevenharrisarchitects.com

01 Kaufmann Residence, Atlantic
Beach, FL, 1987. Photo Steven
Brooke
02 Kaufmann Residence, Atlantic
Beach, FL, 1987. Photo Steven
Brooke
03 Surfside Residence, Montauk,
NY, 2010. Photo Scott Frances
04 Jane Street, New York, NY,
2007. Photo Jason Schmidt
05 Kinderhook Retreat, Kinderhook,
NY, 2009; in collaboration with
Margie Ruddick Landscape. Photo
Scott Frances
06 Casa Finisterra, Cabo San
Lucas, Mexico, 2001; in col-
laboration with Margie Ruddick
Landscape. Photo Scott Frances

01

03

02

04

05

06

Zack McKown, Calvin Tsao

TsAO & McKOWN Architects, New York City (est. 1985)

Education McKown: University of South Carolina, BA general studies, 1974; Harvard University, MArch, 1979 \\ Tsao: University of California, Berkeley, BArch, 1974; Harvard University, MArch, 1979

Teaching Positions McKown: Syracuse University \\ Tsao: Cooper Union; Harvard University; Parsons The New School for Design; Syracuse University
Notable Honors International Association of Art Critics, Best Thematic Museum Show in New York, 2008; Cooper-Hewitt, National Design Museum, National Design Award, 2009; National AIA, Housing Award, 2009
Website tsao-mckown.com

01 William Beaver House, New York, NY, 2011. © David Sundberg/Esto
02 Qingdao Agora, Qingdao, China, 2012. Photo Kerun Ip
03 Suntec City, Singapore, 1998. Photo Richard Bryant
04 Sagaponac House, Wainscott, NY, 2007. Photo Michael Moran/OTTO
05 Flip Flop, Dinnerware for Swid Powell, 1992. Photo Jen Fong
06 Greenwich Village Townhouse, New York, NY, 1986. Photo Richard Bryant

01

02

William L. Rawn

William Rawn Associates, Boston (est. 1983)

Education Yale University, BA political science, 1965; Harvard University, JD, 1969; Massachusetts Institute of Technology, MArch, 1979

Practice Update Clifford V. Gayley, Douglas C. Johnston, William L. Rawn (principals)
Teaching Positions Harvard University; Massachusetts Institute of Technology
Notable Honors AIA, Fellow, 1994; National AIA, Honor Award, 1995; Boston Society of Architects, Harleston Parker Medal, 2010
Website rawnarch.com

03

04

05

01 Charlestown Navy Yard, Charlestown, MA, affordable housing, 1988. Photo Steve Rosenthal
02 Alice Paul and David Kemp Residence Halls, Swarthmore College, Swarthmore, PA, 2008. Photo Robert Benson
03 Seiji Ozawa Hall, Tanglewood, Lenox, MA, 1994. Photo Steve Rosenthal
04 '62 Center for Theatre and Dance, Williams College, Williamstown, MA, 2005. Photo Robert Benson
05 Back of the Hill, Boston, MA, affordable housing, 1989. Photo Steve Rosenthal

01

02

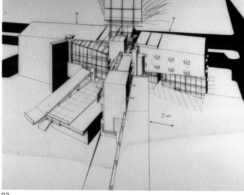

03

04

05

06

Wes Jones,
Peter Pfau

Holt Hinshaw Pfau Jones, San Francisco (est. 1984); Mark Hinshaw, Paul Holt, Wes Jones, Peter Pfau (principals)

Education Jones: United States Military Academy at West Point, 1976-1978; University of California, Berkeley, AB architecture, 1980; Harvard University, MArch, 1984 \\ Pfau: University of California, Berkeley, BA architecture, 1980; Columbia University, MArch, 1984

Practice Update Jones, Partners: Architecture, Los Angeles (est. 1993); Wes Jones (principal) \\ Pfau Architecture, San Francisco (1991-2008); Peter Pfau (principal) \\ Pfau Long Architecture, San Francisco (est. 2008); Dwight Long, Peter Pfau (principals)
Teaching Positions Jones: Columbia University; Harvard University; Princeton University; SCI-Arc; University of California, Berkeley \\ Pfau: California College of the Arts; Columbia University
Notable Honors *See page 296*
Websites jonespartners.com \\ pfaulong.com

01 **Holt Hinshaw Pfau Jones** Harn Museum, Gainesville, FL, competition entry, 1985
02 **Holt Hinshaw Pfau Jones** Harn Museum, Gainesville, FL, competition entry, 1985
03 **Holt Hinshaw Pfau Jones** Harn Museum, Gainesville, FL, competition entry, 1985
04 **Pfau Long Architecture** Strategic Planning and Urban Research Center (SPUR), San Francisco, CA, 2009. Photo Iwan Baan
05 **Pfau Architecture** Swatch 98 Expo, Lisbon, Portugal, 1998. Photo Mark Darley
06 **Pfau Architecture** Wine Country Retreat, St. Helena, CA, 2007. Photo Matthew Millman

01

02

04

03

05

06

John Keenen, Terry Riley

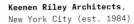

Keenen Riley Architects, New York City (est. 1984)

Education Keenen: Georgetown University, BA history, 1979; Columbia University, MArch, 1983 \\ Riley: University of Notre Dame, BArch, 1978; Columbia University, MS architecture and urban design, 1982

Practice Update K/R, Miami, New York City
Teaching Positions Keenen: Columbia University; Harvard University; Parsons The New School for Design; Rhode Island School of Design \\ Riley: Harvard University; University of Miami
Notable Honors International Association of Art Critics, Best Architecture or Design Show, 2001; AIA Florida, Honor Award for Design, 2011; AIA Florida, Honor Award for Unbuilt Work, 2011
Website krnyc.com

01 Mill House Casino, Lambertville, NJ, 1988. Photo Eduard Hueber
02 Parque de Levante Master Plan, Murcia, Spain, 2011
03 Court House, Miami, FL, 2005. Photo Annie Schlechter
04 Aviary, Dominican Republic, 1998. Photo Andrew Bush
05 Split House, Sagaponack, NY, 2010. Photo Michael Moran
06 Field House, Western New Jersey, 1990. Photo Peter Aaron/Esto

Julie Eizenberg, Hank Koning

Koning Eizenberg Architecture, Santa Monica, CA (est. 1981)

Education Eizenberg: University of Melbourne, BArch, 1978; University of California, Los Angeles, MArch, 1981 \\ Koning: University of Melbourne, BArch, 1977; University of California, Los Angeles, MArch, 1981

Practice Update Nathan Bishop, Julie Eizenberg, Hank Koning, Brian Lane (principals)

Teaching Positions Eizenberg: Harvard University; SCI-Arc; University of California, Los Angeles; University of Melbourne; Yale University \\ Koning: Harvard University; University of California, Los Angeles; University of Hong Kong; Yale University

Notable Honors AIA California, Firm of the Year, 2009; AIA Los Angeles, Gold Medal, 2012; World Architecture Festival, Housing Winner, 2013

Website kearch.com

01

02

03

01 Hollywood Duplex, Los Angeles, CA, 1987. Photo Tim Street-Porter

02 28th Street Housing, Los Angeles, CA, 2012. © Eric Staudenmaier

03 Children's Museum of Pittsburgh, Pittsburgh, PA, 2004. Photo Albert Večerka/Esto

04 Hancock Lofts, West Hollywood, CA, 2009. © Eric Staudenmaier

04

01

02

03

04

05

Coleman Coker, Samuel Mockbee

Mockbee/Coker Architects, Canton, MS, and Memphis, TN (est. 1986)

Education Coker: Memphis College of Art, MFA studio arts, 1984 \\ Mockbee: United States Army, 1966-1969; Auburn University, BArch, 1974

Practice Update Auburn University Rural Studio, Hale County, AL (est. 1993); Samuel Mockbee, D.K. Ruth (founders); Andrew Freear (director) \\ buildingstudio, New Orleans (est. 1999); Coleman Coker (principal)
Teaching Positions Coker: Memphis Center of Architecture (director, 1997-2001); Tulane University; University of Arkansas; University of Texas at Austin \\ Mockbee: Auburn University; Mississippi State University; University of California, Berkeley; University of Virginia; Yale University
Notable Honors Coker: Memphis College of Art, Honorary Doctor of Fine Arts, 2008 \\ Mockbee: MacArthur Foundation, Fellow, 2000; Mississippi Governor's Lifetime Achievement Award for Artistic Excellence, 2001; AIA, Gold Medal, posthumous, 2004 \\ Mockbee/ Coker Architects: *Progressive Architecture*, P/A Award, 1987; National AIA, National Design Award, 1992, 1994
Websites buildingstudio.net \\ ruralstudio.org

Samuel Mockbee died in 2001.

01 Mockbee/Coker Architects Barton House, Madison County, MS, 1991. Photo Tim Hursley
02 Auburn University Rural Studio Butterfly/Harris House, Mason's Bend, AL, 1996. © Tim Hursley
03 buildingstudio Bridges Educational Facility, Memphis, TN, 2005. Photo Tim Hursley
04 buildingstudio Alligator House, New Orleans, LA, 2009. Photo Will Crocker Photography
05 Auburn University Rural Studio Haybale/Bryant House, Mason's Bend, AL, 1995. © Tim Hursley

01

03

05

02

04

06

Ralph Johnson

Perkins+Will, Chicago (est. 1935; Johnson, 1978-present)

Education University of Illinois at Urbana-Champaign, BArch, 1971; Harvard University, MArch, 1973

Practice Update Twenty-four offices worldwide; 122 principals
Teaching Positions Illinois Institute of Technology; University of Illinois; University of Wisconsin
Notable Honors National AIA, Honor Award, 2004, 2005; World Architecture Festival, Category Winner, 2013
Website perkinswill.com

01 Chevron International Trading Company, Nanjing, China, 2007. Photo Wu Pei Jun/Chun Shang Advertising and Arts Co., Ltd.
02 100 North Riverside Plaza (Morton International Building), Chicago, IL, 1990. Photo Nick Merrick © Hedrich Blessing
03 Troy High School, Troy, MI, 1992. Photo Nick Merrick © Hedrich Blessing
04 Universidade Agnostino Neto, Luanda, Angola, 2010. Photo James Steinkamp © Steinkamp Photography
05 Contemporaine, Chicago, IL, 2004. Photo James Steinkamp © Steinkamp Photography
06 Desert View Elementary School, Sunland Park, NM, 1988. © Robert Reck

Walter Chatham

Walter Chatham Architect,
New York City (est. 1986)

Education New York
Studio School, painting;
Philadelphia College of
Art, painting; University
of Maryland, BArch, 1978;
Institute for Architecture
and Urban Studies, post-
graduate studies, 1979

Notable Honors American
Academy in Rome, Fellow,
1989; National AIA,
Distinguished Architecture
Award, 1989, 1995
Website wfchatham.com

01 Delta Pineland Guest House,
   Scott, MS, 1995. Photo Langdon
   Clay
02 Pugin House, Seaside, FL, 1990.
   Photo Michael Moran
03 Ruskin House, Seaside, FL,
   1989. Photo Michael Moran
04 Bowes House, St. Barts, 1998.
   Photo Todd Eberle
05 Stealth House, Aspen, CO, 2010.
   Photo Deborah Cota

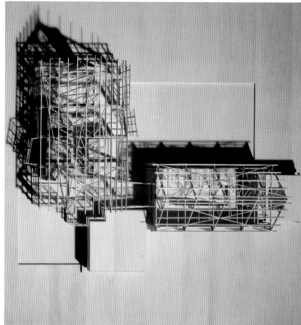

Karen Bausman, Leslie Gill

Bausman Gill Associates, New York City (est. 1982)

Education Bausman: Cooper Union, BArch, 1982 \\ Gill: Cooper Union, BArch, 1982

Practice Update Karen Bausman + Associates, New York City (est. 1995); Karen Bausman, Karla Bausman (principals) \\ Leslie Gill Architect, New York City (est. 1995)
Teaching Positions Bausman: City College of New York; Columbia University; Harvard University; Yale University \\ Gill: Architectural Association; Columbia University; Cooper Union (trustee, 2000-2004); Cornell University; Harvard University
Notable Honors Bausman: American Academy in Rome, Rome Prize, 1994; Cooper Union, President's Citation for Outstanding Contributions to the Field of Architecture, 1994; New York Foundation for the Arts, Fellow, 1996 \\ Bausman Gill Associates: The Architectural League of New York, Young Architects Forum, 1987 \\ Gill: New York Foundation for the Arts, Fellow, 1992; *Architectural Record*, Record Houses, 1998; Cooper Union, John Q. Hejduk Award for Architecture, 2013
Websites karenbausman.com; karenbausmanstudio.com; thewallproject.tumblr.com \\ lesliegill.com

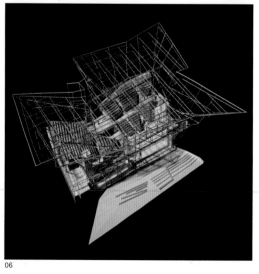

01 **Leslie Gill Architect** Chelsea Townhouse, New York, NY, 2009; with Melissa Neel, associate in charge
02 **Bausman Gill Associates** Conanicut Island House, Jamestown, RI, 1991. Photo Jock Pottle
03 **Bausman Gill Associates** Warner Bros. Records, New York, NY, 1992. Photo Scott Frances/Esto
04 **Leslie Gill Architect** West Side Townhouse, New York, NY, 2003
05 **Karen Bausman + Associates** The Wall Project, New York, NY, 2011. Photo Jock Pottle
06 **Karen Bausman + Associates** Performance Theater, Los Angeles, CA, 1999. Photo Jock Pottle

01

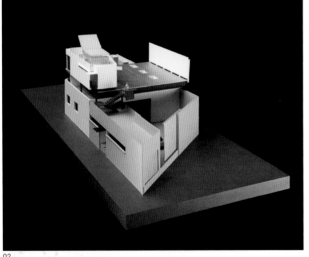

02

03

04

05

Ron Golan,
Eric A. Kahn,
Russell N. Thomsen

Central Office of Architecture, Los Angeles (est. 1986)

Education Golan: California Polytechnic State University, San Luis Obispo, BArch, 1981; SCI-Arc, MArch, 1986 \\ Kahn: California Polytechnic State University, San Luis Obispo, BArch, 1981 \\ Thomsen: California Polytechnic State University, San Luis Obispo, BArch, 1981

Practice Update IDEA, Los Angeles (est. 2009); Eric A. Kahn, Russell N. Thomsen (principals)
Teaching Positions Kahn: Arizona State University; SCI-Arc; University of Arkansas; University of California, Berkeley; University of Michigan \\ Thomsen: Arizona State University; SCI-Arc; University of Michigan
Notable Honors National AIA, Education Honor Award, 2007; *Architect*, Annual Design Review, 2009; Graham Foundation for Advanced Studies in the Fine Arts, grant recipient, 2013
Website ideaoffice.net

Eric A. Kahn died in 2014.

01 **Central Office of Architecture** Brix Restaurant, Los Angeles, CA, 1990. Photo Tom Bonner
02 **Central Office of Architecture** Hawkes Studio, Los Angeles, CA, 1992-1995. Photo William Hawkes
03 **Central Office of Architecture** *Stentorian*, Los Angeles, CA, 2005. Photo Josh White
04 **Central Office of Architecture** Y House, Saitama, Japan, 2008; with associate architect Masao Yahagi & Associates. Photo Kouichi Torimura
05 **IDEA** Room for London, London, England, competition entry, 2010; in collaboration with Jason Payne/Hirsuta

01

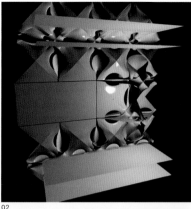

02

03

04

Sulan Kolatan, William Mac Donald

Kolatan/Mac Donald Studio, New York City (est. 1988)

Education Kolatan: Rheinisch-Westfälische Technische Hochschule Aachen Universität, Dipl.Ing.Arch, 1983; Columbia University, MS architecture and building design, 1984 \\ Mac Donald: Architectural Association, 1978; Syracuse University, BArch, 1979; Columbia University, MS architecture and urban design, 1982

Practice Update KOL/MAC
Teaching Positions Kolatan: Columbia University; Cornell University; Pratt Institute; SCI-Arc; University of Pennsylvania \\ Mac Donald: Columbia University (director, MS Architecture Post-Professional Program, Graduate School of Architecture, Planning and Preservation, 1985-1988; codirector, MArch Core Program, 2002-2005); Ohio State University; Pratt Institute (chair, graduate architecture, 2005-present); University of Pennsylvania; University of Virginia (acting chair, undergraduate program, School of Architecture, 1985)
Notable Honors *40 Under 40: A Guide to New Young Talent with Seductive Ideas for Living Today*, 1995; Venice Architecture Biennale, exhibitor, 2004; HRH The Crown Prince of Denmark, INDEX Award, 2008
Website kolmacllc.com

01 Resi Rise, New York, NY, 1999
02 INVERSABRANE, INDEX, Copenhagen, Denmark, competition finalist, 2008
03 OK Apartment, New York, NY, 1997. Photo Michael Moran
04 Moss Loft, New York, NY, 1992. Photo Michael Moran

01

02

03

04

05

Ted Flato,
David Lake

Lake|Flato Architects,
San Antonio, TX (est. 1984)

Education Flato: Stanford
University, BA architecture,
1977 \\ Lake: University
of Texas at Austin, BS
architecture, 1976

Practice Update Ted Flato,
Karla Greer, Robert Harris,
Andrew Herdeg, David Lake,
Kim Monroe, Matt Morris, Greg
Papay (principals)
Notable Honors National AIA,
Firm Award, 2004; Texas
Cultural Trust, Texas Medal
of Arts, 2009; the LOCUS
Fund, Global Award for
Sustainable Architecture,
2013
Website lakeflato.com

01 School of Nursing, University
of Texas Health Science Center,
Houston, TX, 2004. Photo Hester
+ Hardaway
02 Alamo Cement House, Kyle, TX,
1990. Photo Hester + Hardaway
03 World Birding Center, Mission,
TX, 2004. Photo Hester +
Hardaway
04 Polytechnic Academic Campus,
Arizona State University,
Tempe, AZ, 2008. Photo Bill
Timmerman
05 Lasater Ranch, Hebbronville,
TX, 1986

Adrian Luchini

02

01

03

04

05

Schwetye Luchini Maritz Architects, St. Louis (est. 1988); Adrian Luchini, Thomas Schwetye (principals); Alice Maritz (investor)

Education Universidad Católica de Córdoba, Dipl. Arch., 1981; University of Cincinnati, MS architecture, 1983; Harvard University, MArch, 1985

Practice Update LuchiniAD, St. Louis (est. 2001)
Teaching Position Washington University in St. Louis (director, graduate architecture program, Sam Fox School of Design & Visual Arts, 2003-2008)
Notable Honors *Progressive Architecture*, P/A Award, 1992; Buenos Aires Architecture Biennale, exhibitor, 2010; AIA St. Louis, Honor Award, 2011
Website luchiniad.com

01 Denison Luchini Architects Piku Residence, Bloomfield Hills, MI, 1999. Photo Balthazar Korab
02 LuchiniAD William S. Clay Education Center, Harris-Stowe State University, St. Louis, MO, 2009. Photo Sam Fentress, Photography
03 LuchiniAD Montessori Children's School, St. Louis, MO, 2013. Photo Patrick Brown
04 LuchiniAD Headmaster's Residence, The Principia, St. Louis, MO, 2000. Photo Sam Fentress
05 Schwetye Luchini Maritz Architects Maritz Residence, St. Louis, MO, 1988. Photo Sam Fentress, Photography

Toshiko Mori

Toshiko Mori Architect,
New York City (est. 1981)

Education Cooper Union,
BArch, 1976; Harvard
University, MArch, 1996

Teaching Positions Cooper
Union; Harvard University
(chair, Department of
Architecture, Graduate School
of Design, 2002-2008); Yale
University
Notable Honors Cooper Union,
John Q. Hejduk Award for
Architecture, 2003; AIA
New York Chapter, Medal
of Honor, 2005; American
Academy of Arts and Letters,
Arts and Letters Award in
Architecture, 2005
Website tmarch.com

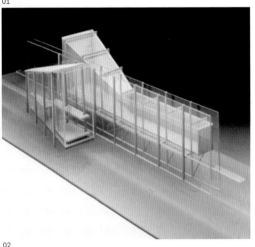

01 SHIRT Store, Comme des Garçons,
New York, NY, 1988. © Paul
Warchol
02 Glass House, prototype, 1989
03 House on Martha's Vineyard,
Chilmark, MA, 2011. © Iwan Baan
04 Syracuse Center of Excellence
in Environmental and Energy
Systems Headquarters Building,
Syracuse, NY, 2010. © Iwan Baan
05 House in Columbia County, NY,
2009. © Iwan Baan

01

02

03

04

05

06

David Piscuskas, Juergen Riehm

1100 Architect, New York City (est. 1983)

Education Piscuskas: Brown University, BA art, 1979; University of California, Los Angeles, MArch, 1982 \\ Riehm: Fachhochschule Rheinland-Pfalz, Diploma architecture, 1977; Staatliche Hochschule für Bildende Künste-Städelschule, MArch, 1982

Practice Update Frankfurt, New York City
Teaching Position Parsons The New School for Design
Notable Honors AIA New York Chapter, Design Award, 2001; AIA and American Library Association, Building Award, 2009; Municipal Art Society of New York, MASterworks Award, 2012
Website 1100architect.com

01 Greenwich Village Duplex, New York, NY, 1989. © Michael Moran/OTTO
02 Children's Library Discovery Center, Queens Central Library, Queens, NY, 2011. © Michael Moran/OTTO
03 Long Island House, Long Island, NY, 2012. © Nikolas Koenig
04 A/D Gallery, New York, NY, 1989. © Michael Moran/OTTO
05 Brooklyn Detention Center, Brooklyn, NY, 2010; joint venture with RicciGreene Associates. Rendering © Vize
06 Lichtenstein Studio and Residence, New York, NY, 1989. © Michael Moran/OTTO

01

02

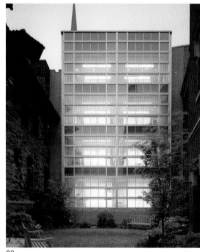

03

04

05

Peggy Deamer, Scott Phillips

Deamer + Phillips, Architecture, New York City (est. 1986)

Education Deamer: Oberlin College, BA philosophy, 1972; Cooper Union, BArch, 1977; Princeton University, PhD architecture history, criticism, and theory, 1988 \\ Phillips: Trinity College, BA history, 1971; University of Washington, MArch, 1977

Practice Update Deamer Studio, Brooklyn (est. 2004) \\ Phillips Gelfand Architects, New York City (est. 2004); Lisa Gelfand, Scott Phillips (principals) \\ Gelfand Partners Architects, San Francisco; Chris Duncan, James Fagler, Lisa Gelfand, Tobin Kendrick, Scott Phillips (2009-2012), Lawrence Schadt (principals) \\ Scott N. Phillips Architect, New Canaan, CT (est. 2013)
Teaching Positions Deamer: Barnard College; Parsons The New School for Design; Princeton University; University of Kentucky; Yale University
Notable Honors Deamer: Yale University, A. Whitney Griswold Faculty Research Grant, 2005 \\ Deamer + Phillips, Architecture: AIA New York Chapter, Interior Architecture Award, 1991; AIA Tampa Bay, Honor Award for Architecture, 2003
Websites peggydeamer.com \\ scottnphillipsarchitect.com

01 **Deamer + Phillips, Architecture** Sagaponack House 1, Sagaponack, NY, 1992. Photo Lizzie Himmel
02 **Deamer + Phillips, Architecture** Hamilton House, South Hamilton, MA, 1990. Photo Anton Grassl/ Esto
03 **Deamer + Phillips, Architecture** Hillhouse Connection, Yale University, New Haven, CT, 2002. Photo Chuck Choi
04 **Deamer + Phillips, Architecture** Montauk House, Montauk, NY, 1998. Photo Jonathan Wallen
05 **Phillips Gelfand Architects** Windermere Island Club, Eleuthera, the Bahamas, 2008

01

03

Deborah Berke

Deborah Berke Architect,
New York City (est. 1982)

Education Rhode Island School
of Design, BFA, 1975; Rhode
Island School of Design,
BArch, 1977; City University
of New York, MA urban
planning in urban design,
1984

Practice Update Deborah Berke
Partners; Deborah Berke,
Maitland Jones, Marc Leff
(partners); Catherine Bird,
Stephen Brockman, Caroline
Wharton (principals)
Teaching Positions Institute
for Architecture and Urban
Studies; Rhode Island School
of Design; University of
California, Berkeley;
University of Maryland; Yale
University
Notable Honors Rhode Island
School of Design, Honorary
Doctorate of Fine Arts, 2005;
AIA, Fellow, 2008; University
of California, Berkeley,
Berkeley-Rupp Architecture
Professorship and Prize, 2013
Website dberke.com

01 Halley Studio, North Hillsdale,
   NY, 1992. Photo Catherine
   Bogert
02 Modica Market, Seaside, FL,
   1991. Photo Steven Brooke
03 Irwin Union Bank, Creekville
   Branch, Columbus, IN, 2006.
   Photo Catherine Tighe
04 Marianne Boesky Gallery,
   New York, NY, 2006. Photo
   Eduard Hueber
05 48 Bond Street, New York, NY,
   2008. Photo Catherine Tighe
06 21c Museum Hotel Louisville,
   Louisville, KY, 2006. Photo
   Catherine Tighe

02

04

05

06

01

02

03

04

05

Thomas Hanrahan, Victoria Meyers

hanrahan Meyers architects, New York City (est. 1987)

Education Hanrahan: University of Illinois, BArch, 1977; Harvard University, MArch, 1982 \\ Meyers: Lafayette College, AB art history and civil engineering, 1975; Harvard University, MArch, 1982; University of Cambridge, design, 1982

Teaching Positions Hanrahan: Columbia University; Harvard University; Pratt Institute (dean, School of Architecture, 1996-present); Yale University \\ Meyers: City University of New York; Columbia University; University of Cincinnati
Notable Honors Massachusetts Institute of Technology, Eugene McDermott Award in the Arts, 1993; Urban Land Institute, Heritage Award, 2010; AIA New York Chapter, Honor Award, 2013
Websites hanrahanmeyers.com \\ victoriameyers.com

01 Infinity Chapel, New York, NY, 2010. Photo Michael Moran/OTTO
02 Canal Street Waterline, New York, NY, 1993
03 Canal Street Waterline, New York, NY, hand drawing, 1993
04 Won Dharma Center, Claverack, NY, 2011. Photo Michael Moran/OTTO
05 Digital Water i-Pavilion, New York, NY, 2013. Photo Wilk Marketing

01

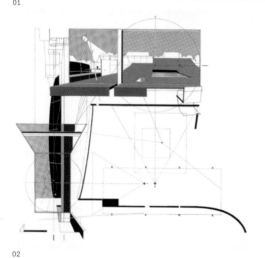

02

03

04

05

06

Joel Sanders

Joel Sanders Architect,
New York City (est. 1989)

Education Columbia
University, BA, 1978;
Columbia University, MArch,
1981

Teaching Positions Parsons
The New School for Design
(director, Graduate Program
in Architecture, 1996-2001);
Princeton University; Yale
University
Notable Honors AIA New York
Chapter, Honor Award, 2009;
AIA New York State, Award of
Excellence, 2010; *Interior
Design*, Best of the Year,
2012
Website joelsandersarchitect
.com

01 Victoria Munroe Gallery,
   New York, NY, 1992. Photo
   Chuck Choi
02 Kyle Residence, Houston, TX,
   1993
03 House on Mt. Merino, Hudson,
   NY, 2008. Photo Peter Aaron/
   OTTO
04 Julian Street Library,
   Princeton University,
   Princeton, NJ, 2011. Photo
   Peter Aaron/OTTO
05 Seongbukdong Residences, Seoul,
   South Korea, 2009. Photo Chai
   Soo Ok
06 Broadway Penthouse, New York,
   NY, 2008. Photo Peter Aaron/
   OTTO

Laszlo Kiss, Todd Zwigard

01

Kiss + Zwigard, New York City (est. 1988)

Education Kiss: James Caldwell High School, West Caldwell, NJ, 1975 \\ Zwigard: Cornell University, BArch, 1983

Practice Update StudioKiss, ASAP-house, Bernardsville, NJ, New York City, and Sag Harbor, NY (est. 2008); Laszlo Kiss (principal) \\ Todd Zwigard Architects, New York City, and Skaneateles, NY (est. 2008)

Teaching Positions Kiss: Columbia University; New York Institute of Technology; Ohio State University; Parsons The New School for Design; Texas A&M University \\ Zwigard: Columbia University; Parsons The New School for Design

Notable Honors *Progressive Architecture*, P/A Award, 1983; *Interiors Magazine*, "30 under 30," 1989; Federal Design Achievement Award, 1995

Websites studiokiss.com; asaphouse.com \\ tzaia.com

02

03

04

05

06

01 **Kiss + Zwigard** Knee Residence, North Caldwell, NJ, 1986; in collaboration with Simon Ungers
02 **Kiss + Zwigard** Private Residence, Remsenburg, NY, 2005
03 **Todd Zwigard Architects** Weimer Winery, Dundee, NY, 2009. Photo Jim Westphalen
04 **Kiss + Zwigard** Jaded Jewelry Store, New York, NY, 1993
05 **ASAP-house** Prefabricated House, Sag Harbor, NY, 2008
06 **Kiss + Zwigard** Hobbs Residence, Lansing, NY, 1983; in collaboration with Simon Ungers. Photo Tim Hursley

01

02

03

04

Thomas Leeser

Leeser Architecture, Brooklyn (est. 1989)

Education Hochschule für Industriedesign und visuelle Kommunikation, industrial design and visual communication, 1975; Technische Universität Darmstadt, BArch, 1979; Cooper Union, thesis-year foreign exchange program, 1981; Technische Universität Darmstadt, MArch, 1985

Teaching Positions Columbia University; Cooper Union; Harvard University; Pratt Institute; Princeton University
Notable Honors New York Foundation for the Arts, Fellowship, 1996; the City of New York, Public Design Commission, Design Award, 2011; Red Dot, Design Award, 2013
Website leeser.com

01 Gieb-Khoso Loft, New York, NY, 1992
02 Eyebeam Atelier Museum of Art and Technology, New York, NY, 2001
03 Twin House, Liberty, NY, 1992
04 World Mammoth and Permafrost Museum, Yakutsk, Russia, 2007
05 Museum of the Moving Image, Queens, NY, 2011. Photo Peter Aaron/Esto, courtesy Museum of the Moving Image

Stan Allen

Stan Allen Architect,
New York City (est. 1991)

Education Brown University,
BA architectural history,
1978; Cooper Union, BArch,
1981; Princeton University,
MArch, 1987

Practice Update SAA/Stan
Allen Architect
Teaching Positions Columbia
University (director,
Advanced Architectural Design
Program, Graduate School of
Architecture, Planning and
Preservation, 1990-2002);
Princeton University (dean,
School of Architecture,
2002-2012)
Notable Honors Cooper Union,
President's Citation for
Outstanding Contributions to
the Field of Architecture,
2003; American Academy of
Arts and Letters, Arts
and Letters Award in
Architecture, 2009; Cooper
Union, John Q. Hejduk Award
for Architecture, 2009
Website stanallenarchitect
.com

01

03

04

05

01 Salim Publishing House, Paju
Book City, South Korea, 2008.
Photo Iroje
02 Busan Opera House, Busan, South
Korea, competition entry, 2011
03 Amy Lipton Gallery, New York,
NY, 1990. Photo courtesy Amy
Lipton Gallery
04 Chosen Children's Village
Chapel, Tagaytay, Philippines,
2008. Photo Marvin Dungao
05 Fenster Gallery Installation,
Frankfurt, Germany, 1992. Photo
courtesy Fenster Gallery

1982-1986

1988-1993

1994-1998

1999-2003

2004-2008

2009-2013

It was time to get clean. It was time to get dirty. On the side of cleanliness, Enrique Norten (EV94), Neil Denari (EV95), Gisue Hariri and Mojgan Hariri (EV95), Jesse Reiser and Nanako Umemoto (EV96), Karen Fairbanks and Scott Marble (EV98), Michael Maltzan (EV98), and others—some among them deploying the then-brand-new computational tools that enabled iterative versioning of complex folds and compound curves—unrolled smooth and swoopy terrains of synthetic surfaces and pliant continuities. On the side of dirt, Sheila Kennedy and Frano Violich (EV94), Brigitte Shim and Howard Sutcliffe (EV95), Kathryn Dean and Charles Wolf (EV97), Michael Manfredi and Marion Weiss (EV97), and others combined their interests in craft-driven material practices, in trees and rocks, in hyperarticulate tectonics, and in historical industrial and vernacular typologies—pounding together landscapes of floating planes, revealed edges, and the blackest, steeliest, beamiest black-steel beams, ever.

Time brings convergences. The evermore-thoughtful Weiss and Manfredi have heroically pushed their work to its seemingly opposed extremes, abandoning merely naturalistic craftiness for landscapes of actual nature, sheathed in and balanced by structures of sleek technology. Marble and Fairbanks—alongside peers like Brad Cloepfil (EV96) and Tom Buresh and Danelle Guthrie (EV97)—have meticulously applied computational thinking to the repetitions and inspirations of fabrication (digital and material culture compressed inside a thousand laminations of quivering plywood). And that recondite streak of Stirlingesque Palladianism in those mid-1990s high-tech steel structures? That brooding Pichleresque technoclassicism in those moody cast-concrete beach houses and memorials? That faint residue of Krier? Doesn't it feel like their ecstatic revival is just a heartbeat away, at the fingertips of one's keenest student?

From across a wide watershed of technology and terror, what's true of all recent pasts is particularly true of our own: we see an encounter between real and seeming, between virtually clean and actually dirty. Our recent past is full of unsettling possibilities, where the accelerated certainties compelled by contemporary social media have not yet been directed back to meet the received truths and willfully canonical narratives of consensus history. Somewhere between the computationally linked advent of the World Wide Web and the faux apocalypse of Y2K, between yesterday's Cold War and tomorrow's Drone War, the mid-1990s astonish in both their old newness and new oldness.

James Cutler (EV94), who has long practiced in a venerable Pacific Northwest vernacular modernism, took the last studio taught by Louis Kahn at the University of Pennsylvania in 1974. I think of the luminous shadow of Kahn—that most hokey and yet most irrefutable of architects—casting itself past the follies and furies of postmodernism and deconstructivism, past all wan contingencies of progress, personal and technological, into tomorrow. I think of the vital work of the late Mojdeh Baratloo, a passionate planner and powerful teacher who, along with her design partner, Clifton Balch, was an Emerging Voice in 1996. I think of their *Angst: Cartography*, which superimposed choreography onto geography, diagramming *Invisible Cities* onto old Sanborn maps of an imperial New York and an unremediated Gowanus Canal, "running at night," as that project quoted Italo Calvino, "through an unknown city." I think of Baratloo layering all that cleanliness onto itself until it became dirty enough to see.

01

02

03

04

05

Marc Angélil, Sarah Graham

Angélil/Graham Architecture, Los Angeles, Zurich (est. 1982)

Education Angélil: ETH Zürich, MArch, 1979; ETH Zürich, PhD technical sciences, 1987 \\ Graham: Stanford University, BA art and art history, 1974; Harvard University, MArch, 1982

Practice Update agps architecture, Los Angeles, Zurich; Marc Angélil, Sarah Graham, Manuel Scholl (principals)

Teaching Positions Angélil: ETH Zürich (dean, Department of Architecture, 2009-2012); Harvard University; SCI-Arc; University of Southern California \\ Graham: Nanjing University; University of California, Berkeley; University of Southern California

Notable Honors American Institute of Steel Construction, Presidential Award of Excellence, 2007; AIA California, Honor Award, 2008; Swiss Society of Engineers and Architects, Umsicht - Regards - Sguardi Award for Sustainable Design, 2011

Website agps.ch

01 Hollywood House, Los Angeles, CA, 1993. Photo Julius Shulman
02 Portland Aerial Tram, Portland, OR, 2007. Photo Eric Staudenmaier
03 Lunch Shelters, Los Angeles Unified School District, Los Angeles, CA, 1992. Photo Eduard Hueber
04 Topanga House, Topanga, CA, 1995. Photo Michael Arden
05 SteelHouse, Los Angeles, CA, 2010. Photo Eric Staudenmaier

01

02

03

04

05

06

Carlos Jimenez

Carlos Jimenez Studio, Houston (est. 1983)

Education University of Houston, BArch, 1981

Teaching Positions Harvard University; Rice University; Tulane University; University of California, Berkeley; University of Texas at Austin
Notable Honors Universidad del Diseño, Doctor Honoris Causa, 1998; Rice University, Charles W. Duncan Jr. Award for Outstanding Faculty, 2006; Design Futures Council, Design Intelligence Award, 2013
Website carlosjimenezstudio .com

01 Carlos Jimenez House, Houston, TX, 1983
02 Houston Fine Art Press, Houston, TX, 1987
03 Carlos Jimenez Studio, Houston, TX, 1986
04 Tyler School of Art, Temple University, Philadelphia, PA, 2009
05 Whatley Library, Austin, TX, 2001
06 Data Center, Rice University, Houston, TX, 2007

All images Paul Hester/Hester + Hardaway.

01

02

04

03

05

Gary Cunningham

Cunningham Architects, Dallas
(est. 1981)

Education University of Texas
at Austin, BArch, 1976

Notable Honors AIA, Fellow,
1992; Texas Society of
Architects/AIA, Design Award,
2012; AIA Dallas, Design
Award, 2013
Website cunninghamarchitects
.com

01 Addison Conference and Theatre
   Centre, Addison, TX, 1992.
   Photo James F. Wilson
02 Casa Caja, Dallas, TX, 2002.
   Photo James F. Wilson
03 Texas Utilities Customer
   Service Center, Waco, TX, 1999.
   Photo James F. Wilson
04 Wimberley Residence, Wimberley,
   TX, 2010. Photo Tre Dunham
05 Cistercian Abbey Church,
   Irving, TX, 1992. Photo James
   F. Wilson

01

02
03

04

Nicholas Goldsmith

FTL Happold, New York City (est. 1991); Todd Dalland, Nicholas Goldsmith (principals)

Education Cornell University, BArch, 1975

Practice Update FTL Design Engineering Studio, New York City (est. 2002); Nicholas Goldsmith, Joseph Schedlbauer, Ashish Soni (principals)
Teaching Positions Pratt Institute; University of Innsbruck; University of Pennsylvania
Notable Honors AIA New York Chapter, Design Award, 1997; DuPont Benedictus Award for Glass, 2000; Building Stone Institute, Tucker Design Award, 2010
Website ftlstudio.com

01 **FTL Happold** Carlos Moseley Pavilion, Metropolitan Opera and New York Philharmonic, 1990. Photo Jeff Goldberg/Esto
02 **FTL Happold** Winter Garden, World Financial Center, New York, NY, 1989. Photo Durston Saylor
03 **FTL Happold** DKNY World Headquarters, New York, NY, 1993. Photo Elliott Kaufman
04 **FTL Design Engineering Studio** Shaded Center, Arizona State University, Scottsdale, AZ, 2009. Photo Matt Winquist

01

02

03

04

James Cutler

James Cutler Architects, Bainbridge Island, WA (est. 1977)

Education University of Pennsylvania, BA cultural anthropology, 1971; University of Pennsylvania, MArch, 1973; University of Pennsylvania, Louis I. Kahn Studio, 1974

Practice Update Cutler Anderson Architects, Bainbridge Island, WA (est. 2001); Bruce Anderson, James Cutler (principals)
Teaching Positions Dartmouth College; Harvard University; Middlebury College; University of California, Berkeley; University of Oregon
Notable Honors National AIA, Honor Award, 1993, 1994, 2001
Website cutler-anderson.com

05

01 **James Cutler Architects** Medina Guest House, Medina, WA, 1993. Photo Art Grice
02 **Cutler Anderson Architects** Grace Episcopal Church, Bainbridge Island, WA, 2003. Photo Art Grice
03 **Cutler Anderson Architects** Ohana House, Niulii, HI, 2005. Photo Art Grice
04 **Cutler Anderson Architects** Edith Greene Wendell Wyatt Federal Building, Portland, OR, 2012; joint venture with SERA Architects. Photo Nic Lehoux
05 **James Cutler Architects** Bridge House, Bainbridge Island, WA, 1987. Photo Peter Aaron

01

02

03

04

05

Sheila Kennedy, Frano Violich

Kennedy & Violich Architecture (KVA), Boston (est. 1988)

Education Kennedy: Wesleyan University, BA history, philosophy, and literature, 1979; Ecole Nationale Supérieure des Beaux-Arts, architecture, 1980; Harvard University, MArch, 1984 \\ Violich: University of California, Berkeley, BA architecture, 1980; Harvard University, MArch, 1984

Teaching Positions Kennedy: Harvard University; Massachusetts Institute of Technology; SCI-Arc; University of Michigan; University of Oklahoma \\ Violich: Cornell University; Rhode Island School of Design; University of California, Berkeley; University of Michigan; University of Virginia
Notable Honors Parsons The New School for Design, Michael Kalil Endowment for Smart Design, 2010; Boston Society of Architects, Honor Award for Design Excellence, 2013; Internationale Bauausstellung IBA, IBA Excellence, 2013
Websites kvarch.net \\ portablelight.org

01 Golkin Hall, University of Pennsylvania Law School, Philadelphia, PA, 2012. Photo Halkin Architectural Photography
02 Soft House, Hamburg, Germany, 2013. Photo Michael Moser
03 Temporary Museum, Boston Center for the Arts, Boston, MA, 1990. Photo Bruce T. Martin Photography
04 34th Street Ferry Terminal, New York, NY, 2012. Photo John Horner
05 Boston Children's Museum, Boston, MA, 1992. Photo Steve Rosenthal

01

02

03

04

05

William Leddy, Marsha Maytum, Richard Stacy, James L. Tanner

Tanner Leddy Maytum Stacy Architects, San Francisco (est. 1989)

Education Leddy: University of Oregon, BArch, 1975 \\ Maytum: Royal Danish Academy of Fine Arts, architecture, 1976; University of Oregon, BArch, 1977 \\ Stacy: Rice University, BA art and architecture, 1977, BArch, 1979 \\ Tanner: University of Houston, BArch, 1968

Practice Update LEDDY MAYTUM STACY Architects, San Francisco (est. 2000); William Leddy, Marsha Maytum, Richard Stacy (principals) \\ TannerHecht Architecture, San Diego, San Francisco (est. 2001); David Hecht, James L. Tanner (principals) **Teaching Positions** Leddy: California College of the Arts; SCI-Arc; University of California, Berkeley \\ Maytum: California College of the Arts; University of California, Berkeley **Notable Honors** LEDDY MAYTUM STACY Architects: National AIA, Honor Award, 2009; Urban Land Institute, Global Award for Excellence, 2011; National AIA, Top Ten Green Projects, 2013 \\ TannerHecht Architecture: AIA California, Citation, 2005; AIA San Diego, Committee on the Environment Award, 2009; National AIA, Housing Award, 2009 **Websites** lmsarch.com \\ tannerhecht.com

01 **Tanner Leddy Maytum Stacy Architects** Datamart, San Francisco, CA, 1989. Photo Richard Barnes
02 **LEDDY MAYTUM STACY Architects** Nueva School Hillside Learning Complex, Hillsborough, CA, 2007. Photo Tim Griffith
03 **TannerHecht Architecture** Cannery Lofts, Newport Beach, CA, 2004. Photo Toby Ponnay
04 **Tanner Leddy Maytum Stacy Architects** Corson-Heinser Live/Work, San Francisco, CA, 1992. Photo Thomas Heinser
05 **Tanner Leddy Maytum Stacy Architects** Haight Street Lofts, San Francisco, CA, 1994. Photo Sharon Risedorph

01

02

03

04

Enrique Norten

TEN Arquitectos, Mexico City
(est. 1986)

Education Universidad
Iberoamericana, BArch, 1978;
Cornell University, MArch,
1980

Practice Update Mexico City,
New York City; Fernando
Alanis, Melissa Fukumoto,
Enrique Norten, Andrea Steele
(principals)
Teaching Positions Harvard
University; University of
Michigan; University of
Pennsylvania
Notable Honors Fundació Mies
van der Rohe, Mies van der
Rohe Award for Latin American
Architecture, 1998; World
Cultural Council, Leonardo da
Vinci World Award of Arts,
2005; The Smithsonian Latino
Center, Legacy Award, 2007
Website ten-arquitectos.com

01 National Laboratory of Genomics
for Biodiversity, Irapuato,
Mexico, 2010. Photo Luis Gordoa
02 National School of Theater,
Mexico City, Mexico, 1994.
Photo Luis Gordoa
03 Emblematic Monument of Puebla's
Battle, Puebla, Mexico, 2012.
Photo Pablo Crespo
04 MUSEVI (Elevated Museum of
Villahermosa), Villahermosa,
Mexico, 2011. Photo Luis Gordoa
05 Televisa Services Building,
Mexico City, Mexico, 1994.
Photo Luis Gordoa

05

01

02

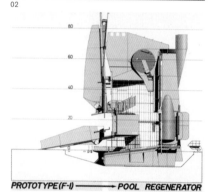

PROTOTYPE(F-I) ──────► POOL REGENERATOR

03

04

Neil Denari

Cor-Tex Architecture,
Los Angeles (est. 1988)

Education University of
Houston, BArch, 1980; Harvard
University, MArch, 1982

Practice Update Neil M.
Denari Architects (NMDA),
Los Angeles (est. 1998)
Teaching Positions Harvard
University; Princeton
University; SCI-Arc
(director, 1997-2001);
University of California,
Berkeley; University of
California, Los Angeles
Notable Honors American
Academy of Arts and
Letters, Arts and Letters
Award in Architecture,
2008; California Community
Foundation, Fellow, 2010; AIA
Los Angeles, Gold Medal, 2011
Website denari.co

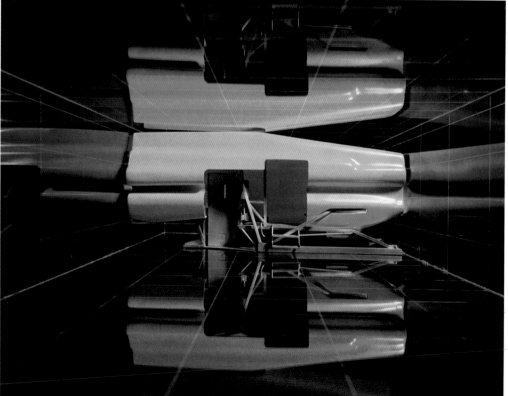

05

01 **Cor-Tex Architecture** Massey
   Residence, Los Angeles, CA,
   1994
02 **Cor-Tex Architecture**
   Interrupted Projections, Tokyo,
   Japan, 1996. Photo Fujitsuka
   Mitsumasa
03 **Cor-Tex Architecture** Pool
   Regenerator, ink and Zip-a-Tone
   on Mylar, 1988
04 **Neil M. Denari Architects
   (NMDA)** HL23, New York, NY,
   2012. Photo Benny Chan/
   Fotoworks
05 **Cor-Tex Architecture** Details
   Design Studio, model, 1993.
   Photo Benny Chan/Fotoworks

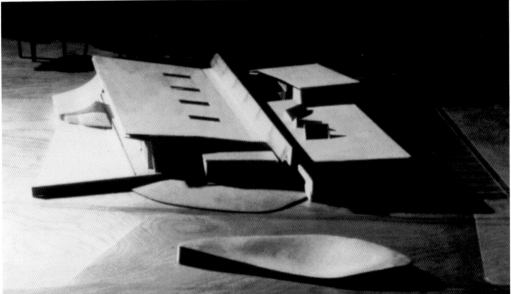

01

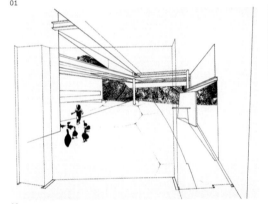

02

03

04

05

06

Homa Farjadi

Farjadi/Mostafavi Associates, Cambridge, MA, and London (est. 1987); Homa Farjadi, Mohsen Mostafavi (principals)

Education Tehran University, MArch, 1977; Architectural Association, AA graduate diploma, 1979; University of London, MA history of film and visual media, 2008

Practice Update Farjadi Architects, Cambridge, MA, and London (est. 1997)
Teaching Positions Architectural Association; Harvard University; University of Edinburgh; University of Pennsylvania; Yale University
Notable Honors *Progressive Architecture*, P/A Award, 1996; Hackney Empire Theatre Architectural Design Competition, first prize and commission with Tim Ronalds, 1997; Museum of Modern Art (New York City), *The Un-Private House*, exhibitor, 1999
Website farjadi.com

01 Headstart Childcare Center, Princeton, NJ, 1997
02 Headstart Childcare Center, Princeton, NJ, 1997
03 Wawu Mountain Resort, Sichuan, China, 2011. Rendering Farjadi Architects and Turenscape
04 Block 100 Apartment, Madison, WI, 2002
05 Kunming Research Library and Museum, Yunnan, China, 2011. Rendering Farjadi Architects and Turenscape
06 BV House, Lancashire, England, 2000

All projects by Farjadi Architects.

01

02

Gisue Hariri, Mojgan Hariri

Hariri & Hariri, New York City (est. 1986)

Education Gisue Hariri: Cornell University, BArch, 1980 \\ Mojgan Hariri: Cornell University, BArch, 1981; Cornell University, MAUD, 1983

Teaching Positions Gisue Hariri: Columbia University; Cornell University; McGill University; Parsons The New School for Design

Notable Honors American Academy of Arts and Letters, Arts and Letters Award in Architecture, 2005; *Interior Design*, Hall of Fame, 2005; *Architectural Digest*, AD100, 2012

Website haririandhariri.com

03

04

05

01 Soho Loft, New York, NY, 1988. Photo John M. Hall
02 Barry's Bay Cottage, Ontario, Canada, 1994. Photo John M. Hall
03 Aqua House, Miami Beach, FL, 2005. Photo Michael Moran
04 Salzburg Residential Complex, Salzburg, Austria, 2014
05 Sagaponac House, East Hampton, NY, 2004. Photo Paul Warchol

01

02

03

Chuck Hoberman

Hoberman Associates, New York City (est. 1990)

Education Brown University, 1974-1976; Cooper Union, BFA sculpture, 1979; Columbia University, MS mechanical engineering, 1984

Practice Update Hoberman Associates \\ Hoberman Designs, New York City (est. 1993); Chuck Hoberman (principal) \\ Adaptive Building Initiative, New York City (est. 2008); Chuck Hoberman, Craig Schwitter (principals)
Teaching Positions Harvard University; Massachusetts Institute of Technology
Notable Honors Chrysler Group, Chrysler Design Award, 1997; Cooper-Hewitt, National Design Museum, National Design Award Finalist, 2000; Cooper Union, Augustus Saint-Gaudens Award, 2002
Websites adaptivebuildings .com \\ hoberman.com

04

05

01 Hoberman Sphere Toy, 1995
02 Expanding Sphere, Otaru Bay City Center, Otaru, Japan, 1999
03 Iris Dome, *The Elaine Dannheisser Projects Series #45*, Museum of Modern Art, New York, NY, rendering, 1994
04 Expanding Video Screen, U2 360° World Tour, 2009. Photo Mark Fisher
05 Transformable Facade, Simons Center for Geometry and Physics, Stony Brook University, Stony Brook, NY, 2010

Susan Lanier, Paul Lubowicki

Lubowicki Lanier Architecture, El Segundo, CA (est. 1990)

Education Lanier: Pitzer College, BA psychology, 1971; SCI-Arc, MArch, 1988 \\ Lubowicki: Cooper Union, BArch, 1977

Teaching Positions Harvard University; Tulane University; University of Southern California; University of Texas at Arlington

Notable Honors *Architectural Record*, Record Houses, 1994; AIA Los Angeles, Honor Award, 1998; AIA Los Angeles, Decade Award, 2006

Website lalarc.com

01 Stringfellow Residence, Los Angeles, CA, 1993. Photo Tom Bonner

02 *Angels & Franciscans*, Castelli/ Gagosian Gallery, New York, NY, 1992. Photo Michael Moran

03 O'Neill Guesthouse, Los Angeles, CA, 1998. Photo Eric Koyama

04 Laidley Residence, Belvedere, CA, 2010. Photo Michael Moran

05 Hardy Residence, West Hollywood, CA, 1995. Photo Tim Street-Porter

01

02

03

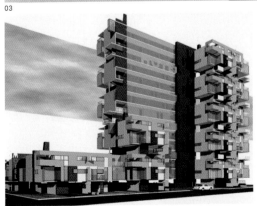

04

05

Mark Rakatansky

Mark Rakatansky Studio,
Ames, IA (est. 1982)

Education University of
California, Santa Cruz, BA
design aesthetics, 1979;
University of California,
Berkeley, MArch, 1982

Practice Update Brooklyn
Teaching Positions Columbia
University; Parsons The New
School for Design; Pratt
Institute
Notable Honors *Progressive
Architecture*, P/A Award,
1992; Graham Foundation for
Advanced Studies in the Fine
Arts, grant recipient, 2009;
New York State Council on the
Arts, grant recipient, 2009
Website mr-studio.com

01 A/Partments, Chicago, IL, 1994.
Photo Karant and Associates
02 Summer Reading Pavilion (for
Banned Books), Gwangju Design
Biennale, Gwangju, South Korea,
2009. Photo Wooseop Hwang
03 Adult Day, Des Plaines,
IL, 1992. Photo Karant and
Associates
04 Urbia, Far Rockaway, NY, 2001
05 Open Shelves, Little Free
Library/NYC, University
Settlement, New York, NY, 2013;
in collaboration with Aaron
White. Photo Alexandra Hay/
The Architectural League of
New York and PEN World Voices
Festival

01

02

03

04

05

Brigitte Shim, Howard Sutcliffe

Shim-Sutcliffe Architects, Toronto (est. 1994)

Education Shim: University of Waterloo, BArch, BES, 1983 \\ Sutcliffe: University of Waterloo, BArch, BES, 1983

Teaching Positions Shim: Ecole polytechnique fédérale de Lausanne; Harvard University; University of Toronto; Yale University
Notable Honors Royal Architectural Institute of Canada, Governor General's Medal in Architecture, 2010, 2012; National AIA, Honor Award, 2012
Website shim-sutcliffe.com

01 Laneway House, Toronto, Canada, 1993. Photo Steve Evans
02 Integral House, Toronto, Canada, 2009. Photo Ed Burtynsky
03 Garden Pavilion and Reflecting Pool, Toronto, Canada, 1988. Photo James Dow
04 Moorelands Camp Dining Hall, Lake Kawagama, Ontario, Canada, 2000
05 Congregation Bet Ha'am, Portland, ME, 2009. Photo James Dow

Wellington Reiter

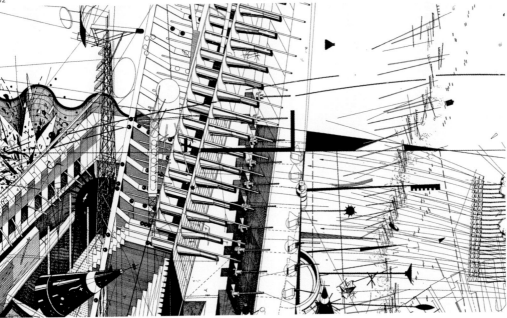

Urban Instruments, Boston
(est. 1995)

Education Tulane University,
BArch, 1981; Harvard
University, MArch, 1986

Practice Update Urban
Instruments \\ Arizona State
University Foundation,
Phoenix (senior vice
president and managing
director, 2011-present)
Teaching Positions Arizona
State University (dean,
College of Design, 2003-2008,
2010-present); Massachusetts
Institute of Technology;
School of the Art Institute
of Chicago (president,
2008-2010)
Notable Honors Harvard
University, Wheelwright
Prize, 1990; AIA Arizona,
Arizona Architects Medal,
2007; AIA, Fellow, 2008
Website urbaninstruments.com

01 *Empty Vessel*, Boston Visions
competition, winning entry,
Boston, MA, 1988
02 Subdivision, Artpark, Lewiston,
KY, 1990
03 Visitor's Station, DeCordova
Museum and Sculpture Park,
Lincoln, MA, 2003. Photo
Clements-Howcroft
04 *12 Battles of New Orleans*,
Institute of Contemporary Art,
Boston, MA, drawing detail,
1988

Brad Cloepfil

Allied Works, Portland, OR (est. 1994)

Education University of Oregon, BArch, 1980; Columbia University, MS architecture, 1985

Practice Update New York City and Portland, OR; Brad Cloepfil, Kyle Lommen (principals)
Teaching Positions Cornell University; Rice University; University of California, Berkeley; Washington University in St. Louis
Notable Honors AIA Northwest & Pacific Region, Honor Award, 2009; National AIA, Honor Award, 2011; AIA New York Chapter, Honor Award, 2012
Website alliedworks.com

01 Maryhill Overlook (first of the Sitings Project), Goldendale, WA, 1998. Photo Sally Schoolmaster
02 Dutchess County Residence Guest House, Stanfordville, NY, 2007. Photo Dean Kaufman
03 Clyfford Still Museum, Denver, CO, 2011. Photo Jeremy Bittermann
04 Contemporary Art Museum, St. Louis, MO, 2003. Photo Hélène Binet
05 National Music Centre of Canada, Calgary, Canada, in progress. Rendering MIR
06 Wieden + Kennedy Agency World Headquarters, Portland, OR, 2000. Photo Sally Schoolmaster

01

02

03

04

05

06

07

Audrey Matlock

Audrey Matlock Architect,
New York City (est. 1993)

Education Syracuse
University, BFA experimental
studios, 1973; Yale
University, MArch, 1979

Teaching Positions City
University of New York;
Syracuse University;
University of Texas at
Austin; Yale University
Notable Honors AIA New York
Chapter, Vice President's
Certificates of Excellence,
2010; AIA, Fellow, 2011
Website audreymatlock.com

01 Armstrong Industries Exhibition
   Center, Lancaster, PA, 2000
02 Tian Shan Mountain House,
   Almaty, Kazakhstan, 2009. Photo
   Artetra
03 New York Aquarium Discovery
   Cove, Brooklyn, NY, 1997
04 Medeu Sports Center, Medeu,
   Kazakhstan, in progress
05 Chelsea Modern, New York, NY,
   2008
06 57 Irving Place, New York, NY,
   2012. Rendering Arch Partners
07 Yokohama International Port
   Terminal, Yokohama, Japan,
   competition entry, 1994

01

02

03

04

05

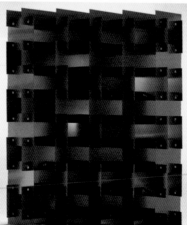

06

Clifton Balch, Mojdeh Baratloo

Baratloo-Balch Architects, New York City (est. 1984)

Education Balch: University of Illinois, BS architectural studies, 1975; University of Michigan, MArch, 1977 \\ Baratloo: University of Michigan, BS, 1976; University of Michigan, MArch, 1978; University of Copenhagen, postgraduate studies in housing and urban design, 1978

Practice Update Clifton Balch, Architect, New York City (2002-present); WEISS/MANFREDI Architecture/Landscape/Urbanism, New York City (Balch, senior project manager, 2003-present) \\ Mojdeh Baratloo Architects, New York City (2002-2013)
Teaching Positions Balch: Cornell University; Harvard University; Rhode Island School of Design; Royal Danish Academy of Fine Arts \\ Baratloo: Columbia University; Cornell University; Harvard University; Parsons The New School for Design; University of Michigan
Notable Honors See page 296
Website mojibaratloo.com

Mojdeh Baratloo died in 2013.

01 Shamana, New York, NY, 1989. Photo Paul Warchol
02 JOOP! Jeans USA Showroom and Headquarters, New York, NY, 1995. Photo Paul Warchol
03 *Object Lessons, 100 Years of Collecting at Cooper-Hewitt, National Design Museum*, Park Avenue Armory, New York, NY, 1997. Photo Paul Warchol
04 Wolf-Gordon Showroom, New York, NY, 1999. Photo Paul Warchol
05 *ANGST: Cartography (Field Dreams)*, The Rotunda Gallery, Brooklyn, NY, 1993. Photo Paul Warchol
06 Resinated Canvas Screen, 1993, 2002. Photo Paul Warchol

All projects by Baratloo-Balch Architects.

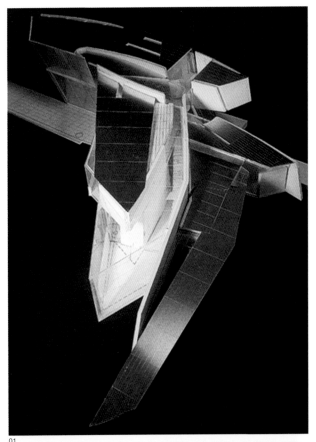

01

02

03

04

05

Carlos Zapata

Carlos Zapata Design Studio (CZDS), Boston (est. 1991)

Education Pratt Institute, BArch, 1984; Columbia University, MArch, 1989

Practice Update Wood + Zapata, Boston (est. 1996); Benjamin Wood, Carlos Zapata (principals) \\ Carlos Zapata Studio, New York City (est. 2004); Melissa Koff, Carlos Zapata (principals)
Notable Honors AIA Illinois, Design Award, 2003; Biennale XII Buenos Aires, Argentina, International Works Award, 2009; CNN, "25 Great Skyscrapers: Icons of Construction," 2013
Website cz-studio.com

01 **Carlos Zapata Design Studio (CZDS)** Private House, Quito, Ecuador, 1996. Photo Undine Prohl
02 **Carlos Zapata Studio** Cooper Square Hotel, New York, NY, 2009. Photo courtesy Cooper Square Hotel Group
03 **Carlos Zapata Studio** Airport Concourse, Miami International Airport, Miami, FL, 2009. Photo Esto
04 **Carlos Zapata Studio** Bitexco Financial Tower, Ho Chi Minh City, Vietnam, 2010
05 **Carlos Zapata Design Studio (CZDS)** Private House and Guest House, Golden Beach, FL, 1994. Photo Peter Aaron/Esto

01

Craig Konyk

Konyk Architecture, Brooklyn
(est. 1989)

Education Catholic University
of America, BA architecture,
1981; University of Virginia,
MArch, 1983

Teaching Positions Columbia
University; Pratt Institute
Notable Honors American
Academy in Rome, Rome
Prize Finalist, 2006;
Cooper-Hewitt, National
Design Museum, National
Design Triennial, exhibitor,
2006; AIA New York Chapter,
Award of Merit, 2009
Website konyk.net

02

03

04

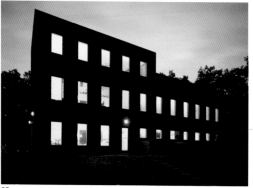

05

01 House on Fiji Island, Vanua
Levu, Fiji, 1991
02 *Church of the Year 2000*, The
Architectural League of New
York, New York, NY,
installation design, 1995
03 Malin+Goetz, New York, NY,
2004. Photo Eric Laignel
04 *Rise & Fall of Apartheid*, Haus
der Kunst, Munich, Germany,
installation design, 2013.
Photo Wilfried Petzi
05 The 52 Window House, Noyac, NY,
2000. Photo Marco Senti

Linda Lindroth, Craig Newick

Lindroth + Newick, New Haven, CT \\ **Newick Architects**, New Haven, CT (est. 1991)

Education Lindroth: Rutgers University, BA studio art, 1968; Rutgers University, MFA, 1979 \\ Newick: Lehigh University, BArch, 1982; Yale University, MArch, 1987

Teaching Position Lindroth: Quinnipiac University
Notable Honors Foundation for Contemporary Arts, grant recipient, 1989; New England Foundation for the Arts, New Forms Regional Initiative, participant, 1993 \\ Newick: The Architectural League of New York, Young Architects Forum, 1991
Websites lindalindroth.com \\ newickarchitects.com

01

03

04

05

01 *Simultaneous Space*, Wesleyan University, Middletown, CT, 1990
02 The Offices of Towers-Golde, New Haven, CT, 2005. Photo Frank Poole
03 *Articulating Wing*, The Hartford Ballet, Hartford, CT, 1989. Photo T. Charles Erickson
04 Water House, Branford, CT, 2011. Photo Robert Benson
05 The Firestone Pavilion, Longmeadow, MA, 2010

01

Louise Braverman

Louise Braverman, Architect, New York City (est. 1991)

Education University of Michigan, BA, 1970; Yale University, MArch, 1977

Notable Honors AIA, Fellow, 2008; Venice Architecture Biennale, exhibitor, 2012, 2014

Website louisebravermanarch.com

02

03

04

05

01 House at Ninevah Beach, Sag Harbor, NY, 1994. Photo Scott Frances
02 Apartment Residence, New York, NY, 1993. Photo Scott Frances
03 Village Health Works Staff Housing, Kigutu, Burundi, 2013. Photo Iwan Baan
04 Centro de Artes Nadir Afonso, Boticas, Portugal, 2013. Photo FG+SG Architectural Photography
05 Poets House, New York, NY, 2009. Photo Michael Moran

Jesse Reiser, Nanako Umemoto

01

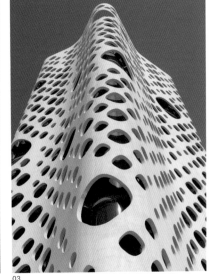

02

03

04

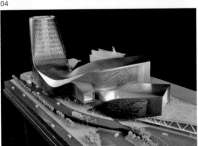

05

06

Reiser + Umemoto, New York City (est. 1986)

Education Reiser: Cooper Union, BArch, 1981; Cranbrook Academy of Art, MArch, 1984 \\ Umemoto: Osaka University of Arts, BA urban design, 1975; Cooper Union, BArch, 1983

Practice Update RUR Architecture, New York City (est. 1996)

Teaching Positions Reiser: Princeton University \\ Umemoto: Columbia University; Ecole polytechnique fédérale de Lausanne; SCI-Arc; University of Hong Kong; University of Pennsylvania

Notable Honors Chrysler Group, Chrysler Design Award, 1999; American Academy of Arts and Letters, Arts and Letters Award in Architecture, 2000; AIA New York Chapter, Honor Award, 2013

Website reiser-umemoto.com

01 Graz Music Hall, Graz, Austria, 1998
02 Cardiff Bay Opera House, Cardiff, England, competition entry, 1994
03 O-14, Dubai, United Arab Emirates, 2010. Photo Khalid Al Najjar
04 Taipei Pop Music Center, Taipei, Taiwan, 2014
05 Kaohsiung Port Terminal, Kaohsiung, Taiwan, 2014
06 Shenzhen Bao'an International Airport, Shenzhen, China, 2007

01

03

04

05

Kathryn Dean, Charles Wolf

Dean/Wolf Architects,
New York City (est. 1991)

Education Dean: North
Dakota State University,
BA architecture, 1981;
University of Oregon, MArch,
1983 \\ Wolf: Washington
University in St. Louis,
BA architecture, 1979;
University of Oregon, MArch,
1983

Practice Update Kathryn Dean,
Charles Wolf (principals);
Christopher Kroner (associate
partner)
Teaching Positions Dean:
Columbia University; Harvard
University; Washington
University in St. Louis
(director, Graduate School
of Architecture and Urban
Design, Sam Fox School
of Design & Visual Arts,
2008-2013) \\ Wolf: Columbia
University; Parsons The New
School for Design
Notable Honors American
Academy in Rome, Rome
Prize, 1987; AIA New York
State, Best of State, 2011;
Architect, P/A Award, 2012
Website dean-wolf.com

01 Spiral House, Armonk, NY, 1995.
   Photo Peter Aaron/Esto
02 Urban Interface Loft, New York,
   NY, 1997. Photo Peter Aaron/
   Esto
03 Inside/Outside Studio,
   San Mateo, CA, 1989
04 Contracted Dwelling, Scotch
   Plains, NJ, 2004. Photo
   Elizabeth Felicella
05 Inverted Warehouse Townhouse,
   New York, NY, 2010. Photo Paul
   Warchol

01

02

03

04

Tom Buresh, Danelle Guthrie

Guthrie+Buresh Architects,
Los Angeles (est. 1988)

Education Buresh: Iowa State University, BA architecture, 1978; University of California, Los Angeles, MArch, 1985 \\ Guthrie: University of California, Berkeley, BA architecture, 1981; University of California, Los Angeles, MArch, 1985

Practice Update San Francisco
Teaching Positions SCI-Arc; University of California, Berkeley; University of Michigan
Notable Honors *Architecture*, P/A Award, 1998; University of California, Los Angeles, School of the Arts and Architecture, Distinguished Alumni, 2001 \\ Buresh: University of California, Berkeley, Eva Li Chair in Design Ethics, 2011
Website guthrieburesh.com

01 *Cycles of Expression*, Grand Central Terminal, New York, NY, 1995. Photo Michael Moran Photography
02 King Harbor Marina Boater Facility, Redondo Beach, CA, 1995. Photo Joshua White
03 WorkHouse, West Hollywood, CA, 1996. Photo Tom Bonner Photography
04 WearHouse, Ann Arbor, MI, 2005

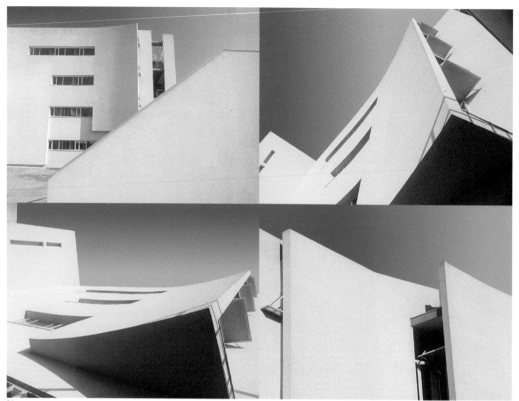

01

Anne Perl de Pal

Perl de Pal Architects,
New York City (est. 1990)

Education North Carolina
State University, BED
architecture, 1980; Columbia
University, MArch, 1986

Teaching Positions Columbia
University; Lehigh
University; North Carolina
State University; Wesleyan
University

Notable Honors National
AIA, Medal of Merit, 1986;
Progressive Architecture, P/A
Award, 1993; New Yorkers for
Parks, Daffodil Award, 2011

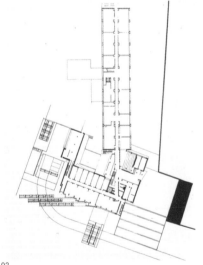

02

03

04

01 Institute of Molecular and
Cellular Biology, Porto,
Portugal, 1997, 2004
02 Institute of Molecular and
Cellular Biology, Porto,
Portugal, 1997, 2004
03 La Valencia Boutique, New York,
NY, 1993
04 Somerset Lodge (Bones Series),
Eastern North Carolina, 2006;
in collaboration with DCF
Consulting Engineers

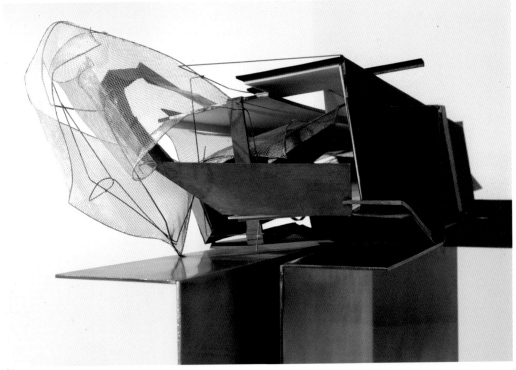

01

02

03

04

05

Michele Saee

SAEE Studio, Los Angeles
(est. 1985)

Education L'Università
degli Studi di Firenze,
MA architecture, 1981;
Politecnico di Milano,
technical urban planning,
1982

Practice Update West
Hollywood, CA
Teaching Positions Otis
College of Art and Design;
Parsons The New School for
Design; SCI-Arc; University
of California, Los Angeles;
University of Southern
California
Notable Honors AIA Los
Angeles, Next LA Award, 1997;
LA12 Award, 2000; City of
Beverly Hills, Architectural
Design Award, 2011
Website michelesaee.com

01 Artist Studio, Los Angeles, CA,
   1997. Photo Marvin Rand
02 Turku Library, Turku, Finland,
   1997. Photo Marvin Rand
03 Linnie House, Venice, CA, 2004.
   Photo Marvin Rand
04 Publicis Drug Store, Paris,
   France, 2004. Photo Marvin Rand
05 Sky Exhibition Pavilion,
   Beijing, China, 2007. Photo
   Chen Su

Charles Rose, Maryann Thompson

Thompson and Rose Architects, Cambridge, MA (est. 1989)

Education Rose: Princeton University, AB architecture, 1983; Harvard University, MArch, 1987 \\ Thompson: Princeton University, AB architecture, 1983; Harvard University, MArch, MLA, 1989

Practice Update Charles Rose Architects, Somerville, MA (est. 2000) \\ Maryann Thompson Architects, Cambridge, MA (est. 2000)
Teaching Positions Rose: Harvard University; Massachusetts Institute of Technology; Rhode Island School of Design; Rice University; University of Virginia \\ Thompson: Georgia Institute of Technology; Harvard University; Massachusetts Institute of Technology; University of Michigan; University of Virginia
Notable Honors *See page 296*
Websites
charlesrosearchitects.com \\ maryannthompson.com

01 **Thompson and Rose Architects** Atlantic Center for the Arts, Leeper Studio Complex, New Smyrna Beach, FL, 1997. Photo Chuck Choi
02 **Maryann Thompson Architects** Westport Meadow House, Westport, MA, 2005. Photo Chuck Choi
03 **Maryann Thompson Architects** The Children's School, Stamford, CT, 2007. Photo Chuck Choi
04 **Charles Rose Architects** JIB House, Gloucester, MA, 2004. Photo John Linden
05 **Charles Rose Architects** Zero Net Energy Building, John W. Olver Transit Center, Greenfield, MA, 2012. Photo Peter Vanderwarker

01

02

Michael Manfredi, Marion Weiss

WEISS/MANFREDI Architecture/ Landscape/Urbanism, New York City (est. 1989)

Education Manfredi: University of Notre Dame, BArch, 1975; Cornell University, MArch, 1979 \\ Weiss: University of Virginia, BS architecture, 1979; Yale University, MArch, 1984

Teaching Positions Manfredi: Cornell University; Harvard University; Princeton University; University of Pennsylvania; Yale University \\ Weiss: Cornell University; Harvard University; University of Maryland; University of Pennsylvania; Yale University

Notable Honors American Academy of Arts and Letters, Arts and Letters Award in Architecture, 2004; Harvard University, Veronica Rudge Green Prize in Urban Design, 2007; World Architecture Festival, Nature Award, 2008

Website weissmanfredi.com

03

04

05

06

01 Olympia Fields Park and Community Center, Olympia Fields, IL, 1994. Photo Bruce Van Inwegen
02 Women's Memorial and Education Center at Arlington National Cemetery, Arlington, VA, 1997. Photo Jeff Goldberg
03 Olympic Sculpture Park, Seattle Art Museum, Seattle, WA, 2007. Photo Benjamin Benschneider
04 Campus Center, Smith College, Northampton, MA, 2003. Photo Jeff Goldberg
05 Brooklyn Botanic Garden Visitor Center, Brooklyn, NY, 2012. Photo Albert Večerka/Esto
06 College of Architecture and Environmental Design, Kent State University, Kent, OH, in progress

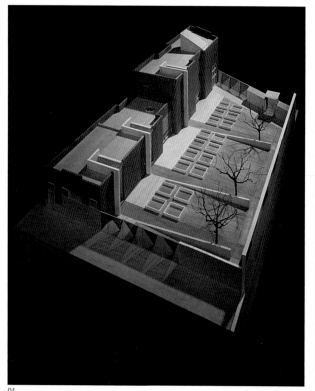

01

02

Sara Caples, Everardo Jefferson

Caples Jefferson Architects, Long Island City, NY (est. 1987)

Education Caples: Smith College, BA art history, 1970; Yale University, MArch, 1974 \\ Jefferson: Pratt Institute, BA industrial design, 1968; Yale University, MArch, 1973

Teaching Positions Caples: City College of New York; Syracuse University; University of Miami \\ Jefferson: Columbia University; New Jersey Institute of Technology; Syracuse University
Notable Honors New York City Minority & Women-Owned Business Enterprise, MWBE of the Year, 2009; AIA New York State, Firm of the Year, 2012; *Architect*, Annual Design Review, Best Cultural Project, 2013
Website capjeff.com

03

04

05

01 Central Harlem Alcoholic Crisis Center, New York, NY, 1994. © Roger Blatz/Preston Photography
02 House for 3 Generations, New York, NY, 1995. © Roger Blatz/Preston Photography
03 Queens Theatre, Queens, NY, 2011. © Nic Lehoux
04 Weeksville Heritage Center, Brooklyn, NY, 2013. Photo Nic Lehoux
05 Marcus Garvey Houses Community Center, Brooklyn, NY, 2011. © Michael Anton

01

02

03

04

05

06

07

François de Menil

François de Menil Architect,
New York City (est. 1991)

Education Cooper Union,
BArch, 1987

Practice Update FdM: Arch
Notable Honors National
AIA, Honor Award, 1999;
National AIA, Honor Award for
Interiors, 1999; AIA, Fellow,
2002
Website fdmarch.com

01 Byzantine Fresco Chapel,
Houston, TX, 1997.
© Paul Warchol Photography
02 Museum Tower Urban Roof Garden,
New York, NY, 2008.
© Paul Warchol Photography
03 Wells BDDP Advertising Agency,
New York, NY, 1996.
© Paul Warchol Photography
04 Lake Guesthouse, Mooresville,
NC, 1998. © Paul Warchol
Photography
05 The Seneca Art and Culture
Center, Victor, NY, 2012.
© Jock Pottle Photography
06 The OneTwo Townhouse, Houston,
TX, 2003. © Paul Warchol
Photography
07 Amagansett House, Amagansett,
NY, 2010. © Michael Moran
Photography

01

03

05

02

04

06

Michael Gabellini

Gabellini Associates, New York City (est. 1991)

Education Rhode Island School of Design, BFA architecture, 1980; Architectural Association, independent exchange program, 1980; Rhode Island School of Design, BArch, 1981

Practice Update Gabellini Sheppard Associates, New York City (est. 1997); Michael Gabellini, Daniel Garbowit, Kimberly Sheppard (partners)
Teaching Position Parsons The New School for Design
Notable Honors AIA, Fellow, 2004; Cooper-Hewitt, National Design Museum, National Design Award for Interior Design, 2006; National AIA, Honor Awards for Interior Architecture and Historic Preservation, 2006
Website gabellinisheppard.com

01 Salvatore Ferragamo Boutique, Venice, Italy, 2001. Photo Paul Warchol
02 Nicole Farhi Boutique/Restaurant/Bar, New York, NY, 1999. Photo Paul Warchol
03 Jil Sander Showroom, Milan, Italy, 1998. Photo Paul Warchol
04 Grant Selwyn Gallery, New York, NY, 1998. Photo Paul Warchol
05 Top of the Rock, New York, NY, 2005. Photo Peter Murdock
06 David Yurman Townhouse, New York, NY, 2010. Photo Paul Warchol

All projects by Gabellini Sheppard Associates.

Julie V. Snow

01

02

03

Julie Snow Architects, Minneapolis (est. 1995)

Education University of Colorado Boulder, BArch, 1970

Practice Update Snow Kreilich Architects, Minneapolis (est. 2014); Matthew Kreilich, Julie V. Snow (principals)

Teaching Positions Harvard University; Syracuse University; University of Minnesota; University of Southern California; Washington University in St. Louis

Notable Honors U.S. General Services Administration, GSA Design Award, 2010; American Academy of Arts and Letters, Arts and Letters Award in Architecture, 2011; *Architect*, P/A Award, 2011

Website snowkreilich.com

04

05

01 Short Run Production, New Richmond, WI, 1990. Photo Don Wong

02 U.S. Land Port of Entry, Warroad, MN, 2010; in collaboration with Coen + Partners. Photo Paul Crosby

03 Weekend House on Lake Superior, Schroeder, MN, 2009. Photo Peter Kerze

04 Fifth Precinct Station, Minneapolis, MN, 1999. Photo Don Wong

05 U.S. Land Port of Entry, Van Buren, ME, 2013. Photo Paul Crosby

01

02

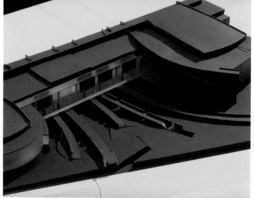
03

04

05

Karen Fairbanks, Scott Marble

Marble Fairbanks, New York City (est. 1990)

Education Fairbanks: University of Michigan, BS architecture, 1981; Columbia University, MArch, 1987 \\ Marble: Texas A&M University, Bachelor of environmental design, 1983; Columbia University, MArch, 1986

Practice Update Brooklyn **Teaching Positions** Fairbanks: Barnard College and Columbia University (chair, Department of Architecture, 1996-present); Columbia University (director, Columbia College Architecture Program, Graduate School of Architecture, Planning and Preservation, 1990-1995); University of Michigan \\ Marble: Columbia University (director, Integrated Design, Graduate School of Architecture, Planning and Preservation, 2010-present); University of Houston; University of Michigan **Notable Honors** *Architectural Review*, AR+D Award for Emerging Architecture, 1999; *Architecture*, P/A Award, 2002; Chicago Athenaeum, American Architecture Awards, 2007 **Website** marblefairbanks.com

01 Chelsea Loft, New York, NY, 1994. Photo Peter Paige
02 Glen Oaks Branch Library, Queens, NY, 2013. Photo Eduard Hueber/Arch Photo
03 Nara Convention Hall, Nara, Japan, 1990. Photo Eduard Hueber/Arch Photo
04 Slide Library, Department of Art History and Archeology, Columbia University, New York, NY, 2005
05 Tenrikyo Mission Center, Queens, NY, 2007

01

02

03

04

05

Marlon Blackwell

Marlon Blackwell Architect, Fayetteville, AR (est. 1990)

Education Auburn University, BArch, 1980; Syracuse University in Florence, MArch, 1991

Teaching Positions Cornell University; University of Arkansas (department head, Fay Jones School of Architecture, 1992-present); University of Michigan; University of Virginia **Notable Honors** American Academy of Arts and Letters, Arts and Letters Award in Architecture, 2012; National AIA, Honor Award, 2012, 2013 **Website** marlonblackwell.com

01 Flynn-Schmitt BarnHouse, Fayetteville, AR, 1994. Photo Richard Johnson
02 L-Stack Residence, Fayetteville, AR, 2006. Photo Tim Hursley
03 Moore Residence, Cashiers, NC, 1990. Photo Richard Johnson
04 Saint Nicholas Eastern Orthodox Church, Springdale, AR, 2010. Photo Tim Hursley
05 Ruth Lilly Visitors Pavilion, Indianapolis, IN, 2010. Photo Tim Hursley

01

02

03

04

05

06

Michael Maltzan

Michael Maltzan Architecture, Los Angeles (est. 1995)

Education Rhode Island School of Design, BFA, 1984; Rhode Island School of Design, BArch, 1985; Harvard University, MArch, 1988

Practice Update Michael Maltzan, Betty Tanaka, Tim Williams (principals)
Teaching Positions Harvard University; Princeton University; Rhode Island School of Design; Rice University; University of Southern California
Notable Honors AIA, Fellow, 2007; Bruner Foundation, Rudy Bruner Award for Urban Excellence, Gold Medal, 2009; American Academy of Arts and Letters, Arts and Letters Award in Architecture, 2012
Website mmaltzan.com

01 Feldman Horn Center for the Arts, Harvard Westlake School, Los Angeles, CA, 1998. Photo Tom Bonner
02 Inner-City Arts, Phase 3, Los Angeles, CA, 2008. Photo Iwan Baan
03 MoMA-QNS, Queens, NY, 2002. Photo Christian Richters
04 Napa Valley Residence, Napa, CA, 1998. Photo Iwan Baan
05 New Carver Apartments, Los Angeles, CA, 2009. Photo Iwan Baan
06 Pittman Dowell Residence, La Crescenta, CA, 2009. Photo Iwan Baan

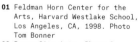

01

02

03

04

05

Vincent James

Vincent James Associates, Minneapolis (est. 1995)

Education University of Wisconsin-Milwaukee, MArch, 1978

Practice Update VJAA, Minneapolis (est. 1998); Vincent James, Jennifer Yoos (principals); Nathan Knutson (managing principal)
Teaching Positions Harvard University; Illinois Institute of Technology; University of Minnesota
Notable Honors AIA, Fellow, 2005; *Architect*, Top 10 Award-Winning Firms, first place, 2010; National AIA, Firm Award, 2012
Website vjaa.com

01 **Vincent James Associates** Dayton House, Minneapolis, MN, 1997. Photo Don Wong
02 **VJAA** Minneapolis Rowing Club, Minneapolis, MN, 2001. Photo Mary Ludington
03 **VJAA** Blessed Sacrament Chapel, Saint John's Abbey and Monastery, Collegeville, MN, 2008. Photo Paul Crosby
04 **VJAA** Charles Hostler Student Center, American University of Beirut, Beirut, Lebanon, 2008. Photo Paul Crosby
05 **Vincent James Associates** Type/Variant House, Northern Wisconsin, 1997. Photo Mary Ludington

COMMENTARY Paul Makovsky

1982-1986
1988-1993
1994-1998

1999-2003

2004-2008
2009-2013

From the theoretical to the eminently buildable, work produced by Emerging Voices at the turn of the twenty-first century varied in terms of design and scale. Formal invention continued to preoccupy the profession and its publications, the digital revolution began to make its way from the edge to the center, the craft of making and material exploration resurfaced, and, most significantly, sustainable practices gained traction among practitioners and clients.

Frank Gehry's Guggenheim Museum Bilbao (1997) and Walt Disney Concert Hall (2003) bookended the millennium's arrival, producing countless signature-style offspring. Digital tools seeped deeper into the architectural psyche, evident in the work of firms such as SHoP Architects (EV01), whose McKinsey-like synthesis of technological and business savvy led the way toward an embrace of digital fabrication. Material investigations, like Office dA's (EV03) modulation of brick and concrete block and Peter Lynch Architect's (EV03) tapered-brick dome and collapsible, wood-and-aluminum structure, produced new tectonic and spatial solutions. But it is this period's deployment of sustainable design strategies and programs that may offer the most enduring legacy.

The Architectural League's yearlong initiative Shades of Green: Architecture and the Natural World coincided, in 2000, with the launch of the U.S. Green Building Council's now-ubiquitous LEED certification system. Two years later architect Edward Mazria launched Architecture 2030, an activist initiative that loudly acknowledged the building sector's outsized contribution to greenhouse gas emissions. And in 2003 the National Building Museum installed *Big & Green*, a show of projects that endeavored to counter their own environmental impacts.

In the context of the League's Shades of Green, Emerging Voices were selected in part for their commitment to rethinking the relationship between the built and natural environments. This work includes the climate-based, low-tech, and passive strategies of Brian MacKay-Lyons Architecture Urban Design (EV00); the passive houses of David Heymann (EV00); the creative responses to local landscapes expressed through the regenerative brownfields of Julie Bargmann's D.I.R.T. studio (EV00); the environmentally

responsive methods of The Miller Hull Partnership (EV00); the artistic interventions of Lisa Rapoport of PLANT Architect (EV00); and the rammed-earth buildings of Rick Joy Architects (EV00).

Other significant sustainability efforts by Emerging Voices during this era include James Corner Field Operations' (EV01) "soft systems" of landscape, ecology, and infrastructure, and Margie Ruddick Landscape's (EV03) storm-water management systems integrated with rigorous design, as seen in her Queens Plaza Pedestrian and Bicycle Improvement project. Still others who made sustainability integral to their architecture while remaining rooted in modernist traditions are Wendell Burnette (EV99), Daly Genik (EV99), Brininstool + Lynch (EV03), and Frank Harmon (EV03).

Taking a different route to the efficient use of resources, Giuseppe Lignano and Ada Tolla of LOT-EK (EV99) applied an innovative, highly idiosyncratic, low-tech approach to adaptive reuse, transforming shipping containers into flexible, functional spaces. Jennifer Siegal's Office of Mobile Design (EV03) reenvisioned the prefabricated trailer as an adaptable, mobile way of living for those seeking to occupy a smaller footprint.

Whether sitting lightly on the land, reimagining age-old construction techniques, or building more efficiently via digital means, Emerging Voices from this period made influential contributions to a pivotal moment in the environmental consciousness of the profession. Much work remains, but some groundwork was laid and ground rules were established.

01

02

Lise Anne Couture, Hani Rashid

Asymptote Architecture,
New York City (est. 1989)

Education Couture: Carleton
University, BArch, 1983; Yale
University, MArch, 1986 \\
Rashid: Carleton University,
BArch, 1983; Cranbrook
Academy of Art, MArch, 1985

Teaching Positions Couture:
Columbia University; Harvard
University; Princeton
University; SCI-Arc; Yale
University \\ Rashid:
Columbia University; Harvard
University; Princeton
University; Swiss Federal
Institute of Technology;
University of Applied Arts
Vienna

Notable Honors AIA New York
Chapter, Design Award,
2002; Austrian Frederick
and Lillian Kiesler Private
Foundation, Prize for
Architecture and Art, 2004;
Chicago Athenaeum, American
Architecture Award, 2004
Website asymptote.net

03

04

05

06

07

01 New York Stock Exchange
   Advanced Trading Floor Command
   Center, New York, NY, 1999
02 New York Stock Exchange Virtual
   Trading Floor (3DTF), New York,
   NY, 1998
03 Yas Island Marina Hotel,
   Abu Dhabi, United Arab
   Emirates, 2008
04 Knoll Furniture System, 2000
05 HydraPier Pavilion,
   Haarlemmermeer, the
   Netherlands, 2002
06 Strata Tower, Abu Dhabi, United
   Arab Emirates, 2009
07 ARC River Culture Multimedia
   Theater Pavilion, Daegu, South
   Korea, 2012

01

02

03

04

05

Brian Healy

Brian Healy Architects,
Boston (est. 1986)

Education Pennsylvania State
University, BS architecture,
1978; Yale University, MArch,
1981

Practice Update Somerville, MA
Teaching Positions City
College of New York; Harvard
University; Massachusetts
Institute of Technology;
Washington University in
St. Louis; Yale University
Notable Honors National
Endowment for the Arts,
Chicago Housing Authority's
design competition for mixed-
income housing, first place,
2001; National Endowment for
the Arts, Design Competition
for The Mill Center for the
Arts, first place, 2005;
Architect, Annual Design
Review, 2010
Website brianhealyarchitects
.com

01 Housing Prototypes, Atlantic
City, NJ, 1996
02 Education and Community Center,
Korean Church of Boston,
Boston, MA, 2010. Photo Paxton
Sheldahl
03 Summer Compound, Barnegat
Light, NJ, 1996; in collabora-
tion with Michael Ryan. Photo
Paul Warchol
04 Grant Recital Hall, Brown
University, Providence, RI,
2008. Photo John Horner
05 Beach House, Loveladies, NJ,
1995; in collaboration with
Michael Ryan. Photo Paul
Warchol

Kevin Daly, Chris Genik

01

02

03

04

05

Daly Genik, Los Angeles
(est. 1990)

Education Daly: University of
California, Berkeley, BArch,
1980; Rice University, MArch,
1985 \\ Genik: Carleton
University, BArch, 1983; Rice
University, MArch, 1985

Practice Update Kevin Daly
Architects, Santa Monica, CA
(est. 2013)
Teaching Positions Daly:
University of California,
Berkeley; University of
California, Los Angeles;
University of Michigan;
University of Southern
California \\ Genik:
NewSchool of Architecture and
Design (dean, 2010-2012);
Rice University; SCI-Arc;
University of California,
Berkeley; University of
Michigan
Notable Honors Bruner
Foundation, Rudy Bruner Award
for Urban Excellence, 2003;
AIA Los Angeles, Firm of the
Year, 2009; National AIA,
Honor Award, 2010
Website kevindalyarchitects
.com

01 Valley Center House, Valley
Center, CA, 1999. Photo Grant
Mudford
02 Topanga Canyon House, Topanga
Canyon, CA, 1992. Photo J.
Scott Smith
03 Music Building Complex,
University of California,
Los Angeles, 2012
04 Camino Nuevo Charter Academy,
Los Angeles, CA, 2000. Photo
Tom Bonner
05 Venice Residence, Venice,
CA, 2010. Photo Benny Chan/
Fotoworks

All projects by Daly Genik.

Evan Douglis

Evan Douglis Studio, New York City (est. 1990)

Education Cooper Union, BArch, 1983; Harvard University, MArch, 1989

Practice Update Troy, NY
Teaching Positions Cooper Union; Columbia University; Pratt Institute (chair, undergraduate program, School of Architecture, 2003-2009); Rensselaer Polytechnic Institute (dean, School of Architecture, 2009-present)
Notable Honors *Architectural Record*, Design Vanguard, 2005; Cooper Union, President's Citation for Outstanding Contributions to the Field of Architecture, 2009; AIA Los Angeles, Restaurant Design Award, 2010
Website evandouglis.com

01 *Auto-braids*, Columbia University, New York, NY, 2002. Photo Michael Moran
02 Moon Jelly, Choice Restaurant, Brooklyn, NY, 2010. Photo Michael Moran
03 REptile, HAKU Restaurant, New York, NY, 2005. Photo Michael Moran
04 Caviar3000, Lanzhou, China, 2012
05 *The Oblique Function*, Columbia University, New York, NY, 1998. Photo Michael Moran

01

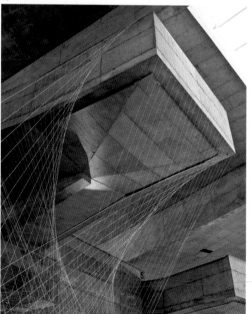

02

03

04

05

06

Raveevarn Choksombatchai, Ralph Nelson

Loom Studio, San Francisco and St. Paul, MN (est. 1991)

Education Choksombatchai: Chulalongkorn University, BArch, 1983; Harvard University, MLA, 1986; Harvard University, MArch, 1987 \\ Nelson: University of Minnesota, BArch, 1988; Yale University, MArch, 1991

Practice Update Loom Studio, St. Paul, MN; Ralph Nelson (principal) \\ VeeV Design, San Francisco (est. 2005); Raveevarn Choksombatchai (principal)

Teaching Positions Choksombatchai: Chulalongkorn University; SCI-Arc; University of California, Berkeley; University of Minnesota; University of Southern California \\ Nelson: California College of Arts; Illinois Institute of Technology; Lawrence Technological University; University of Minnesota

Notable Honors Choksombatchai: Harvard University, Wheelwright Prize, 1996; *Architecture*, P/A Award, 2002; AIA San Francisco, Design Award, 2007 \\ Nelson: Graham Foundation for Advanced Studies in the Fine Arts, grant recipient, 2001; *Architecture*, P/A Award, 2002; *Architect*, R+D Award, 2007

Websites loomstudio.com \\ veevdesign.com

01 **Loom Studio** Knox Garden, Minneapolis, MN, 1995
02 **Loom Studio** Onan Observatory, Norwood-Young America, MN, 1998
03 **VeeV Design** Cut + Fold (Gillis Library/Study), Berkeley, CA, 2007
04 **Loom Studio** Sheep Barn, Nerstrand, MN, 2009
05 **VeeV Design** *Ellipsis Reprise*, Berkeley, CA, 2012
06 **Loom Studio** Lola Pizzeria, Minneapolis, MN, 2011

01

02

Giuseppe Lignano, Ada Tolla

LOT-EK, Naples, Italy, and New York City (est. 1993)

Education Lignano: Università delgi Studi di Napoli Frederico II, masters architecture and urban design, 1989; Columbia University, Graduate School of Architecture, Planning and Preservation, visiting scholar, 1991 \\ Tolla: Università delgi Studi di Napoli Frederico II, Masters architecture and urban design, 1989; Columbia University, Graduate School of Architecture, Planning and Preservation, visiting scholar, 1991

Teaching Positions Columbia University; Massachusetts Institute of Technology; Parsons The New School for Design; Syracuse University **Notable Honors** AIA New York Chapter, Honor Award, 2011; United States Artists, USA Booth Fellows, 2011; Architizer, A+ Award, 2013 **Website** lot-ek.com

03

04

05

01 *Puma City*, installation, Alicante, Spain, Boston, and Tianjin, China, 2008. Photo Danny Bright
02 Mobile Dwelling Unit, Minneapolis, MN, 2003. Photo courtesy Walker Art Center
03 Morton Loft, New York, NY, 2000. Photo Paul Warchol
04 *TV Tank*, New York, NY, 1998. Photo Paul Warchol
05 Sanlitun North, Beijing, China, 2008. Photo Shuhe Architectural Photography

01

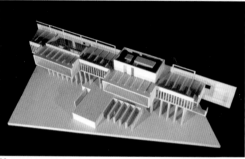

02

03

04

05

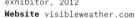

06

Michael Bell

Michael Bell Architecture, New York City (est. 1988)

Education Catholic University of America, BS architecture, 1983; University of California, Berkeley, MArch, 1987

Practice Update Bell / Seong, New York City (est. 2010); Michael Bell, Eunjeong Seong (principals) \\ Visible Weather, New York City (est. 2010); Michael Bell, Eunjeong Seong (principals)
Teaching Positions Columbia University; Harvard University; Rice University; University of California, Berkeley
Notable Honors San Francisco Museum of Modern Art, permanent collection; *Architecture*, P/A Award, 2001; Museum of Modern Art (New York City), *Foreclosed: Rehousing the American Dream*, exhibitor, 2012
Website visibleweather.com

01 **Visible Weather** Simultaneous City (Temple Terrace, FL), *Foreclosed: Rehousing the American Dream*, Museum of Modern Art, New York, NY, 2011. Photo James Ewing
02 **Michael Bell Architecture** Topological Stoa, no man's land between East and West Berlin, Germany, 1989
03 **Michael Bell Architecture** Double Dihedral House, La Cienega, NM, 1992
04 **Michael Bell Architecture** Glass House @ 2 Degrees, Fifth Ward, Houston, TX, 1998
05 **Michael Bell Architecture** Blue House, St. Mary's County, MD, 1989
06 **Michael Bell Architecture** Gefter-Press House (Binocular House), Hudson Valley, NY, 2007. Photo Bilyana Dimitrova

Wendell Burnette

01

02

03

04

05   06

Wendell Burnette Architects, Phoenix (est. 1996)

Education Taliesin, Frank Lloyd Wright School of Architecture, 1980-1983

Teaching Positions Arizona State University; Kansas State University; University of Arkansas; Washington University in St. Louis
Notable Honors *Architectural Record*, Record Houses, 2006; National AIA, Honor Award, 2007; American Academy of Arts and Letters, Arts and Letters Award in Architecture, 2009
Website wendellburnette architects.com

01 Desert Courtyard House, Scottsdale, AZ, 2013
02 Palo Verde Library/Maryvale Community Center, Phoenix, AZ, 2001
03 Field House, Ellington, WI, 2002
04 Desert Courtyard House, Scottsdale, AZ, 2013
05 David Michael Miller Associates, Scottsdale, AZ, 1997
06 Burnette Residence, Phoenix, AZ, 1996

All images Bill Timmerman.

Brian MacKay-Lyons

Brian MacKay-Lyons Architecture Urban Design, Halifax, Canada (est. 1985)

Education Technical University of Nova Scotia, BArch, 1978; University of California, Los Angeles, MAUD, 1982

Practice Update MacKay-Lyons Sweetapple Architects, Halifax, Canada (est. 2005); Brian MacKay-Lyons, Talbot Sweetapple (principals)
Teaching Positions Dalhousie University; Ghost Architectural Laboratory; Harvard University; McGill University; Washington University in St. Louis
Notable Honors *Architectural Record*, Record Houses, 2011; National AIA, Honor Award, 2011; Canadian Wood Council, Ron Thom Award, 2011
Website mlsarchitects.ca

01 **Brian MacKay-Lyons Architecture Urban Design** Rubadoux Studio, Nova Scotia, Canada, 1989. Photo James Steeves
02 **Brian MacKay-Lyons Architecture Urban Design** Howard House, Nova Scotia, Canada, 1999. Photo James Steeves
03 **Brian MacKay-Lyons Architecture Urban Design** Kutcher House, Nova Scotia, Canada, 2001. Photo James Steeves
04 **MacKay-Lyons Sweetapple Architects** Two Hulls House, Nova Scotia, Canada, 2011. Photo Greg Richardson
05 **MacKay-Lyons Sweetapple Architects** Sliding House, Upper Kingsburg, Canada, 2007. Photo Greg Richardson

David Heymann

01

04

05

02

03

06

David Heymann, Architect, Austin, TX (est. 1991) \\ **Michael Underhill, David Heymann, and Laura J. Miller, Architects**, Ames, IA, Austin, TX, and Phoenix (est. 1988)

Education Cooper Union, BArch, 1984; Harvard University, MArch, 1988

Practice Update David Heymann, Architect
Teaching Positions Iowa State University; University of Texas at Austin (associate dean, undergraduate programs, School of Architecture, 1998-2003)
Notable Honors Association of Collegiate Schools of Architecture, Distinguished Professor, 2007; National ASLA, Bradford Williams Medal, 2012; AIA, Fellow, 2014

01 **David Heymann, Architect** Prairie Chapel House, Crawford, TX, 2001
02 **David Heymann, Architect** Hill House, Austin, TX, 2009
03 **David Heymann, Architect** Hill House, Austin, TX, 2009
04 **Michael Underhill, David Heymann, and Laura J. Miller, Architects** Oakwood Road Church, Ames, IA, 2007. Photo Cameron Campbell
05 **Michael Underhill, David Heymann, and Laura J. Miller, Architects** Unitarian Fellowship, Ames, IA, 1994
06 **David Heymann, Architect** Cravens House, Houston, TX, 2004. Photo Hester + Hardaway

01

02

03

04

05

Julie Bargmann

D.I.R.T. studio,
Charlottesville, VA
(est. 1992)

Education Carnegie Mellon
University, BFA sculpture,
1980; Harvard University,
MLA, 1987

Teaching Positions Columbia
University; Harvard
University; University of
Virginia (director, graduate
programs for landscape
architecture, School of
Architecture, 2007-2009);
Yale University
Notable Honors American
Academy in Rome, Rome Prize,
1990; Cooper-Hewitt, National
Design Museum, National
Design Award, 2001; United
States Artists, USA Target
Fellow, 2009
Website dirtstudio.com

01 Ford River Rouge Plant,
   Dearborn, MI, 2000
02 Vitondale Reclamation Park,
   Vintondale, PA, 2004
03 MASS MoCA, North Adams, MA,
   1997. Photo Kevin Kenneflick
04 Brooklyn Navy Yard Visitor's
   Center, Brooklyn, NY, 2011
05 Urban Outfitters Headquarters,
   Philadelphia Navy Yard,
   Philadelphia, PA, 2006

01

02

03

04

05

Robert Hull, David Miller

The Miller Hull Partnership, Seattle (est. 1977)

Education Hull: Washington State University, BArch, 1968 \\ Miller: Washington State University, BArch, 1968; University of Illinois, MArch, 1972

Practice Update San Diego, Seattle; David Miller (founding partner); Craig Curtis, Sian Roberts, Ron Rochon, Norman Strong, Scott Wolf (partners); Ruth Baleiko, Brian Court, Mike Jobes, Robert Misel, Margaret Sprug, Rich Whealan (principals)

Teaching Positions Hull: University of Washington; Washington State University \\ Miller: University of Maryland; University of Oregon; University of Washington (chair, Department of Architecture, College of Built Environments, 2006-present)

Notable Honors National AIA, Firm Award, 2003; Washington State University, Regents' Distinguished Alumni Award, 2007; AIA Seattle, Gold Medal, 2010 \\ Miller: *Residential Architect*, Leadership Award, 2009

Website millerhull.com

Robert Hull died in 2014.

01 LOTT Clean Water Alliance Regional Services Center, Olympia, WA, 2009. © Nic Lehoux
02 156 West Superior, Chicago, IL, 2006. © Nic Lehoux
03 Michaels/Sisson Residence, Mercer Island, WA, 1998. © James Housel
04 Vancouver Community Library, Vancouver, WA, 2011. © Benjamin Benschneider
05 Olympic College, Shelton, WA, 1995. © Chris Eden

01

02

03

04

05

Lisa Rapoport

PLANT Architect, Toronto
(est. 1995); Chris Pommer,
Lisa Rapoport, Mary Tremain
(principals)

Education University of
Waterloo, BArch, 1988

Teaching Positions Illinois
Institute of Technology;
University of Toronto;
University of Waterloo
Notable Honors University
of Waterloo, Faculty of
Engineering, Team Alumni
Achievement Medal, 2012;
Environmental Design
Research Association, Great
Places Award, 2013; Royal
Architectural Institute of
Canada, Fellowship, 2013
Website branchplant.com

01 Dublin Grounds of Remembrance,
   Dublin, OH, 2009. Photo Steven
   Evans
02 Nathan Phillips Square Podium
   Roof Garden, Toronto, Canada,
   2010. Photo Steven Evans
03 Sweet Farm, Sutton, Canada,
   1997. Photo Steven Evans
04 Le Jardin du Repos, Les Jardins
   de Métis, Grand-Métis, Canada,
   2003
05 Conversation Piece, Toronto,
   Canada, 2004

Rick Joy

01

02

03

04

Rick Joy Architects, Tucson
(est. 1993)

Education University of
Maine, music, 1976-1978;
Portland School of Art,
photography, 1982-1984;
University of Arizona, BArch,
1990

Teaching Positions
Architecture Foundation
Australia; Harvard
University; Massachusetts
Institute of Technology; Rice
University; University of
Arizona
Notable Honors American
Academy of Arts and Letters,
Arts and Letters Award in
Architecture, 2002; Cooper-
Hewitt, National Design
Museum, National Design
Award, 2004; Universidad
Anáhuac, Mario Pani Award,
2009
Website rickjoy.com

01 Convent Studios, Tucson, AZ,
1999. Photo Bill Timmerman
02 Tubac House, Tubac, AZ, 2000.
Photo Bill Timmerman
03 400 Rubio Studio, Tuscon, AZ,
1999. Photo Bill Timmerman
04 Adobe Canyon House, Patagonia,
AZ, 2006. Photo Bill Timmerman
05 Woodstock Farmhouse, Woodstock,
VT, 2008. Photo Jean-Luc Laloux

01

02

03

04

05

06

Winka Dubbeldam

ARCHI-TECTONICS, New York City (est. 1994)

Education Rotterdam Academy of Architecture and Urban Design, MA architecture, 1990; Columbia University, MArch advanced architectural design, 1992

Teaching Positions Columbia University; Cornell University; Harvard University; Rotterdam Academy of Architecture and Urban Design; University of Pennsylvania (chair, Department of Architecture, School of Design, 2013-present)
Notable Honors *Esquire Magazine*, Best and Brightest, 2004; International Interior Design Association and *Metropolis*, Smart Environments Award, 2006; *Retail Week* Interiors Award, Shopfitting Excellence Award, second place, 2010
Website archi-tectonics.com

01 Aida Hair Salon, New York, NY, 2000. Photo Paul Warchol
02 Aida Hair Salon, New York, NY, 2000. Photo Paul Warchol
03 V33 Residential Building, New York, NY, 2013
04 PORTS1961, Shanghai, China, 2011. Photo Jiang Yang
05 Residence, Kent, NY, 2003. Photo Floto+Warner Studio
06 Greenwich Street Building, New York, NY, 2004. Photo Floto+Warner Studio

01

Stephen Cassell, Adam Yarinsky

Architecture Research Office (ARO), New York City (est. 1993)

Education Cassell: Princeton University, BArch, 1986; Harvard University, MArch, 1992 \\ Yarinsky: University of Virginia, BS architecture, 1984; Princeton University, MArch, 1987

Practice Update Stephen Cassell, Kim Yao, Adam Yarinsky (principals)
Teaching Positions Cassell: Harvard University; Massachusetts Institute of Technology; Princeton University; University of California, Berkeley; University of Virginia \\ Yarinsky: Harvard University; Princeton University; University of Michigan; University of Virginia; Yale University
Notable Honors American Academy of Arts and Letters, Arts and Letters Award in Architecture, 2010; Cooper-Hewitt, National Design Museum, National Design Award, 2011
Website aro.net

02

03

04

05

01 Colorado House, Telluride, CO, 2000. © Paul Warchol
02 Martha's Vineyard House, Chilmark, MA, 2007. © Thomas Brodin
03 New Urban Ground, *Rising Currents: Projects for New York City's Waterfront*, Museum of Modern Art, New York, NY, 2010; in collaboration with Dlandstudio architecture and landscape architecture
04 U.S. Armed Forces Recruiting Station, New York, NY, 1999. © David Joseph
05 School of Architecture Addition, Princeton University, Princeton, NJ, 2007. © Paul Warchol

Douglas Garofalo

Garofalo Architects, Chicago (est. 1992)

Education University of Notre Dame, BArch, 1981; Yale University, MArch, 1987

Teaching Position University of Illinois at Chicago (interim director, School of Architecture, 2001-2003)
Notable Honors AIA Chicago, Young Architect Award, 1995; Richard H. Driehaus Foundation, Award for Architectural Excellence in Community Design, 2007; United States Artists, USA Target Fellow, 2008; University of Illinois at Chicago, School of Architecture, Douglas A. Garofalo Fellowship, established 2013
Website garofaloarchitects .com

Douglas Garofalo died in 2011.

01

03   04

01 Sanders Residence, Jefferson City, MO, 2009
02 Suburban Houses, Chicago metropolitan area, 1993
03 Bhatt Residence, Oak Brook, IL, 2010
04 Markow House, Prospect Heights, IL, 1998
05 Manilow Residence, Lake Geneva, WI, 2002
06 Nothstine Residence, Green Bay, WI, 2004

05   06

02

01

03

04

05

Mario Gooden, Ray Huff

Huff + Gooden Architects, Charleston, SC (est. 1997)

Education Gooden: Clemson University, BS design, 1987; Columbia University, MArch, 1990 \\ Huff: Clemson University, BArch, 1971

Practice Update New York City **Teaching Positions** Gooden: Columbia University (codirector, Global Africa Lab, Graduate School of Architecture, Planning and Preservation, 2011-present); SCI-Arc; University of Florida; Yale University \\ Huff: Clemson Architecture Center in Charleston (director, 2010-present); Yale University
Notable Honors Virginia Key Beach Park Museum Competition, winning entry, 2005; Venice Architecture Biennale, exhibitor, 2006; NYC Department of Design and Construction, Design and Construction Excellence Shortlist, 2009
Website huffgooden.com

01 Beach Residence, Sullivan's Island, SC, 1993. Photo Starling Photography
02 Mary Ford Elementary School, North Charleston, SC, 2003. Photo Robert E. Mikrut
03 *un | Spoken Spaces: Inside and Outside the Boundaries of Class, Race and Space*, Gibbes Museum of Art, Charleston, SC, 2005. Photo William Struhs
04 Herbert Hasell Aquatic Facility, Charleston, SC, 2001. Photo Robert E. Mikrut
05 Memminger Theater, Charleston, SC, 2008
06 1890 Conference Center, Orangeburg, SC, 1993

01

02

03

04

James Corner

James Corner Field Operations, New York City (est. 1998)

Education Manchester Metropolitan University, BA architecture and landscape architecture, 1983; University of Pennsylvania, MLA/Dipl urban design, 1986

Practice Update London, New York City, Shenzhen; Tatiana Choulika, James Corner, Keith O'Connor, Lisa Switkin (principals)
Teaching Position University of Pennsylvania (chairman, Department of Landscape Architecture, School of Design, 2000-2013)
Notable Honors Chrysler Group, Chrysler Design Award, 2000; American Academy of Arts and Letters, Arts and Letters Award in Architecture, 2004; Cooper-Hewitt, National Design Museum, National Design Award, 2010
Website fieldoperations.net

01 Freshkills Park, Staten Island, NY, 2001
02 Queen Elizabeth Olympic Park, London, England, 2011-2014
03 Tongva Park, Santa Monica, CA, 2011-2013. Photo Tim Street-Porter
04 High Line, New York, NY, 2004-2016. Photo Iwan Baan

01

03

02

04

05

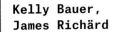

Kelly Bauer,
James Richärd

richärd + bauer, Phoenix
(est. 1996)

Education Bauer: University
of Arizona, BS interior
design, 1982 \\ Richärd:
University of Arizona, BArch,
1985

Practice Update Phoenix and
Solana Beach, CA; Kelly
Bauer, Stephen Kennedy, James
Richärd (principals)
Notable Honors *Contract
Magazine*, Designer of the
Year, 2007; AIA Arizona,
Firm of the Year, 2013 \\
Richärd: AIA Arizona, Arizona
Architects Medal, 2008
Website richard-bauer.com

01 Student Services and
Administration Building,
Glendale Community College,
Glendale, AZ, 2003
02 Arabian Library, Scottsdale,
AZ, 2007
03 Meinel Optical Sciences
Building, Tucson, AZ, 2006
04 Estrella Hall, Avondale, AZ,
2013
05 Mesquite Library, Phoenix, AZ,
1998

All photos Bill Timmerman.

01

02

04

05

06

Jonathan Marvel, Robert Rogers

Rogers Marvel Architects, New York City (est. 1992)

Education Marvel: Dartmouth College, BA geography and visual studies, 1982; Harvard University, MArch, 1986 \\ Rogers: Rice University, BA architecture, BArch, 1983; Harvard University, MA design studies, 1989

Practice Update Marvel Architects, New York City (est. 2013); Guido Hartray, Jonathan Marvel, Lissa So (partners) \\ Rogers Partners Architects+Urban Designers, New York City (est. 2013); Robert Rogers (partner)
Teaching Positions Marvel: Columbia University; Cornell University; Harvard University; Parsons The New School for Design; Washington University in St. Louis \\ Rogers: Columbia University; Harvard University; Pratt Institute; Rice University; Washington University in St. Louis
Notable Honors *See page 296*
Websites marvelarchitects.com \\ rogersarchitects.com

01 Rogers Partners Architects+Urban Designers SandRidge Energy Commons, Oklahoma City, OK, 2011. Rendering dbox and Rogers Partners
02 Rogers Marvel Architects Elevated Acre at 55 Water Street, New York, NY, 2008. © Nathan Sayers Photography
03 Rogers Marvel Architects State Street, 14 Townhouses, Brooklyn, NY, 2007. © David Sundberg/Esto
04 Marvel Architects Pierhouse and 1 Hotel at Brooklyn Bridge Park, Brooklyn, NY, 2012
05 Rogers Marvel Architects Tanya Bonakdar Gallery, New York, NY, 1997. © Reto Halme
06 Rogers Marvel Architects Studio Museum in Harlem, New York, NY, 2001. © Albert Verčerka/Esto

01

02

03

04

05

André Perrotte, Gilles Saucier

Saucier + Perrotte architectes, Montréal
(est. 1988)

Education Perrotte: Université Laval, BArch, 1982 \\ Saucier: Université Laval, BArch, 1982

Teaching Positions Perrotte: McGill University; Université de Montréal; Université du Québec à Montréal; University of Toronto; University of Waterloo \\ Saucier: Massachusetts Institute of Technology; McGill University; University of British Columbia; University of Toronto; University of Washington
Notable Honors *Architecture*, P/A Award, 2001; Royal Architectural Institute of Canada, Architectural Firm Award, 2009; Royal Architectural Institute of Canada, Governor General's Medal in Architecture, 2014
Website saucierperrotte.com

01 First Nations Garden Pavilion, Montréal Botanical Garden, Montréal, Canada, 2000
02 Perimeter Institute for Theoretical Physics, Waterloo, Canada, 2004
03 Private Residence, Laurentian Mountains, Canada, 2007
04 Scandinave Les Bains Vieux-Montréal, Montréal, Canada, 2009
05 Gerald-Goldin College, Sainte-Geneviève, Canada, 1997

All photos Marc Cramer.

01

02

03

04

05

06

Kimberly Holden, Gregg Pasquarelli, Christopher Sharples, Coren Sharples, William Sharples,

SHoP Architects, New York City (est. 1996)

Education Holden: University of Vermont, BA art history, 1988; Columbia University, MArch, 1994 \\ Pasquarelli: Villanova University, BS business, 1987; Columbia University, MArch, 1994 \\ Christopher Sharples: Dickinson College, BA history, BFA, 1987; Columbia University, MArch, 1990 \\ Coren Sharples: University of Maryland, BS business and management, 1987; Columbia University, MArch, 1994 \\ William Sharples: Pennsylvania State University, BA architectural engineering, 1988; Columbia University, MArch, 1994

Practice Update SHoP Architects \\ SHoP Construction (est. 2007); Vishaan Chakrabarti, Kimberly Holden, Jonathan Mallie, Gregg Pasquarelli, Christopher Sharples, Coren Sharples, William Sharples (principals)
Teaching Positions See *page 296*
Notable Honors Cooper-Hewitt, National Design Museum, National Design Award, 2009; AIA New York State, Firm of the Year Award, 2013; *Fast Company*, "The World's Top 10 Most Innovative Companies in Architecture," first place, 2014
Websites shoparc.com \\ shop-construction.com

01 *Dunescape*, MoMA PS1 Young Architects Program, Queens, NY, winning proposal, 2000. © David Joseph
02 South Street Seaport, New York, NY, 2012
03 Carousel House, Mitchell Park, Greenport, NY, 2001. Photo Seong Kwon
04 Pier 15, East River Waterfront, New York, NY, 2012
05 Barclays Center, Brooklyn, NY, 2012. Photo Bruce Damonte
06 Domino Sugar Refinery, Brooklyn, NY, in progress

01

02

03

04

05

06

Mehrdad Yazdani

Yazdani Studio of Cannon Design, Los Angeles (est. 2000)

Education University of Texas at Austin, BA architecture, 1984; Harvard University, MArch, 1987

Practice Update Boston, Los Angeles
Teaching Positions University of Oregon; University of Texas at Arlington; University of Texas at Austin
Notable Honors Museum of Modern Art (New York City), permanent collection; *Progressive Architecture*, P/A Award, 1992; National AIA and American Hospital Association, Design Award, 2013
Website yazdanistudio.com

01 Lloyd D. George U.S. Courthouse, Las Vegas, NV, 1999. Photo Peter Aaron/Esto
02 Gates Vascular Institute, Buffalo, NY, 2012. Photo Bjorg Magnea
03 Los Angeles Metro, Red Line Station, Los Angeles, CA, 1995. Photo Tim Hursley
04 Price Center East, University of California, San Diego, 2008. Photo Tim Hursley
05 Chaparral Science Hall, California State University, Northridge, 2010. Photo Tim Hursley
06 Only One Research and Development Center, CJ Corporation, Seoul, South Korea, 2012

Thom Faulders

01

Beige Design, San Francisco (est. 1998)

Education California Polytechnic State University, San Luis Obispo, BArch, 1986; Cranbrook Academy of Art, MArch, 1993

Practice Update Faulders Studio, Oakland (est. 2008)
Teaching Positions California College of the Arts; KTH Royal Institute of Technology; University of California, Berkeley
Notable Honors San Francisco Museum of Modern Art, Experimental Design Award, 2001; AIA San Francisco, New Practices Award, 2009; FRAC Centre, permanent collection, 2012
Website faulders-studio.com

02

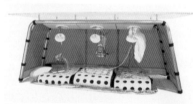

03

04

05

01 Beige Design *Particle Reflex*, San Francisco Museum of Modern Art, San Francisco, CA, 2001. Photo Kallan Nishimoto
02 Beige Design *Undercover Table*, 1999; in collaboration with Anna Rainer
03 Faulders Studio *Entrium Light Cloud*, Science, Teaching and Research Center, Portland State University, Portland, OR, 2014
04 Faulders Studio *BAMscape*, Berkeley Art Museum and Pacific Film Archive, University of California, Berkeley, 2010. Photo Marion Brenner
05 Beige Design *Airspace Tokyo*, Tokyo, Japan, 2007; in collaboration with Hajime Masubuchi, Proces2, Studio M

Byron Kuth, Elizabeth Ranieri

02

03

05

01

04

Kuth|Ranieri Architects, San Francisco (est. 1990)

Education Kuth: California Institute of the Arts, BA industrial design, 1972; Rhode Island School of Design, BFA architecture, BArch, 1986 \\ Ranieri: Rhode Island School of Design, BFA architecture, BArch, 1986

Practice Update Kuth|Ranieri Architects \\ Deep Green Design Alliance (dgda), San Francisco (est. 2005); Byron Kuth (founder)
Teaching Positions California College of the Arts; Harvard University; University of California, Berkeley
Notable Honors San Francisco Bay Conservation and Development Commission, Rising Tides Competition, winner, 2009; National ASLA, Honor Award with Andrea Cochran, 2011 \\ Kuth: AIA, Fellow, 2007 \\ Ranieri: AIA, Fellow, 2010
Websites dgda.com \\ kuthranieri.com

06

01 Nob Hill Residence, San Francisco, CA, 2001. Photo Cesar Rubio
02 Guesthouse/Gallery, San Francisco, CA, 2004. Photo Joe Fletcher
03 Hillsborough Residence, Hillsborough, CA, 2006. Photo Joe Fletcher
04 *Fabrications: Body in Repose*, San Francisco Museum of Modern Art, San Francisco, CA, 1998. © San Francisco Museum of Modern Art
05 Lodi Bunkhouse, St. Helena, CA, 2002. Photo Joe Fletcher
06 Private Residence and LEF Foundation Offices, Napa Valley, CA, 1994. Photo Sharon Risedorph

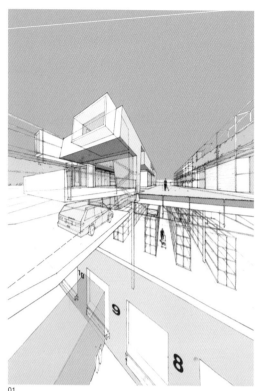

01

02

03

04

05

06

David Lewis, Paul Lewis, Marc Tsurumaki

Lewis Tsurumaki Lewis Architects (LTL Architects), New York City (est. 1997)

Education David Lewis: Carleton College, BA political science, 1988; Cornell University, MA history of architecture and urbanism, 1992; Princeton University, MArch, 1995 \\ Paul Lewis: Wesleyan University, BA art, 1988; Princeton University, MArch, 1992 \\ Tsurumaki: University of Virginia, BS architecture, 1987; Princeton University, MArch, 1991

Teaching Positions David Lewis: Cornell University; Ohio State University; Parsons The New School for Design (director, MArch Program, 2002-2007; interim dean, School of Constructed Environments, 2012-2013); University of Limerick; University of Pennsylvania \\ Paul Lewis: Barnard College; Cooper Union; Ohio State University; Parsons The New School for Design; Princeton University (director, Graduate Studies, School of Architecture, 2003-2009) \\ Tsurumaki: Columbia University; Cornell University; Massachusetts Institute of Technology; Syracuse University; Yale University
Notable Honors See page 296
Website LTLarchitects.com

01 New Suburbanism, speculative neighborhood, 2000
02 Fluff Bakery, New York, NY, 2004. Photo Michael Moran
03 Arthouse at the Jones Center, Austin, TX, 2010. Photo Michael Moran
04 Bornhuetter Hall, College of Wooster, Wooster, OH, 2004. Photo Michael Moran
05 Lozoo Restaurant, New York, NY, 2002. Photo Michael Moran
06 Administrative Campus Center, Claremont University Consortium, Claremont, CA, 2011. Photo Michael Moran

01

02

03

04

06

05

Marwan Al-Sayed

Marwan Al-Sayed Architects (MASA), Phoenix (est. 1997)

Education Vassar College, BA art and architectural history, 1983; Columbia University, MArch, 1986

Practice Update Marwan Al-Sayed, Inc., Los Angeles (est. 2012)
Teaching Positions Arizona State University; New York Institute of Technology
Notable Honors *Esquire* magazine, Best and Brightest, 2004; American Academy of Arts and Letters, Arts and Letters Award in Architecture, 2006; *Travel + Leisure*, T+L Design Awards, Best Small Resort, 2010
Website masastudio.com

01 House of Earth + Light, Phoenix, AZ, 2001. Photo Bill Timmerman
02 House of Earth + Light, Phoenix, AZ, 2001. Photo Bill Timmerman
03 Desert City House, Paradise Valley, AZ, 2005. Photo Matt Winquist
04 Kinderhorn Residence, Sun Valley, ID, 2004. Photo Bill Timmerman
05 Amangiri, Canyon Point, UT, 2009; in collaboration with Wendell Burnette Architects and Rick Joy Architects. Photo Joe Fletcher
06 Desert City House, Paradise Valley, AZ, 2005. Photo Matt Winquist

01

Alan Koch,
Lyn Rice,
Galia Solomonoff,
Linda Taalman

OpenOffice, New York City
(est. 1998)

Education Koch: Parsons The
New School for Design, BFA
sculpture, 1990; Cornell
University, BArch, 1995 \\
Rice: University of Oklahoma,
BArch, BS environmental
design, 1984; Columbia
University, MSAAD, 1994 \\
Solomonoff: City College
of New York, BSArch, 1991;
Columbia University, MArch,
1994 \\ Taalman: Cooper
Union, BArch, 1997

Practice Update RICE+LIPKA
ARCHITECTS, New York City
(est. 2004); Astrid Lipka,
Lyn Rice (principals) \\
Solomonoff Architecture
Studio, New York City (est.
2004); Galia Solomonoff
(principal) \\ Taalman Koch
Architecture, Los Angeles
(est. 2003), IT House, Inc.,
Los Angeles (est. 2010);
Alan Koch, Linda Taalman
(principals)
Teaching Positions *See page
296*
Notable Honors *See page 296*
Websites ricelipka.com \\
solomonoff.com \\
taalmankoch.com; tkithouse
.com

02

03

04   05

01 OpenOffice Dia:Beacon, Beacon,
NY, 2003; in collaboration with
Robert Irwin. © Richard Barnes
02 OpenOffice *Defective Brick
Project*, New York, NY, 2000.
© Lily Wang
03 RICE+LIPKA ARCHITECTS Sheila C.
Johnson Design Center, Parsons
The New School for Design, New
York, NY, 2009. © Michael Moran
04 Solomonoff Architecture Studio
Mini Marfa, New York, NY, 2012.
© Alex Guerrero
05 Taalman Koch Architecture Off-
Grid IT House, Pioneertown, CA,
2006. © Undine Prohl

01

02

03

04

Ali Tayar

Parallel Design Partnership, New York City (est. 1993)

Education University of Stuttgart, Dipl. Ing., architecture, 1983; Massachusetts Institute of Technology, MS architectural studies, 1986

Teaching Positions Harvard University; Parsons The New School for Design; Royal College of Art; Syracuse University
Notable Honors National Endowment for the Arts, grant recipient, 1995; Cooper-Hewitt, National Design Museum, National Design Award Finalist in Interior Design, 2009; *Interior Design*, Best of the Year, 2011
Website alitayar.com

01 Gansevoort Gallery Gate, New York, NY, 1996. © Joshua McHugh
02 Carbon Fiber House, Switzerland, 2014. © Simon B. Opladen
03 Queen of Greene, New York, NY, 2011. © Joshua McHugh
04 PoP Burger, New York, NY, 2007. © Joshua McHugh
05 Ellen's Brackets, 1994. © Joshua McHugh

01

02

03

04

05

Louise Harpman, Scott Specht

Specht Harpman, New York City
(est. 1995)

Education Harpman: Harvard
University, AB East Asian
studies, 1987; Cambridge
University, MPhil in social
anthropology, 1988; Yale
University, MArch, 1993
\\ Specht: University of
Florida, BA design, 1985;
Yale University, MArch, 1993

Practice Update Specht
Harpman | Architecture,
Austin, TX, and New York City
Teaching Positions Harpman:
New York University;
University of Pennsylvania;
University of Texas at Austin
(associate dean, School of
Architecture, 2003-2009);
Yale University
Notable Honors AIA New York
Chapter, Honor Award, 2003;
Wallpaper*, Architects
Directory, Top 50 Emerging
Practices, 2008; Architizer,
A+ Award, 2012
Website spechtharpman.com

01 Concrete Incorporated National
Headquarters, New York, NY,
1999. Photo Michael Moran
02 Stirratt Residence, New Canaan,
CT, 2010. Photo Elizabeth
Felicella
03 Manhattan Micro-Loft, New
York, NY, 2012. Photo Taggart
Sorensen
04 Funny Garbage, New York, NY,
1998. Photo Michael Moran
05 Doyle Hall, St. Edward's
University, Austin, TX, 2009.
Photo Taggart Sorensen

01

02

Andrew Zago

Zago Architecture, Detroit
(est. 1991)

Education University of
Michigan, BFA painting, 1980;
Harvard University, MArch,
1986

Practice Update Los Angeles
Teaching Positions City
College of New York;
Cornell University; Ohio
State University; SCI-Arc;
University of Illinois at
Chicago
Notable Honors American
Academy in Rome, Franklin
D. Israel Rome Prize, 2002;
American Academy of Arts and
Letters, Arts and Letters
Award in Architecture, 2003;
United States Artists, USA
Target Fellow, 2008
Website zagoarchitecture.com

03

01 The Greening of Detroit
   Pavilion, Detroit, MI, 2001.
   Photo Raimund Koch
02 Cornell Synthesis Studio,
   Cornell University, Ithaca,
   NY, 1997
03 Property with Properties,
   *Foreclosed: Rehousing the
   American Dream*, Museum of
   Modern Art, New York, NY, 2011
04 Fine Venture Office Tower,
   Seoul, South Korea, 2002; in
   collaboration with Minoru
   Yamasaki Associates
05 Korean Presbyterian Church
   of Metropolitan Detroit,
   Southfield, MI, 2001. Photo
   Balthazar Korab

04

05

01

David Brininstool, Brad Lynch

Brininstool + Lynch, Chicago
(est. 1989)

Education Brininstool:
University of Michigan,
BS architecture, 1974;
University of Michigan,
MArch, 1976 \\ Lynch:
University of Wisconsin,
BA art, 1985

Teaching Positions
Brininstool: Illinois
Institute of Technology \\
Lynch: Archeworks; Illinois
Institute of Technology;
Syracuse University
Notable Honors AIA Chicago,
Distinguished Building Award,
1992; Chicago Athenaeum,
American Architecture
Award, 2002; AIA Chicago,
Sustainability Leadership
Award, 2012
Website brininstool-lynch.com

02

03

04

05

01 Racine Art Museum, Racine,
WI, 2003. Photo Christopher
Barrett/Hedrich Blessing
02 Yamamoto Residence,
McCordsville, IN, 2000. Photo
Christopher Barrett/Hedrich
Blessing
03 1720 South Michigan, Chicago,
IL, 2007. Photo Jamie Padgett/
Padgett and Company, Inc.
04 Claremont House, Chicago,
IL, 2007. Photo Christopher
Barrett/Hedrich Blessing
05 Coffou Cottage, Michigan City,
IN, 2008. Photo Christopher
Barrett/Hedrich Blessing

Frank Harmon

Frank Harmon Architect,
Raleigh, NC (est. 1985)

Education North Carolina
State University, College of
Design, 1961; Architectural
Association, 1967

Teaching Positions
Architectural Association;
Auburn University; North
Carolina State University
Notable Honors AIA North
Carolina, Kamphoefner Prize,
1995; National AIA, Housing
Award, 2009; AIA North
Carolina, F. Carter Williams
Gold Medal, 2013
Websites frankharmon.com \\
nativeplaces.tumblr.com

01

02

03

01 Frank and Judy Harmon
Residence, Raleigh, NC, 1994.
Photo Tom Aldi
02 Taylor Vacation Home, Abaco,
the Bahamas, 2000. Photo James
West/J. West Productions
03 JC Raulston Arboretum Lath
House, Raleigh, NC, 2010
04 North Carolina Botanic Garden
Education Center, Chapel Hill,
NC, 2009
05 Strickland Ferris Residence,
Raleigh, NC, 2005. Photo Tim
Hursley

04

05

01

02

04

03

05

Margie Ruddick

Margie Ruddick Landscape, New York City, Philadelphia (est. 1995)

Education Bowdoin College, BA English literature, 1979; Harvard University, MLA, 1988

Practice Update Margie Ruddick Landscape, New York City, Philadelphia (1995-2004; 2007-present) \\ Wallace Roberts and Todd, Miami, Philadelphia, San Diego, San Francisco (Ruddick, partner, 2004-2007) **Teaching Positions** Harvard University; Parsons The New School for Design; Princeton University; University of Pennsylvania; Yale University **Notable Honors** Architects/ Designers/Planners for Social Responsibility, Lewis Mumford Award, 2002; National Audubon Society, Rachel Carson Award, 2006; Cooper-Hewitt, National Design Museum, National Design Award, 2013 **Website** margieruddick.com

01 Casa Cabo, Cabo, Mexico, 2003; in collaboration with Steven Harris Architects. Photo David Kelly
02 Queens Plaza, Queens, NY, rendering, 2003; in collaboration with Marpillero Pollak Architects
03 Queens Plaza, Queens, NY, 2012; in collaboration with Marpillero Pollak Architects
04 Urban Garden, New York, NY, 2009; in collaboration with Dorothy Ruddick and WRT Design. Photo Sam Oberter
05 Kinderhook Retreat, Kinderhook, NY, 2009; in collaboration with Steven Harris Architects. Photo Scott Frances

01

02

03

04

05

Monica Ponce de Leon, Nader Tehrani

Office dA, Boston (est. 1991)

Education Ponce de Leon: University of Miami, BArch, 1989; Harvard University, MArch urban planning, 1991 \\ Tehrani: Rhode Island School of Design, BFA, BArch, 1986; Architectural Association, postgraduate degree in history and theory, 1987; Harvard University, MArch urban planning, 1991

Practice Update MPdL Studio, Ann Arbor, Boston, New York City (est. 2011); Monica Ponce de Leon (principal) \\ NADAAA, Boston, New York City (est. 2011); Katherine Faulkner, Daniel Gallagher, Nader Tehrani (principals)
Teaching Positions Ponce de Leon: Georgia Institute of Technology; Harvard University; Northeastern University; Rhode Island School of Design; University of Michigan (dean, A. Alfred Taubman College of Architecture and Urban Planning, 2008-present) \\ Tehrani: Harvard University; Massachusetts Institute of Technology (head, Department of Architecture, School of Architecture + Planning, 2010-2014); Northeastern University; Rhode Island School of Design; University of Melbourne
Notable Honors *See page 296*
Websites monicaponcedeleon .com \\ NADAAA.com

01 **MPdL Studio** Conrad Hilton, New York, NY, 2012. Photo John Horner
02 **Office dA** Tongxian Gatehouse, Beijing, China, 2003
03 **Office dA** Inter-Faith Spiritual Center, Northeastern University, Boston, MA, 1998
04 **NADAAA** Samsung Model Home Gallery, Seoul, South Korea, 2012
05 **NADAAA** Faculty of Architecture, Building, and Planning, University of Melbourne, Australia, in progress. Rendering John Wardle Architects and NADAAA

01

02

03

04

05

06

Jennifer Siegal

Office of Mobile Design,
Los Angeles (est. 1998)

Education Hobart and
William Smith Colleges, BA
architectural studies, 1987;
SCI-Arc, MArch, 1994

Teaching Positions Arizona
State University; Taliesin,
Frank Lloyd Wright School
of Architecture; University
of North Carolina at
Charlotte; University of
Southern California; Woodbury
University
Notable Honors Harvard
University, Loeb Fellowship,
2003; SCI-Arc, Distinguished
Alumna Award, 2009; USA
Network, Character Approved
Award, 2009
Website designmobile.com

01 Ecolab, 1998. Photo Benny Chan
02 Hydra House, 2003
03 KCRW Mobile, 2012
04 iMobile, 2000
05 Seatrain Residence,
   Los Angeles, CA, 2003. Photo
   Undine Prohl
06 Taliesen Mod.Fab, Scottsdale,
   AZ, 2009. Photo Bill Timmerman

01

02

03

04

05

Peter Lynch

Peter Lynch Architect,
New York City (est. 1991)

Education Cooper Union,
BArch, 1984

Practice Update Studio THEM,
New York City (est. 2006);
Gustavo Crembil, Peter Lynch
\\ Lynch+Song, Beijing,
Brooklyn, Stockholm (est.
2010); Peter Lynch, Lydia
Fangzhou Song (principals)
Teaching Positions City
College of New York;
Cranbrook Academy of Art
(director, Architecture
Department, 1996-2005);
Harvard University; Parsons
The New School for Design;
Rhode Island School of Design
Notable Honors American
Academy in Rome, Rome Prize,
2005; *Architecture*, P/A
Award, 2005; Association
of Collegiate Schools of
Architecture, JAE Award,
Best Design as Scholarship
Article, coauthored with
Gustavo Crembil, 2010
Website studiothem.com

01 **Peter Lynch Architect** Villa for
   an Industrialist, Shenzhen,
   China, 2008; in collaboration
   with Ahlaiya Yung
02 **Peter Lynch Architect** Villa for
   an Industrialist, Shenzhen,
   China, 2008; in collaboration
   with Ahlaiya Yung
03 **Lynch+Song** House for a
   Classicist and Antiques
   Restorer, Sea Cliff, NY, 2012
04 **Peter Lynch Architect** Dome
   Structure Research, Cranbrook
   Academy of Art, Bloomfield
   Hills, MI, 2003. Photo Tim
   Thayer
05 **Peter Lynch Architect** Bamboo
   construction research for emer-
   gency housing, American Academy
   in Rome, Rome, Italy, 2004
06 **Peter Lynch Architect** Bushwick
   Community College, High School,
   and Day Care, Brooklyn, NY,
   1992

1982-1986
1988-1993
1994-1998
1999-2003

2004-2008

2009-2013

The biggest architecture story of 2013 was an insult from 1991. When Robert Venturi won the Pritzker Architecture Prize that year, the jury citation mentioned his partner and wife, Denise Scott Brown, in the fifth paragraph. Asked about the Pritzker by the *Architects' Journal* in March 2013, Scott Brown said, "They owe me not a Pritzker Prize but a Pritzker inclusion ceremony. Let's salute the notion of joint creativity." It is important for Scott Brown to be recognized, because she deserves it. But the second part of her quote is more meaningful for the future of the field.

More than making a place for women, Scott Brown's emphasis on "joint creativity" means making a place for partners. Looking at the Emerging Voices across the decades reveals a program that has evolved in order to reflect new definitions of both "architecture" and "practice." These new definitions make the Pritzker, still fighting the idea of admitting a wrong, seem fundamentally out-of-date, despite the fact that it has honored two partnerships (Jacques Herzog and Pierre de Meuron of Herzog & de Meuron in 2001, and Ryue Nishizawa and Kazuyo Sejima of SANAA in 2010). Even the AIA has (belatedly) recognized the importance of partnerships, voting in new rules for the Gold Medal that allow it to be awarded to pairs as of 2014.

Starting in the late 1990s the ratio of individuals to partnerships in the Emerging Voices program slowly began to change. The period from 2004 to 2008 is, if not a watershed, clear evidence of that shift. In 2004 John Friedman Alice Kimm Architects was the only partnership honored. A year later more than half the winners were firms with two or more principals. In 2006 half of the winners were partnerships. By 2007 partnerships, including brothers Mark Anderson and Peter Anderson of Anderson Anderson Architecture, outnumbered individuals. And in 2008 nearly all the selected firms were led by multiple voices, including the five-person partnership of el dorado, the four-person Onion Flats (three brothers among them), and siblings Granger Moorhead and Robert Moorhead of Moorhead & Moorhead.

The rise of partnerships is an acknowledgment that one person isn't doing it all; togetherness may be the only way to have it all. Partners have different but equal talents. Partners cover for each other during life events (births, deaths, illnesses). Partners write and partners design. Partners set up the plumbing inspection and partners manipulate the 3-D model. And sometimes partners stay home two days a week to take care of the kids.

The future of a sustainable, inclusive, and creative architectural profession also requires expanding the definition of "architecture practice." Freecell (EV05), Lead Pencil Studio (EV06), and Höweler + Yoon Architecture/MY Studio (EV07) sustain themselves through both conventional and alternative projects, including installations. The "and" in many-handed firms means different skills, not all learned in architecture school: design and construction for Bercy Chen Studio (EV06) and design and development for then-partnership Della Valle Bernheimer (EV07).

The makeup of Emerging Voices mid-aught reflects reality. My own jury experience in 2011 involved no predetermined agenda to select firms helmed by multiple principals, yet there were no sole practitioners among the winners. I sifted through the portfolios, waiting to be drawn into the work. I never counted the names on the title page.

It is as important to recognize Scott Brown's role in what remains Venturi's Pritzker as it is to acknowledge that a single person is no longer expected to have all the talent or shoulder all the responsibility. To succeed, one shouldn't have to do everything. Putting two, three, four, or five names on the door makes a tremendous difference and diminishes no one.

01

02

03

04

05

Pierre Thibault

Atelier Pierre Thibault,
Québec City (est. 1988)

Education Université Laval,
BArch, 1982

Teaching Positions Ecole de design
Nantes Atlantique; Ecole des hautes
études appliquées du Droit;
Ecole nationale supérieure
d'architecture de Nancy;
Massachusetts Institute of
Technology; Université Laval
Notable Honors Fonds
d'études et de recherches en
design intérieur de l'Est
(FERDIE) and *Intérieurs*,
Prix Intérieurs FERDIE,
2009; Ordre des architects
du Québec, finaliste, 2009;
Ordre des architects du
Québec, Prix d'excellence,
2011
Website atelier.pthibault.com

01 Musée des Abénakis, Odanak,
Canada, 2003
02 Winter Gardens, Parc des
Grands-Jardins, Canada, 2001
03 The Black House, Lac des Deux
Montagnes, Canada, 2009
04 Villa du lac du Castor,
Grandes-Piles, Canada, 1999
05 Cistercian Abbey, Saint-Jean-
de-Matha, Canada, 2005

All photos Alain Laforest.

Rand Elliott

01

02

03

04

05

06

Elliott + Associates Architects, Oklahoma City (est. 1976)

Education Oklahoma State University, BArch, 1973

Notable Honors National AIA, Honor Award, 2007; Oklahoma State University, Distinguished Alumni Award, 2010; AIA Oklahoma, Lifetime Achievement Award, 2012
Website e-a-a.com

01 Morris Agency, Oklahoma City, OK, 1994. Photo Robert Shimer/ Hedrich Blessing
02 KJ McNitt, Oklahoma City, OK, 1996. Photo Robert Shimer/ Hedrich Blessing
03 Devon Boathouse, Oklahoma City, OK, 2010. Photo Scott McDonald/ Hedrich Blessing
04 POPS, Arcadia, OK, 2007. Photo Scott McDonald/Hedrich Blessing
05 Chesapeake Finish Line Tower, Oklahoma City, OK, 2011. Photo Scott McDonald/Hedrich Blessing
06 American Bank, Edmond, OK, 1997. Photo Robert Shimer/ Hedrich Blessing

01

John Friedman, Alice Kimm

**John Friedman Alice Kimm
Architects**, Los Angeles
(est. 1996)

Education Friedman:
Massachusetts Institute of
Technology, BS architecture,
1983; University of Oxford,
MA philosophy, politics,
and economics, 1986; Harvard
University, MArch, 1990 \\
Kimm: Cornell University,
BA economics, 1986; Harvard
University, MArch, 1990

Teaching Positions Friedman:
SCI-Arc; University of
Southern California \\
Kimm: University of
Southern California (chair,
Undergraduate Architecture,
School of Architecture,
2010-2014)
Notable Honors National
AIA, Institute Honor Award,
2004; Bruner Foundation,
Rudy Bruner Award for Urban
Excellence, 2008
Website jfak.net

02

03

04

05

01 LA Design Center, Los Angeles,
CA, 2003
02 Graduate Aerospace Labs,
California Institute of
Technology, Pasadena, CA, 2009
03 Los Angeles Police Department,
Main Street Parking and Motor
Transport Division,
Los Angeles, CA, 2010
04 Ehrlich Retreat +,
Santa Monica, CA, 2012
05 Irolo Elderly Housing,
Los Angeles, CA, 2002

All photos Benny Chan/Fotoworks.

01

02

Lorcan O'Herlihy

Lorcan O'Herlihy Architects,
Los Angeles (est. 1990)

Education California
Polytechnic State University,
San Luis Obispo, BArch, 1981;
Architectural Association, MA
histories and theories, 2009

Teaching Positions
Architectural Association;
Parsons The New School for
Design; SCI-Arc; University
of Southern California
Notable Honors National AIA,
Housing Award, 2008, 2010;
AIA Los Angeles, Firm of the
Year, 2010
Website loharchitects.com

03

04

05

01 Gardner1050, West Hollywood,
CA, 2007. Photo Lawrence
Anderson
02 Vertical House, Los Angeles,
CA, 2004. Photo Juergen Nogai
03 Formosa 1140, West Hollywood,
CA, 2009. Photo Lawrence
Anderson
04 Cloverdale749, Los Angeles, CA,
2014. Photo Lawrence Anderson
05 Flynn Mews House, Dublin,
Ireland, 2013. Photo Enda
Cavanagh

01

02

03

04

Tom Kundig

Olson Kundig Architects, Seattle (est. 1996); Tom Kundig, Jim Olson (principals)

Education University of Washington, BA environmental design, 1977; University of Washington, MArch, 1981

Practice Update Tom Kundig, Alan Maskin, Kirsten Murray, Jim Olson (principals)
Teaching Positions Syracuse University; University of Arkansas; University of Oregon in Kyoto; University of Southern California; University of Washington
Notable Honors American Academy of Arts and Letters, Arts and Letters Award in Architecture, 2007; Cooper-Hewitt, National Design Museum, National Design Award, 2008; National AIA, Firm Award, 2009
Website olsonkundigarchitects.com

05

01 Shadowboxx, San Juan Islands, WA, 2009. Photo Michael Burns
02 The Pierre, San Juan Islands, WA, 2010. Photo Dwight Eschliman
03 Studio Sitges, Sitges, Spain, 2010. Photo Nikolas Koenig
04 Chicken Point Cabin, Hayden Lake, ID, 2003. Photo Benjamin Benscheider
05 Delta Shelter, Mazama, WA, 2002. Photo Tim Bies

Preston Scott Cohen

01

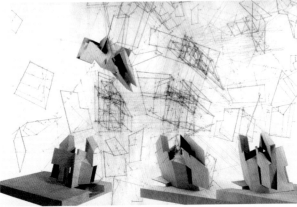

02

03

04

05

06

Preston Scott Cohen Studio, Cambridge, MA (est. 1989)

Education Rhode Island School of Design, BFA architecture, BArch, 1983; Harvard University, MArch, 1985

Teaching Positions Harvard University (chair, Department of Architecture, Graduate School of Design, 2008-2013); Ohio State University; Princeton University; University of California, Los Angeles; University of Toronto
Notable Honors *Architect*, P/A Award, 2010; *Travel + Leisure*, Best Museum, 2011; Bengbu City Opera House Competition, first prize, 2013
Website pscohen.com

01 Cornered House, Sarasota, FL, 1992
02 Taiyuan Museum of Art, Taiyuan, China, 2012
03 Arcade Canopy, New York, NY, 2009; in association with Pei Cobb Freed and Partners
04 Stilicho Duplex, Paris, France, 1994
05 Herta and Paul Amir Building, Tel Aviv Museum of Art, Tel Aviv, Israel, 2011
06 Herta and Paul Amir Building, Tel Aviv Museum of Art, Tel Aviv, Israel, 2011. Photo Amit Geron, courtesy Tel Aviv Museum of Art

Lawrence Scarpa

Pugh + Scarpa, Los Angeles (est. 1991); Angela Brooks, Gwynne Pugh, Lawrence Scarpa (principals)

Education University of Florida, BA design, 1981; University of Florida, MArch, 1987

Practice Update Brooks + Scarpa, Los Angeles (est. 2011); Angela Brooks, Lawrence Scarpa (principals)
Teaching Positions Harvard University; University of California, Berkeley; University of Michigan; University of Southern California; Washington University in St. Louis
Notable Honors *Interior Design*, Hall of Fame, 2008; National AIA, Firm Award, 2010; Cooper-Hewitt, National Design Museum, National Design Award, 2014
Website brooksscarpa.com

01 Colorado Court Affordable Housing SRO, Santa Monica, CA, 2002. Photo John Linden
02 Solar Umbrella House, Venice, CA, 2005. Photo Marvin Rand
03 Bergamot Station Arts Center, Santa Monica, CA, 2000. Photo Marvin Rand
04 XAP Corporation, Culver City, CA, 2009. Photo Benny Chan
05 Cherokee Studios, West Hollywood, CA, 2010. Photo John Linden

All projects by Pugh + Scarpa.

01

03

04

02

05

06

Ken Smith

WORKSHOP: Ken Smith Landscape Architect, New York City (est. 1992)

Education Iowa State University, BS landscape architecture, 1976; Harvard University, MLA, 1986

Teaching Positions City College of New York; Harvard University

Notable Honors Bruner Foundation, Rudy Bruner Award for Urban Excellence, 2011; National ASLA, Landmark Award, 2012; California Preservation Foundation, Design Award, 2013

Website kensmithworkshop.com

01 Santa Fe Railyard Park and Plaza, Santa Fe, NM, 2007. © Peter Mauss/Esto
02 East River Waterfront, New York, NY, 2006. © Peter Mauss/Esto
03 Time Warner Center, New York, NY, 2003. © Peter Mauss/Esto
04 P.S. 19, Queens, NY, 2006. © Paul Warchol
05 Palm Court Arts Complex/North Lawn, Orange County Great Park, Irvine, CA, 2006-present. © Grant Mudford
06 Glowing Topiary Garden, New York, NY, 1997. Photo John Back

Taryn Christoff, Martin Finio

Christoff:Finio, New York City (est. 1999)

Education Christoff: Illinois Institute of Technology, BArch, 1985 \\ Finio: Cooper Union, BArch, 1988

Teaching Positions Finio: Columbia University; Yale University
Notable Honors National AIA, Honor Award, 2009; Chicago Athenaeum, American Architecture Award, 2010; American Academy of Arts and Letters, Arts and Letters Award in Architecture, 2014
Website christofffinio.com

01 Carriage House, New York, NY, 2006. Photo Jan Staller
02 Heckscher Foundation for Children, New York, NY, 2006. Photo Elizabeth Felicella
03 Donghia Materials Study Center, New York, NY, 2003. Photo Elizabeth Felicella
04 Sagaponack House, Sagaponack, NY, 2010; original renovation by Tod Williams. Photo Scott Frances/Esto
05 House on a Barrier Island, Long Beach Island, NJ, 2002. Photo Elizabeth Felicella

Claude Cormier

Claude Cormier architectes paysagistes, Montréal
(est. 1994)

Education University of Guelph, BA agronomy, 1982; University of Toronto, BA landscape architecture, 1986; Harvard University, MA history and theory of design, 1994

Practice Update Claude Cormier et Associés
Notable Honors National Order of Quebec, Knight, 2009; National ASLA, Design Award, 2012; Canadian Society of Landscape Architects, National Honor, 2013
Website claudecormier.com

01 Blue Tree, Sonoma, CA, 2004. Photo Cornerstone Garden
02 Parc Hydro-Québec, Montréal, Canada, 2012. Photo Guillaume Paradis
03 Pink Balls, Montréal, Canada, 2011-2013. Photo Marc Cramer
04 Place d'Youville, Montréal, Canada, 2008. Photo Jean-François Vézina
05 Blue Stick Garden, Les Jardins de Métis, Grand-Métis, Canada, 2000
06 Canadian Museum of Civilizations Plaza, Gatineau, Canada, 2010

01

02

03

04

05

06

Lauren Crahan, John Hartmann

Freecell, New York City
(est. 2000)

Education Crahan: Rhode
Island School of Design, BFA,
BArch, 1996 \\ Hartmann:
Cooper Union, BArch, 2000

Teaching Positions Crahan:
China Academy of Art;
Parsons The New School for
Design; Rhode Island School
of Design; University of
Pennsylvania \\ Hartmann:
Cooper Union; New Jersey
Institute of Technology;
Parsons The New School for
Design; Rhode Island School
of Design
Notable Honors Hartmann:
American Academy in Rome,
Rome Prize, 2005; MacDowell
Colony, Resident, 2010
Website frcll.com

01 *moistSCAPE*, Henry Urbach
 Architecture Gallery, New York,
 NY, 2004. Photo Ron Amstuz
02 *LightHearted*, New York, NY,
 2011
03 NYCVelo, New York, NY, 2005.
 Photo Christopher Payne
04 *Point to Line*, Akron, OH, 2012.
 Photo Warren Darius Aftahi
05 Pearl Street Apartment,
 New York, NY, 2005. Photo
 Christopher Payne
06 Pearl Street Apartment,
 New York, NY, 2005. Photo
 Christopher Payne

01

02

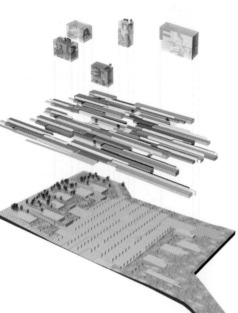

03

04

05

06

John Ronan

John Ronan Architects,
Chicago (est. 1999)

Education University of
Michigan, BS architecture,
1985; Harvard University,
MArch, 1991

Teaching Position Illinois
Institute of Technology
Notable Honors National
AIA, Honor Award, 2009,
2012; Art Institute of
Chicago, *Iterations: John
Ronan's Poetry Foundation*,
exhibition, 2013
Website jrarch.com

01 Poetry Foundation, Chicago,
IL, 2011
02 Chapel of St. Ignatius Loyola,
Christ the King Jesuit College
Preparatory School, Chicago,
IL, 2010. Photo Nathan Kirkman
03 High School, Perth Amboy, NY,
2003
04 Gary Comer College Prep,
Chicago, IL, 2010.
© Steve Hall/Hedrich Blessing
05 Gary Comer Youth Center,
Chicago, IL, 2006.
© Steve Hall/Hedrich Blessing
06 House on the Edge of a Forest,
Northbrook, IL, 2002.
© Steve Hall/Hedrich Blessing

01

02

03

04

05

Pablo Castro, Jennifer Lee

OBRA Architects, New York City (est. 2000)

Education Castro: Universidad Nacional de San Juan, BArch, 1987; Columbia University, MS building design, 1989 \\ Lee: Harvard University, BA, 1990; Cooper Union, BArch, 1997

Practice Update Beijing, New York City, Seoul
Teaching Positions Castro: Barnard College; Cranbrook Academy of Art; Parsons The New School for Design; Pratt Institute; Rhode Island School of Design \\ Lee: Cooper Union; Cranbrook Art Academy; Korea National University of Arts; Pratt Institute
Notable Honors MoMA PS1, Young Architects Program, competition winner, 2006; AIA New York Chapter, Design Merit Award, 2014 \\ Castro: American Academy in Rome, Rome Prize, 2012
Website obraarchitects.com

01 Freedom Park Museum and Witness Memorial, Pretoria, South Africa, 2003. Photo Adriana Miranda
02 *Architettura Povera: Wall of Lessons*, BEB Gallery, Rhode Island School of Design, Providence, RI, 2004. Photo Adriana Miranda
03 *BEATFUSE!*, MoMA PS1 Young Architects Program, Queens, NY, winning proposal, 2006
04 Oxymoron Pavilion, Shenzhen Biennale for Urbanism and Architecture, Shenzhen, China, 2011
05 Casa Osa, Cerra Osa, Costa Rica, 2013. Photo Peter Lynch

01

02

03

05

04

06

John Frane,
Hadrian Predock

Predock_Frane Architects,
Los Angeles (est. 2000)

Education Frane: University of Texas at Austin, BArch, 1993 \\ Predock: University of New Mexico, BArch, 1990; Harvard University, MArch, 1993

Practice Update Venice, CA
Teaching Positions Frane: Tulane University; University of California, Berkeley; University of Southern California \\ Predock: Tulane University; University of California, Berkeley; University of California, Los Angeles; University of Southern California (director, undergraduate architecture, School of Architecture, 2014-present)
Notable Honors National AIA, Honor Award, 2004; Venice Architecture Biennale, exhibitor, 2004; AIA California, Monterey Design Conference, Emerging Talent Award, 2009
Website predockfrane.com

01 Center of Gravity Foundation Hall, Jemez Springs, NM, 2004
02 Twin Houses, Pacific Palisades, CA, 2008
03 Acqua Alta, *Transcending Type*, Venice Architecture Biennale, Venice, Italy, 2004. Photo Elliott Kaufman
04 Getty Family Room, J. Paul Getty Center, Los Angeles, CA, 2005. Photo Elon Schoenholz
05 Habitat 15, Los Angeles, CA, 2008. Photo Elon Schoenholz
06 Optic Clouds, commissioned for *Material Matters*, Pacific Design Center, West Hollywood, CA, 2012

01

02

03

04

05

Gary Hilderbrand, Douglas Reed

Reed Hilderbrand Landscape Architecture, Watertown, MA (est. 1993)

Education Hilderbrand: State University of New York College of Environmental Science and Forestry, Bachelor of landscape architecture, 1979; Harvard University, MLA, 1985 \\ Reed: Louisiana State University, Bachelor of landscape architecture, 1978; Harvard University, MLA, 1981

Teaching Position Hilderbrand: Harvard University
Notable Honors National ASLA, Award of Excellence in Communications, 2013; National ASLA, Firm Award, 2013
Website reedhilderbrand.com

01 Charles River Pier, Spaulding Hospital, Boston, MA, 2003. Photo Alan Ward
02 Old Quarry, Guilford, CT, 2011. Photo Millicent Harvey
03 Children's Therapeutic Garden, Institute for Child and Adolescent Development, Wellesley, MA, 1993. Photo Steve Dunwell
04 Stone Hill Center, The Clark Art Institute, Williamstown, MA, 2008. Photo Alex MacLean
05 Maple Avenue, Mount Auburn Cemetery, Cambridge, MA, 2000. Photo Alan Ward

01

02

03

04

05

Zoltan Pali

Studio Pali Fekete architects (SPF:a), Los Angeles (est. 1988); Judit Méda Fekete, Zoltan Pali (principals)

Education University of California, Los Angeles, BArch, 1981

Teaching Position University of Southern California
Notable Honors National AIA, Honor Award, 2004; Chicago Athenaeum, American Architecture Award, 2007; *LA Business Journal*, Commercial Real Estate Awards, Gold Award, 2014
Website spfa.com

01 Zireing Residence, Pacific Palisades, CA, 2012. Photo Bruce Damonte Photography
02 Brosmith House, Los Angeles, CA, 2005. Photo John Edward Linden Photography
03 Oberfeld Residence, Los Angeles, CA, 2010. Photo John Edward Linden Photography
04 MODAA Building, Culver City, CA, 2007. Photo John Edward Linden Photography
05 Blue Jay Residence, Hollywood Hills, CA, 2004. Photo John Edward Linden Photography

01

03

02

04

05

Thomas Bercy, Calvin Chen

Bercy Chen Studio, Austin, TX (est. 2001)

Education Bercy: La Pontificia Universidad Catolica de Chile, urbanism studies, 1997; University of Texas at Houston, BArch, 1999; University of Texas at Houston, Bachelor architectural engineering, 2000 \\ Chen: University of Texas at Austin, BArch, 1998

Practice Update Austin, TX; Los Angeles; Monterrey, Mexico; Taipei, Taiwan
Notable Honors *Architectural Record*, Design Vanguard, 2006; Chicago Athenaeum and The European Centre for Architecture, Art, Design and Urban Studies, 40 Under 40 Award, 2009; GA Gallery, Tokyo, exhibitor, 2014
Website bcarc.com

01 Lago Vista Lake House, Austin, TX, 2004
02 Shore Vista Boat Dock, Austin, TX, 2011
03 Edgeland Residence, Austin, TX, 2010
04 Annie Residence, Austin, TX, 2003
05 East Village Studios, Austin, TX, 2009

01

02

03

04

05

Mark Goulthorpe

dECOi Architects, Boston, London, Paris (est. 1991)

Education University of Liverpool, BA architecture, 1984; University of Liverpool, BArch, 1988

Practice Update dECOi Architects \\ HypoSurface, Boston (est. 2006) \\ Zero+, Boston (est. 2009)
Teaching Positions Architectural Association; Ecole spéciale d'architecture; Escola tècnica superior d'arquitectura; Massachusetts Institute of Technology; University of Kassel
Notable Honors Far Eastern Group and National Chiao Tung University, Far Eastern International Digital Architecture Design Award, 2004; *Architectural Record*, Design Vanguard, 2005; ADC Global Network, Tomorrow Award, 2012
Websites decoi-architects.org \\ hyposurface.org

01 Galerie Miran, Paris, France, 2003
02 HypoSurface, Chicago, IL, 2007
03 Glaphyros Apartment, Paris, France, 2004. Photo Marc Kicherer
04 Robotically Milled Door, Boston, MA, 2011
05 One Main Office Interior, Cambridge, MA, 2009. Photo Eric Grossl/Esto

01

02

04

03

05

06

Frank Escher,
Ravi GuneWardena

Escher GuneWardena,
Los Angeles (est. 1995)

Education Escher: ETH Zürich,
Diploma architecture,
1987 \\ GuneWardena:
California State Polytechnic
University, Pomona, BArch,
1984; California State
University, International
Program, Florence, art and
architectural history, 1984

Teaching Positions Escher:
California State Polytechnic
University, Pomona;
University of Southern
California \\ GuneWardena:
California State Polytechnic
University, Pomona
Notable Honors Cooper-Hewitt,
National Design Museum,
National Design Triennial,
exhibitor, 2003; Art Center
College of Design and Vitra
Design Museum, *Open House:
Intelligent Living by Design*,
participant, 2006; Swiss Art
Awards, finalist, 2013
Website egarch.net

01 *Lunch Break*, Secession Gallery,
   Vienna, Austria, 2008;
   installation designed in
   collaboration with Sharon
   Lockhart. Photo Alex Slade
   © Sharon Lockhart.
   Reproductions of Sharon
   Lockhart's work appear courtesy
   of the artist and Blum & Poe,
   Los Angeles; Gladstone Gallery,
   New York and Brussels; and
   neugerriemschneider, Berlin
02 Chemosphere Restoration, Los
   Angeles, CA, 2000; original
   design by John Lautner, 1960.
   Photo Josh White
03 Sola/Wright Residence, Los
   Angeles, CA, 2008. Photo Jonas
   Lara
04 Tyre Residence Restoration,
   Los Angeles, CA, 2012; original
   design by A. Quincy Jones,
   1957. Photo Nicolas Valencia
05 Cleantech Corridor,
   Los Angeles, CA, 2011
06 Jamie Residence, Pasadena, CA,
   2000. Photo Gene Ogami

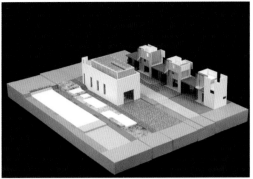

01

02

03

04

05

06

Teddy Cruz

Estudio Teddy Cruz, San Diego (est. 2000)

Education Universidad Rafael Landívar, BA architectural studies, 1982; California Polytechnic State University, San Luis Obispo, BArch, 1987; Harvard University, MDes, 1997

Teaching Positions University of California, San Diego (founder and director, Center for Urban Ecology, 2010-present; codirector, Blum Cross-Border Initiative, 2013-present)
Notable Honors American Academy in Rome, Rome Prize, 1991; Canadian Centre for Architecture and London School of Economics, James Stirling Memorial Lecture on the City, lecturer, 2011; American Academy of Arts and Letters, Arts and Letters Award in Architecture, 2013
Websites estudioteddycruz.com \\ politicalequator.org

01 Casa Familiar Living Rooms at the Border: Housing and Social Infrastructure for Small Parcels, San Ysidro, CA, 2001-present
02 Casa Familiar Living Rooms at the Border: Housing and Social Infrastructure for Small Parcels, San Ysidro, CA, 2001-present
03 Mike Davis Studio, San Diego, CA, 2007
04 Infosite: Portable Public Space, San Diego, CA, 2005
05 Manufactured Sites: A Housing Urbanism Made of Waste, Tijuana, Mexico, 2005-present
06 Manufactured Sites: A Housing Urbanism Made of Waste, Tijuana, Mexico, 2005-present

01

02

03

04

05

George Yu

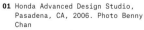

George Yu Architects,
Los Angeles (2002-2007)

Education University of
British Columbia, BA urban
geography, 1985; University
of California, Los Angeles,
MArch, 1988

Teaching Positions Florida
International University;
SCI-Arc; University of
British Columbia; University
of Texas at Austin
Notable Honors *Architectural
Record*, Design Vanguard,
2000; Canada Council for the
Arts, Prix de Rome, 2000;
Venice Architecture Biennale,
U.S. Pavilion, exhibitor,
2004

George Yu died in 2007.

01 Honda Advanced Design Studio,
Pasadena, CA, 2006. Photo Benny
Chan
02 Honda Advanced Design Studio,
Pasadena, CA, 2006. Photo Benny
Chan
03 *Shoplift*, Venice Architecture
Biennale, Venice, Italy, 2004
04 *Blow Up*, SCI-Arc Gallery,
Los Angeles, CA, 2004
05 Gardens by the Bay, Singapore,
competition entry, 2006;
in collaboration with AHBE
Landscape Architects

01

02

03

04

05

Annie Han, Daniel Mihalyo

Lead Pencil Studio, Seattle (est. 1997)

Education Han: University of Oregon, BArch, 1993 \\ Mihalyo: University of Oregon, BArch, 1994

Teaching Position University of Washington
Notable Honors Creative Capital Foundation, Visual Arts Grant Recipient, 2005; American Academy in Rome, Rome Prize, 2008; Van Alen Institute, New York Prize Fellowship, 2010
Website leadpencilstudio.org

01 *Stair*, Sand Point Arts and Cultural Exchange, Seattle, WA, 2003
02 *Maryhill Double*, Biggs, OR, 2006
03 *Non-Sign II*, U.S.-Canada border crossing, Blaine, WA, 2010
04 *Minus Space*, Henry Art Gallery, Seattle, WA, 2005. Photo Eduardo Calderon
05 *Inversion Plus Minus*, Portland, OR, 2013

01

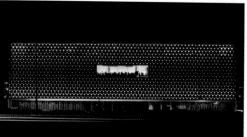

02

03

04

05

Eric Bunge, Mimi Hoang

nARCHITECTS, New York City (est. 1999)

Education Bunge: McGill University, BArch, 1991; Harvard University, MArch, 1996 \\ Hoang: Massachusetts Institute of Technology, BS architecture, 1993; Harvard University, MArch, 1998

Teaching Positions Bunge: Columbia University; Harvard University; Parsons The New School for Design; Rhode Island School of Design; Yale University \\ Hoang: Columbia University; Harvard University; University of California, Berkeley; Yale University

Notable Honors AIA New York Chapter, Design Honor Award, 2005; AIA New York Chapter, Building Type Merit Award, 2009; AIA New York Chapter, Design Merit Award, 2013

Website narchitects.com

01 Ply Loft, New York, NY, 2005. Photo Frank Oudeman
02 My Micro NY, New York, NY, in progress. Rendering Mir
03 Switch Building, New York, NY, 2007. Photo Frank Oudeman
04 ABC Dbayeh Department Store, Beirut, Lebanon, 2012. Photo Joe Kesrouani
05 Wyckoff Farmhouse Museum, Brooklyn, NY, in progress; in collaboration with Nancy Owens Studio
06 Forest Pavilion, Hualien, Taiwan, 2011. Photo Iwan Baan

06

01

02

03

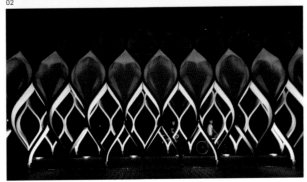

04

Jeanne Gang

Studio Gang Architects,
Chicago (est. 1997)

Education University of
Illinois at Urbana-Champaign,
BS architecture, 1986; ETH
Zürich, urban design studies,
1989; Harvard University,
MArch, 1993

Teaching Positions Harvard
University; Illinois
Institute of Technology;
Princeton University; Rice
University; Yale University
Notable Honors John D. and
Catherine T. MacArthur
Foundation, Fellow, 2011;
Cooper-Hewitt, National
Design Museum, National
Design Award, 2013;
University of Chicago,
Rosenberger Medal, 2013
Website studiogang.net

01 Aqua Tower, Chicago, IL, 2010.
Photo Steve Hall © Hedrich
Blessing
02 Bengt Sjostrom Starlight
Theatre, Rockford, IL, 2003.
© Greg Murphey
03 *Marble Curtain*, National
Building Museum, Washington DC,
2003. Photo Harry Zernike
04 Nature Boardwalk, Lincoln Park
Zoo, Chicago, IL, 2010. Film
still courtesy Spirit of Space
05 WMS Boathouse at Clark Park,
Chicago, IL, 2013. Photo Steve
Hall © Hedrich Blessing

01

02

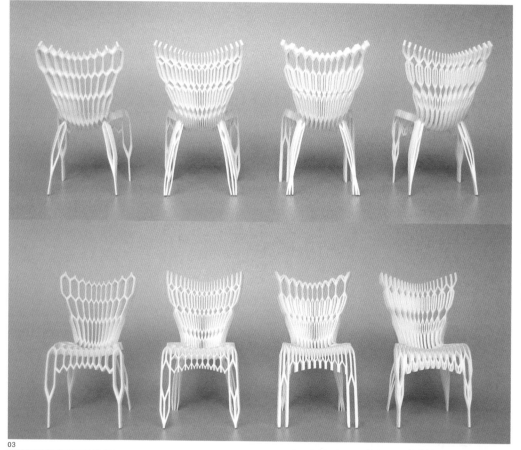

03

04

05

Ammar Eloueini

Ammar Eloueini Digit-all Studio, New Orleans, Paris (est. 1997)

Education Ecole d'architecture Paris-Villemin, Diplôme d'architecte, 1994; Columbia University, MArch, 1996

Teaching Positions California College of the Arts; cole nationale supérieure de création industrielle; Syracuse University; Tulane University; University of Illinois at Chicago
Notable Honors CoReFab Chairs, permanent collections of Canadian Centre for Architecture, Centre Pompidou, Disseny Hub Barcelona, Museum of Modern Art (New York City), Ogden Museum of Southern Art; French Ministry of Culture, Nouveaux Albums des Jeunes Architectes, lauréat, 2002; MoMA PS1, Young Architects Program, competition finalist, 2012
Website digit-all.net

01 *Le Tramway*, Pavillon de l'Arsenal, Paris, France, 2008. Photo Christian Richters
02 J House, New Orleans, LA, in progress
03 CoReFab#71, 2006
04 Issey Miyake *me* Boutique, Paris, France, 2006. Photo Gitty Garugar
05 *California*, stage set for John Jasperse, traveling performance, 2003. Photo Melissa Urcan

01

02

03

04

05

An Te Liu

An Te Liu, Toronto
(est. 1999)

Education University of
Toronto, BA fine art history
and Renaissance studies,
1990; SCI-Arc, MArch, 1995

Teaching Positions University
of British Columbia;
University of Toronto
(director, BA architectural
studies, John H. Daniels
Faculty of Architecture,
Landscape, and Design,
2000-2002; director, MArch
Program, 2002-2007, 2012-
2013)
Notable Honors Canada Council
for the Arts, International
Residency at Künstlerhaus
Bethanien, Berlin, 2008
Website anteliu.com

01 *Title Deed*, the Leona Drive
   Project, Toronto, Canada, 2009
02 *Cloud*, Venice Architecture
   Biennale, Venice, Italy, 2008
03 *Pattern Language: Levittown
   (white)*, silk-screen ink on
   paper, Galerie Ben Kaufmann,
   Berlin, Germany, 2007
04 *White Dwarf*, 2012
05 *No Molestar*, cotton T-shirts
   and silk-screen ink, Witte de
   With Center for Contemporary
   Art, Rotterdam, the
   Netherlands, 2006

01

02

03

04

05

06

Mark Anderson, Peter Anderson

Anderson Anderson Architecture, San Francisco (est. 1983)

Education Mark Anderson: Pacific Lutheran University, BA history and Asian studies, 1982; Harvard University, MArch, 1986 \\ Peter Anderson: Pacific Lutheran University, BA French literature, 1983; Harvard University, MArch, 1988

Teaching Positions Mark Anderson: University of California, Berkeley; University of Hawaiʻi at Mānoa \\ Peter Anderson: California College of the Arts; University of Hawaiʻi at Mānoa

Notable Honors Venice Architecture Biennale, U.S. Pavilion, exhibitor, 2006; AEDES Gallery, Holcim Awards exhibition, participant, 2010; Museum für Kunst und Gewerbe Hamburg, Klimakapseln Exhibition, participant, 2010

Website andersonanderson.com

01 Child Care Center, Harvard University, Cambridge, MA, 2010
02 Prairie Hopper, Fort Worth, TX, 2009. Photo David Williams
03 *Sponge Combs*, Venice Architecture Biennale, Venice, Italy, 2006
04 Net-Positive Energy Modular Classroom Building, Honolulu, HI, 2012
05 Lips Tower, San Francisco, CA, 2011
06 Chameleon House, Bridgeport, MI, 2006. Photo Anthony Vizzari

01

02

03

05

04

06

Andrew Bernheimer, Jared Della Valle

Della Valle Bernheimer, Brooklyn (est. 1996)

Education Bernheimer: Williams College, BA art history, 1990; Washington University in St. Louis, MArch, 1994 \\ Della Valle: Lehigh University, BA architecture and urban studies, 1993; Washington University in St. Louis, MArch, MS construction management, 1996

Practice Update Alloy Development, Brooklyn and Fairfield, NJ (est. 2006); Jared Della Valle, Katherine McConvey, A.J. Pires, Abelardo de la Teja (principals) \\ Bernheimer Architecture, Brooklyn (est. 2011); Andrew Bernheimer (principal)
Teaching Positions Bernheimer: City College of New York; Lehigh University; Parsons The New School for Design; Rhode Island School of Design; Syracuse University \\ Della Valle: Columbia University; Lehigh University; Parsons The New School for Design; Syracuse University; Washington University in St. Louis
Notable Honors *See page 296*
Websites alloyllc.com \\ bernheimerarchitecture.com

01 **Della Valle Bernheimer** 459 West 18th Street, New York, NY, 2008
02 **Della Valle Bernheimer** 450 Golden Gate Avenue Federal Plaza, San Francisco, CA, 2000. Photo Richard Barnes
03 **Alloy Development** 192 Water Street, Brooklyn, NY, 2011
04 **Bernheimer Architecture** Boy's Club of New York, Brooklyn, NY, 2011. Rendering by-encore nyc
05 **Bernheimer Architecture** Malin + Goetz Apothecary and Lab, Los Angeles, CA, 2012. Photo Eric Laignel
06 **Alloy Development** Hudson Yards Tower, New York, NY, 2008. Rendering by-encore nyc

Eric Höweler,
Meejin Yoon

Höweler + Yoon Architecture/ MY Studio, Boston (Höweler + Yoon Architecture, est. 2005; MY Studio, est. 2001)

Education Höweler: Cornell University, BArch, 1994; Cornell University, MArch, 1996 \\ Yoon: Cornell University, BArch, 1995; Harvard University, MAUD, 1997

Teaching Positions Höweler: Harvard University \\ Yoon: Massachusetts Institute of Technology (director, Undergraduate Program in Architecture, School of Architecture + Planning, 2009-2014; head, Department of Architecture, 2014-present)
Notable Honors Audi Urban Future Award, 2012; *Architectural Review*, AR+D Awards for Emerging Architecture, Highly Commended, 2013 \\ Yoon: American Academy in Rome, Rome Prize, 2005; Rhode Island School of Design, Athena Award, 2008; United States Artist, USA Target Fellow, 2008
Websites hyarchitecture.com \\ mystudio.us

01 *LoRez HiFi*, Washington DC, 2007
02 Chengdu Skycourts, Chengdu, China, 2011
03 Uni Project, New York, NY, 2011
04 BSA Space, Boston Society of Architects, Boston, MA, 2011
05 *White Noise White Light*, Athens, Greece, 2004

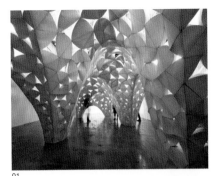

01

03

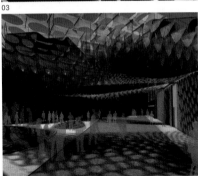

04

02

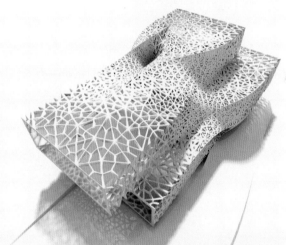

05

Lisa Iwamoto,
Craig Scott

IwamotoScott Architecture,
San Francisco (est. 2000)

Education Iwamoto: University
of Colorado Boulder, BS
structural engineering, 1985;
Harvard University, MArch,
1993 \\ Scott: Syracuse
University, BArch, 1986;
Harvard University, MArch,
1994

Teaching Positions Iwamoto:
Harvard University; SCI-Arc;
University of California,
Berkeley; University of
Michigan \\ Scott: California
College of the Arts; Harvard
University; SCI-Arc;
University of Michigan
Notable Honors History
Channel, IBM, and Infiniti,
City of the Future
Competition, Grand Prize
winner, 2008; *Architectural
Record*, Design Vanguard,
2011; San Francisco Museum
of Modern Art, permanent
collection, 2011
Website iwamotoscott.com

01 *Voussoir Cloud*, Los Angeles,
 CA, 2008
02 2:1 House, Berkeley, CA, 2004
03 Obscura Digital Headquarters,
 San Francisco, CA, 2011. Photo
 Rien van Rijthoven
04 *REEF*, MoMA PS1 Young Architects
 Program, Queens, NY, competition finalist, 2007
05 Jellyfish House, San Francisco,
 CA, 2006; in collaboration with
 proces2
06 Heavybit Industries,
 San Francisco, CA, 2012.
 Photo Bruce Damonte

01

02

03

04

Sharon Johnston, Mark Lee

Johnston Marklee, Los Angeles (est. 1998)

Education Johnston: Stanford University, BA history, 1988; Harvard University, MArch, 1995 \\ Lee: University of Southern California, BArch, 1991; Harvard University, MArch, 1995

Teaching Positions Johnston: Harvard University; Rice University; SCI-Arc; University of California, Los Angeles \\ Lee: ETH Zürich; Harvard University; Rice University; Technische Universität Berlin; University of California, Los Angeles

Notable Honors AIA Los Angeles, Next LA Award, 2011; *Architect*, P/A Award, 2012; AIA Los Angeles, Presidential Board Honoree for Emerging Practice, 2013

Website johnstonmarklee.com

05

01 Pavilion of Six Views, Shanghai, China, 2013. Photo Heng Zhong
02 Vault House, Los Angeles, CA, 2013. Photo Eric Staudenmaier
03 Menil Drawing Institute, Houston, TX, in progress. Rendering Johnston Marklee/ Nephew
04 View House, Rosario, Argentina, 2009. Photo Eric Staudenmaier
05 Walden-Wilson Studio, Los Angeles, CA, 2002. Photo Eric Staudenmaier

01

02

03

04

05   06

Victor F. "Trey" Trahan III

Trahan Architects,
Baton Rouge (est. 1992)

Education Louisiana State
University, BArch, 1983

Practice Update Baton Rouge,
Chicago, New Orleans, New
York City
Teaching Position
Massachusetts Institute of
Technology
Notable Honors *Architect*,
P/A Award, 2010; *Architect*,
Annual Design Review, Honor
Award, 2013; *Interior Design*,
Best of Year Award, 2013
Website trahanarchitects.com

01 Louisiana State Museum
   and Sports Hall of Fame,
   Natchitoches, LA, 2013.
   Photo Tim Hursley
02 Magnolia Mound Visitor's
   Center, Baton Rouge, LA, 2012
03 Louisiana State Museum
   of Sports Hall of Fame,
   Natchitoches, LA, 2013.
   Photo Tim Hursley
04 Holy Rosary Catholic Church,
   St. Amant, LA, 2004. Photo Tim
   Hursley
05 Academic Center for Student
   Athletes, Louisiana State
   University, Baton Rouge, LA,
   2002. Photo Tim Hursley
06 River Center Library, Baton
   Rouge, LA, 2008

01

Hagy Belzberg

Belzberg Architects,
Santa Monica, CA (est. 1997)

Education Arizona State
University, BS architecture,
1987; Harvard University,
MArch, 1991

Teaching Positions SCI-Arc;
University of California,
Los Angeles; University of
Southern California
Notable Honors AIA, Fellow,
2010; National AIA, Honor
Award, 2011, 2014
Website belzbergarchitects
.com

02

03

04

05

01 Mataja Residence, Malibu, CA,
2001
02 9800 Wilshire, Los Angeles,
CA, 2012
03 Los Angeles Museum of the
Holocaust, Los Angeles, CA,
2011. Photo Iwan Baan
04 Kona Residence, Kona, HI, 2010.
Photo Benny Chan/Fotoworks
05 Conga Room, Nokia Theater
at L.A. Live, Los Angeles,
CA, 2008. Photo Benny Chan/
Fotoworks

01

02

03

04

05

Jamie Darnell,
David Dowell,
Dan Maginn,
Josh Shelton,
Douglas Stockman

el dorado, Kansas City, MO
(est. 1996)

Education Darnell: Kansas
State University, BArch,
1989 \\ Dowell: Washington
University in St. Louis,
BA architecture, 1989;
University of California,
Berkeley, MArch, 1994 \\
Maginn: Tulane University,
BArch, MArch, 1989 \\
Shelton: University of
Tennessee, BArch, 1995 \\
Stockman: Kansas State
University, BArch, 1993

Practice Update Chris French
Metal, Oakland, CA; Jamie
Darnell (designer) \\ el
dorado, Kansas City, MO, and
Wichita, KS; David Dowell,
Dan Maginn, Josh Shelton,
Douglas Stockman (principals)
Teaching Positions Dowell:
Kansas State University;
Technische Universität
Dresden; University of
Kansas; Washington University
in St. Louis \\ Shelton:
University of Kansas \\
Stockman: Kansas State
University
Notable Honors *Architect*,
Annual Design Review, 2012;
Azure Magazine, AZ Award,
2012; *Residential Architect*,
Design Award, 2012 \\ Maginn:
AIA, Fellow, 2012
Website eldo.us

01 Cox Communications, Topeka,
   KS, 2007
02 Finn Lofts, Wichita, KS, 2010
03 Broadway Overpass, Kansas City,
   MO, 2011
04 Cellar I, Boulevard Brewer,
   Kansas City, MO, 2011
05 Hodgdon Powder Facility,
   Herington, KS, 2007

All photos Mike Sinclair.

Brian Johnsen, Sebastian Schmaling

01

02

03

04

05

06

Johnsen Schmaling Architects, Milwaukee (est. 2003)

Education Johnsen: University of Wisconsin-Milwaukee, BS architectural studies, 1994; University of Wisconsin-Milwaukee, MArch, 1997 \\ Schmaling: Technische Universität Berlin, Dipl. Ing. architecture, 1994; University of Wisconsin-Milwaukee, MArch, 1996; Harvard University, MAUD, 2002

Teaching Positions Johnsen: University of North Carolina; University of Oklahoma; University of Wisconsin-Milwaukee \\ Schmaling: Harvard University; University of North Carolina; University of Oklahoma; University of Toronto; University of Wisconsin-Milwaukee

Notable Honors *Architectural Record*, Design Vanguard, 2011; National AIA Committee on the Environment (COTE), AIA COTE Top Ten Green Projects Award, 2011; National AIA, Housing Award, 2014

Website johnsenschmaling.com

01 Camouflage House, Green Lake, WI, 2007. Photo John J. Macaulay
02 Topo House, Blue Mounds, WI, 2013. Photo John J. Macaulay
03 Stacked Cabin, Muscoda, WI, 2011. Photo John J. Macaulay
04 Studio for a Composer, Spring Prairie, WI, 2011. Photo John J. Macaulay
05 The Blatz, Milwaukee, WI, 2007. Photo Kevin Miyazaki
06 Ferrous House, Spring Prairie, WI, 2007. Photo Doug Edmunds

Granger Moorhead, Robert Moorhead

Moorhead & Moorhead, New York City (est. 2000)

Education Granger Moorhead: Yale University, BA architecture, 1991; Yale University, MArch, 1995 \\ Robert Moorhead: Rhode Island School of Design, bachelor's industrial design, 1996

Teaching Position Parsons The New School for Design
Notable Honors Museum of Modern Art (New York City), permanent collection, 2010; New York Foundation for the Arts, Fellows in Architecture + Environmental Structures + Design, 2010; NYC Department of Design and Construction, Design and Construction Excellence Shortlist, 2013
Website moorheadandmoorhead .com

01

02

04

03

05   06

01 Mobile Chaplet, Fargo, ND, 2006
02 *Ice Heart: Times Square Valentine*, New York, NY, 2010
03 *Metropolis* Booth, International Contemporary Furniture Fair, New York, NY, 2005. Photo Katerina Kampiti
04 Barn/Guest House, Washington, CT, 2012
05 *The City We Imagined/The City We Made*, The Architectural League of New York, New York, NY, 2010
06 Beach Pavilion, Jose Ignacio, Uruguay, 2008

Michael Meredith, Hilary Sample

MOS Architects, New York City (est. 2007)

Education Meredith: Syracuse University, BArch, 1994; Harvard University, MArch, 2000 \\ Sample: Syracuse University, BArch, 1994; Princeton University, MArch, 2003

Teaching Positions Meredith: Harvard University; Princeton University (director, graduate studies, School of Architecture, 2011-present); University of Michigan; University of Toronto \\ Sample: Columbia University; University at Buffalo, The State University of New York; University of Toronto; Yale University
Notable Honors *Architect*, P/A Award, 2009; MoMA PS1, Young Architects Program, competition winner, 2009; American Academy of Arts and Letters, Arts and Letters Award in Architecture, 2010
Website mos-office.net

01 *SoftCell*, Henry Urbach Architecture Gallery, New York, NY, 2004. Photo Florian Holzherr
02 Krabbesholm Højskole, Skive, Denmark, 2012. Photo Per Andersen
03 *Afterparty*, MoMA PS1 Young Architects Program, Queens, NY, winning proposal, 2009. Photo Florian Holzherr
04 Element House, Las Vegas, NM, 2014
05 *Pile*, Museum Boijmans Van Beuningen, Rotterdam, the Netherlands, 2008. Photo Florian Holzherr
06 Huyghe Puppet Theater, Cambridge, MA, 2004. Photo Michael Vahrenwald

01

02

03

04

Johnny McDonald, Patrick McDonald, Tim McDonald, Howard Steinberg

Onion Flats, Philadelphia (est. 1997)

Education Johnny McDonald: San Diego State University, BA humanities, in progress \\ Patrick McDonald: Delaware County Community College, engineering and political science, 1982 \\ Tim McDonald: Pennsylvania State University, BArch, 1989; McGill University, MA architectural history and theory, 1994 \\ Steinberg: University of Pennsylvania, BA environmental design, 1987; Washington University in St. Louis, MArch, master's construction management, 1991

Teaching Positions Tim McDonald: Catholic University of America; Temple University; Université de Montréal
Notable Honors Urban Land Institute, Global Award for Excellence, 2010; Greater Philadelphia Chamber of Commerce, Sustainable Business of the Year, 2013; International Passive House Association, Passive House Award, 2014
Website onionflats.com

05

01 Jackhammer, Philadelphia, PA, 2009. Photo Tim McDonald
02 Belfield Homes, Philadelphia, PA, 2012. Photo Tim McDonald
03 Thin Flats, Philadelphia, PA, 2009. Photo Mariko Reed
04 TED House, Syracuse, NY, 2011. Photo Tim McDonald
05 Rag Flats, Philadelphia, PA, 2006. Photo Raimund Koch

01

02

03

04

05

06

Chris Reed

Stoss Landscape Urbanism, Boston (est. 2000)

Education Harvard University, AB urban studies, 1991; University of Pennsylvania, MLA, 1995

Practice Update Scott Bishop, Chris Reed (principals)
Teaching Positions Florida International University; Harvard University; University of Pennsylvania; University of Toronto; University of Wisconsin-Milwaukee
Notable Honors *Architecture*, P/A Award, 2004; *Topos: The International Review of Landscape Architecture and Urban Design*, Topos Landscape Award, 2010; Cooper-Hewitt, National Design Museum, National Design Award, 2012
Website stoss.net

01 Safe Zone, Les Jardins de Métis/Redford Gardens, Grand-Métis, Canada, 2006, 2009
02 Taichung Gateway Park, Taichung, Taiwan, 2011
03 Riverside Park, New Bedford, MA, 2002
04 The Plaza, Harvard University, Cambridge, MA, 2013. Photo Charles Mayer
05 Erie Street Plaza, Milwaukee, WI, 2010. Photo John December
06 CityDeck, Phase 1, Green Bay, WI, 2010. Photo Mike Roemer

01

02

03   04

05

Amale Andraos,
Dan Wood

WORKac, New York City
(est. 2003)

Education Andraos: McGill
University, BArch, 1996;
Harvard University, MArch,
1999 \\ Wood: University of
Pennsylvania, BA film theory,
1989; Columbia University,
MArch, 1992

Teaching Positions Andraos:
Columbia University
(dean, Graduate School of
Architecture, Planning and
Preservation, 2014-present);
Harvard University; Parsons
The New School for Design;
Princeton University;
University of Pennsylvania \\
Wood: Columbia University;
Cooper Union; Ohio State
University; Princeton
University; Yale University
Notable Honors Public Design
Commission of the City of New
York, Award for Excellence in
Design, 2010; AIA New York
Chapter, Merit Award, 2013,
2014
Website work.ac

01 Diane von Furstenberg Studio
    Headquarters, New York, NY,
    2007. Photo Elizabeth Felicella
02 Edible Schoolyard, P.S. 216,
    Brooklyn, NY, 2013. Photo Iwan
    Baan
03 L'Assemblée Radieuse Conference
    Centre, Libreville, Gabon, in
    progress
04 Children's Museum of the Arts,
    New York, NY, 2011. Photo Ari
    Marcopoulos
05 Nature-City, *Foreclosed:
    Rehousing the American Dream*,
    Museum of Modern Art, New York,
    NY, 2012

COMMENTARY Alan G. Brake

1982-1986
1988-1993
1994-1998
1999-2003
2004-2008

2009-2013

The Great Recession, which did its damage between late 2007 and mid-2009, sent countless architects to the unemployment line. While its ranks are beginning to recover as the economy slowly improves, the profession has experienced significant changes in the intervening years. And though the process has been painful for many practitioners, some of those changes are for the better. Unlike previous periods of economic woe, when architecture turned inward, focusing on its own disciplinarity and on speculative forms and futures, throughout the recession many emerging architects and designers faced outward, engaging with other disciplines, the city, new fabrication techniques, the process of making, emerging markets, and our increasingly strained environment.

This diversity of approaches, enabled by technology, is reflective of the attitudes of younger practitioners. Indeed, activist, entrepreneur, and technologist are as likely to be preferred roles of this generation as artist.

Among the selected firms from this period are a significant number of landscape architects and urban designers, which reflects a more integrated relationship between architecture and landscape and a renewed interest in the ameliorative potential of urbanism. WXY Architecture + Urban Design (EV11), a stalwart supporter of the public realm, is increasingly working at the urban scale with projects like the Brooklyn Tech Triangle Plan, a strategic plan for an East Coast Silicon Valley. Interboro Partners' (EV11) community-driven, interventionist designers and planners employ urban design to address social inequalities with projects such as SumCity, a neighborhood development plan for Long Island City, New York, that aims to alter the typical outcomes of gentrification. And Dlandstudio architecture and landscape architecture (EV13) has a growing reputation for innovative green infrastructure, with the Highway Outfall Landscape Detention (HOLD) Systems for storm-water management among its projects. These firms routinely convert urban problems into community amenities, empowering nontraditional clients like neighborhood associations, tenant groups, and pragmatic public agencies.

Operating at a smaller scale, Stephanie Forsythe and Todd MacAllen of Vancouver, Canada-based molo (EV10) have applied their multidisciplinary training to product design, including lighting, freestanding partition walls, seating, and small accessories. Their entrepreneurial approach, driven by material and manufacturing explorations, has resulted in products such as "soft" modular wall systems made of flexible, recyclable materials like paper and polyethylene.

Among recent Emerging Voices technologists is Ball-Nogues Studio (EV11), whose nimble, event-based architectures and installations employ hand- and digital-fabrication techniques that, like molo's product design, are as much about the process of making as they are about the transformation of space. And Oyler Wu Collaborative (EV12) generates complex geometries for building proposals and installations using technologies old and new; its *Netscape*, SCI-Arc Graduation Pavilion, a structure of knitted rope, tube steel, and fabric shade louvers, was designed and constructed with SCI-Arc students using conventional knitting techniques and digital investigations.

While the market for monumentally scaled forms and signature styles has diminished, many practitioners continue to create spatial and visual experiences, albeit on a more modest scale. The Architectural League, for example, recognized the dynamic nature of architecture in Mexico during this period. In Mexico City Emerging Voices are producing work that falls roughly into two categories: hard-edged, neomodern buildings that extend the legacy of Mexican masters like Luis Barragán, such as those designed by Dellekamp Arquitectos (EV09) and Tatiana Bilbao (EV10); and seductive, digitally driven works, rivaling the most eye-catching architecture in Europe and Asia, by the likes of rojkind arquitectos (EV10).

Even in a time of economic crisis, emerging architects are suggesting new formal, spatial, and urban solutions to extend the profession's reach and address the challenges and possibilities of the future. Their adaptability to changing economic and social conditions and new technologies and their mix of activism and entrepreneurial spirit suggest a renewed role for designers in improving everyday life.

01

03

02

05

04

06

Darren Petrucci

A-I-R [Architecture-
Infrastructure-Research],
Scottsdale, AZ (est. 2000)

Education Arizona State
University, BS design, 1990;
Harvard University, MArch,
MAUD, 1996

Teaching Position Arizona
State University (director,
The Design School, 2005–2012)
Notable Honors *Architecture*,
P/A Award, 2002; National
Council of Architectural
Registration Boards, NCARB
Prize, 2008; *Architectural
Record*, Record Houses, 2009
Website a-i-rinc.com

01 Comfort Zone, Phoenix, AZ, 2006
02 Stripscape, Phoenix, AZ, 2005.
Photo Bill Timmerman
03 Dragoon Residence, Paradise
Valley, AZ, 2013
04 Oasis Bus Shelter, Phoenix,
AZ, 2007
05 Diapause House, Portal, AZ,
2013
06 VH R-10 gHouse, Vineyard Haven,
MA, 2008. Photo Bill Timmerman

01

Andrew D. Berman

Andrew Berman Architect,
New York City (est. 1995)

Education Yale University, BA
art and architecture, 1984;
Yale University, MArch, 1988

Notable Honors AIA New York
Chapter, Merit Award, 2012,
2014; AIA, Fellow, 2014
Website
andrewbermanarchitect.com

02

03

04

05

01 Writing Studio, Bellport, NY,
2008. Photo Michael Moran
02 Entrance Building, MoMA PS1,
Queens, NY, 2011. Photo Michael
Moran
03 Watermill Residence, Watermill,
NY, 2012. Photo Michael Moran
04 Stapleton Library, Staten
Island, NY, 2013. Photo Naho
Kubota
05 Center for Architecture, AIA
New York Chapter, New York, NY,
2003. Photo Peter Aaron/Esto

01

02

03

04   05

Julio Amezcua, Francisco Pardo

AT103, New York City
(est. 2001)

Education Amezcua:
Universidad Anáhuac, BArch,
1999; Columbia University,
MS advanced architectural
design, 2001 \\ Pardo:
Universidad Anáhuac, BArch,
1997; Columbia University,
MS advanced architectural
design, 1999

Practice Update Mexico City
Teaching Positions Amezcua:
Columbia University; Pratt
Institute; Universidad
Anáhuac; Universidad
Iberoamericana; University
of Pennsylvania \\ Pardo:
Universidad Anáhuac;
University of California,
Berkeley; Universidad
Iberoamericana; University of
Pennsylvania
Notable Honors Farmani Group,
International Design Awards,
first place, 2009; Mexican
Architecture Biennale, Silver
Medal, 2012; Pan-American
Quito Architecture Biennale,
Grand Jury Prize, 2012
Website at103.com

01 Fire Station, Mexico City,
   Mexico, 2006. Photo Jaime
   Navarro
02 TK139, Mexico City, Mexico,
   2012. Photo Rafael Gamo
03 Azteca TV Sets, Mexico City,
   Mexico, 2012. Photo Enrique
   Macias Martinez
04 Lisboa 7, Mexico City, Mexico,
   2010. Photo Rafael Gamo
05 Azteca TV Sets, Mexico City,
   Mexico, 2012. Photo Enrique
   Macias Martinez

Shane Coen

01

02

04

05

03

06

Coen + Partners, Minneapolis (est. 1992)

Education University of Massachusetts Amherst, AS horticulture, BS landscape architecture, 1990

Practice Update Shane Coen (CEO); Robin Ganser, Bryan Kramer (principals)
Teaching Position Harvard University
Notable Honors *Architecture*, P/A Award, 2003; National ASLA, Honor Award, 2009; U.S. General Services Administration, GSA Design Award, Citation in Landscape Architecture, 2010
Website coenpartners.com

01 Jackson Meadow, Marine on St. Croix, MN, 2000-present; in collaboration with Salmela Architect. Photo Peter Bastianelli Kerze
02 Westminster Presbyterian Church, Minneapolis, MN, 2008. Photo Paul Crosby
03 U.S. Land Port of Entry, Warroad, MN, 2010; in collaboration with Julie Snow Architects. Photo Frank Ooms
04 Mississippi River Pedestrian Bridge, Minneapolis, MN, 2010
05 Lavin-Bernick Center for University Life, Tulane University, New Orleans, LA, 2005; in collaboration with VJAA. Photo Paul Crosby
06 Minneapolis Central Library, Minneapolis, MN, 2006; in collaboration with Pelli Clarke Pelli Architects and Architectural Alliance. Photo Peter Bastianelli Kerze

01

02

03

04

05

Derek Dellekamp

Dellekamp Arquitectos,
Mexico City (est. 1999)

Education Universidad
Iberoamericana, BArch, 1997

Teaching Positions Rice
University; Universidad
Anáhuac; Universidad
Iberoamericana; University of
Texas at Austin
Notable Honors *Wallpaper**,
Architects Directory, 2007;
Centre Pompidou, permanent
collection, 2010; Colegio
de Arquitectos de la Ciudad
de México y Sociedad de
Arquitectos Mexicanos, Best
Young Architect, 2010
Website dellekamparq.com

01 Alfoso Reyes 58, Mexico City,
   Mexico, 2002. Photo Oscar
   Necoechea
02 Desierto de los Leones, Mexico
   City, Mexico, 2003. Photo Lara
   Becerra
03 Cafeteria Mirador, Guadalajara,
   Mexico, 2011
04 CB29, Mexico City, Mexico,
   2006. Photo Oscar Necoechea
05 Michelet, Mexico City, Mexico,
   2010. Photo Sandra Pereznieto

01   02

03

Elizabeth Gray, Alan Organschi

Gray Organschi Architecture, New Haven, CT (est. 1997)

Education Gray: Yale University, BA English and architecture, 1982; Yale University, MArch, 1987 \\ Organschi: Brown University, BA, 1984; Institute for Architecture and Urban Studies, 1985; Yale University, MArch, 1988

Practice Update Gray Design, New Haven, CT (est. 1998); Elizabeth Gray (principal) \\ Gray Organschi Architecture \\ JIG Design Build, New Haven, CT (est. 2011); Alan Organschi (principal)
Teaching Positions Gray: Roger Williams University; Yale University \\ Organschi: Roger Williams University; Wesleyan University; Yale University
Notable Honors *Residential Architect*, Hall of Fame Leadership Award, 2011; American Academy of Arts and Letters, Arts and Letters Award in Architecture, 2012; National AIA, Housing Award, 2012
Website grayorganschi.com

04   05

01 Sachem's Head House, Guilford, CT, 2011. Photo Lisbett Wedendahl
02 Fairfield Jesuit Center, Fairfield, CT, 2009. Photo Robert Benson Photography
03 Storage Barn, Washington, CT, 2008. Photo Bo Crockett
04 Footbridge, Madison, CT, 2001. Photo Robert Benson Photography
05 Cottage, Guilford, CT, 2008. Photo Mark Mahaney

01

02

03

05

04

06

Robert Hutchison, Tom Maul

Hutchison & Maul, Seattle (est. 2001)

Education Hutchison: Drexel University, BS architectural engineering, BS civil engineering, 1990; University of Washington, MArch, 1996 \\ Maul: Bucknell University, BS civil engineering, 1988; University of Washington, MArch, 1996

Practice Update Robert Hutchison Architecture, Seattle (est. 2013) \\ Tom Maul Architecture+Design, Seattle (est. 2013)
Teaching Positions University of Washington; Washington State University
Notable Honors Hutchison: Japan-U.S. Friendship Commission, Creative Artists Program Participant, 2010; City of Seattle, Office of Arts & Culture, CityArtist Project Award, 2014; On the Boards, Ambassador Project, 2014
Websites robhutcharch.com \\ tommauldesign.com

01 Courtyard House on a Steep Site II, Bellevue, WA, 2012
02 Wall + Roof Studio, Seattle, WA, 2006. Photo Lara Swimmer
03 Public Works Administration Building, Bothell, WA, 2011
04 Lake House, Mercer Island, WA, 2007
05 Hole House I, Seattle, WA, 2005
06 Courtyard House on a Steep Site I, Mercer Island, WA, 2007. Photo Alan Abramowitz

All projects by Hutchison & Maul.

01

02

03

04

05

Stella Betts, David Leven

LEVENBETTS, New York City (est. 1997)

Education Betts: Connecticut College, BA fine art and philosophy, 1988; Harvard University, MArch, 1994 \\ Leven: Colgate University, BA fine art, 1986; Yale University, MArch, 1991

Teaching Positions Betts: Columbia University; Cooper Union; Parsons The New School for Design; Syracuse University \\ Leven: City College of New York; Parsons The New School for Design; Syracuse University
Notable Honors *Architectural Record*, Design Vanguard, 2007; AIA New York Chapter, Merit Award, 2008; AIA New York Chapter, Honor Award, 2011
Website levenbetts.com

01 36SML Beach House, Amagansett, NY, 2014
02 *If You Dig a Hole Deep Enough...*, Chengdu Biennale, Chengdu, China, 2011
03 CC01 House, Columbia County, NY, 2006. Photo Michael Moran
04 Taystee Building, New York, NY, in progress
05 Mixed Greens, New York, NY, 2005. Photo Michael Moran

01

02

03

04

05

06

James Dallman, Grace La

LA DALLMAN, Milwaukee
(est. 1999)

Education Dallman: University of Wisconsin-Milwaukee, BS architecture, 1986; Harvard University, MArch, 1992 \\ La: Harvard University, BA visual and environmental studies, 1992; Harvard University, MArch, 1995

Practice Update Boston, Milwaukee
Teaching Positions Dallman: Arizona State University; Harvard University; Syracuse University; University of Wisconsin-Milwaukee \\ La: Harvard University; Syracuse University; University of Wisconsin-Milwaukee
Notable Honors AIA Wisconsin, Design Award, 2006; Bruner Foundation, Rudy Bruner Award for Urban Excellence, Silver Medal, 2007; Rice University, Rice Design Alliance Prize, 2011
Website ladallman.com

01 Hillel Student Center, University of Wisconsin-Milwaukee, 2011
02 Flat Top House, Mequon, WI, 2012
03 Ravine House (Levy House), Fox Point, WI, 2008. Photo Kevin Miyazaki
04 Marsupial Bridge, Crossroads Master Plan, Milwaukee, WI, 2007. Photo Jim Brozek
05 Center for Dance and Wellness, Milwaukee, WI, in progress
06 Bus Shelter, Crossroads Master Plan, Milwaukee, WI, 2004. Photo Greg Murphey

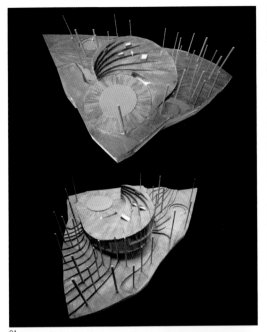

01

02

03

04

05

Ziad Jamaleddine, Makram el Kadi

L.E.FT, New York City
(est. 2001)

Education Jamaleddine:
American University of
Beirut, BArch, 1995; Harvard
University, MArch, 1999 \\
el Kadi: American University
of Beirut, BArch, 1997;
Parsons The New School for
Design, MArch, 1999

Practice Update Beirut,
New York City
Teaching Positions
Jamaleddine: Cornell
University; Massachusetts
Institute of Technology;
University of Pennsylvania;
University of Toronto \\
el Kadi: Columbia University;
Cornell University;
Massachusetts Institute of
Technology; Yale University
Notable Honors
The Architectural League of
New York, Young Architects
Forum, 2002; *Architectural
Record*, Design Vanguard,
2010; Iakov Chernikhov
International Prize for Young
Architects, finalist, 2010
Website leftish.net

01 Baabdat Residence, Baabdat,
Lebanon, 2009
02 Beirut Marina/Zaitunay Bay,
Beirut, Lebanon, 2012; in
collaboration with Steven
Holl Architects. Photo Nathan
Willock
03 Beirut Exhibition Center,
Beirut, Lebanon, 2012. Photo
Pietro Savorelli
04 Vertical Landscape Urbanism,
Holmestrand, Norway, 2009.
Rendering L.E.FT Architects and
Studio HP
05 Loft Barn, Bridgehampton, NY,
2008

Stephanie Forsythe, Todd MacAllen

molo, Vancouver, Canada (est. 2003)

Education Forsythe: Ryerson University, BArchSci, 1991; Sheridan College, glassblowing, metalwork, woodworking, 1992; Aalto University, architecture, ceramics, furniture design, glass, metalwork, 1994; Dalhousie University, BEDS, 1996; Dalhousie University, MArch, 2000; Nova Scotia College of Art and Design University, ceramics, printmaking, 2000 \\ MacAllen: University of Victoria, BFA, 1991; Dalhousie University, BEDS, 1993; Nova Scotia College of Art and Design University, metal casting, stonework, 1994; Dalhousie University, MArch, 2000

Teaching Positions Forsythe: Dalhousie University \\ MacAllen: Dalhousie University; Technical University of Nova Scotia **Notable Honors** City of Aomori, Japan, Aomori Northern Style Housing Competition, first prize, 2001; INDEX: Design to Improve Life, INDEX: Award, 2005; *Architectural Review*, AR+D Award for Emerging Architecture, Highly Commended, 2011 **Website** molodesign.com

01 cloud softlight and soft-wall with LED, Vancouver Art Gallery, Vancouver, Canada, 2011
02 Custom cloud softlight tutu, *Within the Space I Hold*, Jessica Lang Dance, 2013. Photo Karli Cadel, courtesy Jacob's Pillow Dance
03 Nebuta House, Aomori, Japan, 2011
04 Northern Sky Circle, Anchorage, AK, 2009
05 softwall, 2013
06 softblock, 2009

01

Michel Rojkind

rojkind arquitectos,
Mexico City (est. 2002)

Education Universidad
Iberoamericana, BArch and
urban planning, 1994

Practice Update Michel
Rojkind, Gerardo Salinas
(partners)
Teaching Positions Institute
for Advanced Architecture of
Catalonia; SCI-Arc
Notable Honors *Los Angeles
Times*, "Faces to Watch,"
2010; *Wallpaper**, The
Wallpaper* 150, 2011;
Architect, P/A Award, 2014
Website rojkindarquitectos
.com

02

03

04

05

06

01 Nestlé Chocolate Museum,
   Toluca, Mexico, 2007. Photo
   Paul Rivera
02 Tori Tori Restaurant, Mexico
   City, Mexico, 2011. Photo Paul
   Rivera
03 Falcón 2 Headquarters, Mexico
   City, Mexico, 2013; in collabo-
   ration with Gabriela Echegaray.
   Photo Jaime Navarro
04 Liverpool Department Store,
   Mexico City, Mexico, 2014.
   Photo Jaime Navarro
05 Cineteca Nacional, Mexico City,
   Mexico, 2012. Photo Paul Rivera
06 Nestlé Application Group,
   Querérato, Mexico, 2008. Photo
   Paul Rivera

01

02

03

04

05

Hayes Slade, James Slade

Slade Architecture, New York City (est. 2002)

Education Hayes Slade: Cornell University, BS civil and structural engineering, 1988; Cornell University, MEng structural engineering, 1989; University of Pennsylvania, MBA finance, 1998 \\ James Slade: Cornell University, BA, 1988; Columbia University, MArch, 1993

Teaching Positions Hayes Slade: Parsons The New School for Design; Syracuse University \\ James Slade: Barnard College and Columbia University; Florida International University; Parsons The New School for Design; Pratt Institute; Syracuse University

Notable Honors *Architectural Record* and *Businessweek*, Good Design Is Good Business Award, 2009; Public Design Commission of the City of New York, Award for Excellence in Design, 2009; AIA New York Chapter, Design Award, 2014

Website sladearch.com

01 Fight Club, New York, NY, 2010. Photo Tom Sibley
02 Virgin Atlantic JFK Clubhouse, Queens, NY, 2012. Photo Anton Stark
03 Staten Island Zoo, Staten Island, NY, 2014
04 Barbie Shanghai, Shanghai, China, 2009. Photo Iwan Baan
05 Virgin Atlantic EWR Clubhouse, Newark, NJ, 2012. Photo Tom Sibley

01

02

03

04

05

Sunil Bald,
Yolande Daniels

studioSUMO, New York City
(est. 1995)

Education Bald: University
of California, Santa Cruz,
BA biology, 1986; Columbia
University, MArch, 1991 \\
Daniels: City College of New
York, BS architecture, 1987;
Columbia University, MArch,
1990

Teaching Positions Bald:
Columbia University; Cornell
University; Parsons The
New School for Design;
University of Michigan;
Yale University \\ Daniels:
City College of New York;
Columbia University; Howard
University; Massachusetts
Institute of Technology;
University of Michigan
Notable Honors *Architectural
Record*, Design Vanguard,
2006; AIA New York Chapter,
Merit Award, 2008, 2012
Website studiosumo.com

01 School of Business Management,
   Josai University, Sakado,
   Japan, 2006. Photo Nacasa
02 Museum of Contemporary African
   Diasporan Arts, Brooklyn, NY,
   2006. Photo Frank Oudeman
03 School of Business Management,
   Josai University, Sakado,
   Japan, 2006. Photo Nacasa
04 Teatro B32, Sao Paulo, Brazil,
   2012
05 Mizuta Museum of Art, Josai
   University, Sakado, Japan,
   2011. Photo Daichi Ano

01

02

03

04

05

06

Benjamin Ball, Gaston Nogues

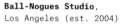

Ball-Nogues Studio,
Los Angeles (est. 2004)

Education Ball: SCI-Arc,
BArch, 1994 \\ Nogues: SCI-
Arc, BArch, 1993

Teaching Positions Ecole
spéciale d'architecture;
SCI-Arc; University of
California, Los Angeles;
University of Southern
California
Notable Honors AIA Los
Angeles, Honor Award, 2006;
MoMA PS1, Young Architects
Program, competition winner,
2007; United States Artists,
USA Target Fellow, 2007
Website ball-nogues.com

01 *Rip Curl Canyon*, Rice Gallery,
Houston, TX, 2006. Photo Nash
Baker
02 *Cradle*, Santa Monica, CA, 2010.
Photo Monica Nouwens
03 *Talus Dome*, Edmonton, Canada,
2012. Photo Dwayne Martineau
04 *Yucca Crater*, near Joshua Tree
National Park, CA, 2011. Photo
Scott Mayoral
05 *Maximilian's Schell*, Los
Angeles, CA, 2005. Photo Neil
Cochran
06 *Table Cloth*, Herb Alpert
School of Music, University of
California, Los Angeles, 2010.
Photo Scott Mayoral

01

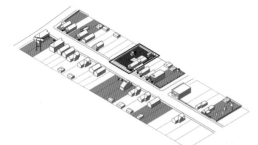

04

02

03

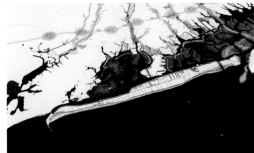

05

06

Tobias Armborst, Dan D'Oca, Georgeen Theodore

Interboro Partners, Brooklyn (est. 2002)

Education Armborst: Rheinisch-Westfälische Technische Hochschule Aachen Universität, Diplom-ingenieur architekt, 1999; Harvard University, MAUD, 2002 \\ D'Oca: Bard College, BA philosophy, 1998; Harvard University, MUP, 2002 \\ Theodore: Rice University, BA architecture, art, and art history, 1992; Rice University, BArch, 1994; Harvard University, MAUD, 2002

Teaching Positions Armborst: Vassar College \\ D'Oca: Harvard University; Maryland Institute College of Art \\ Theodore: New Jersey Institute of Technology (director, Infrastructure Planning Program, College of Architecture and Design, 2010-present); Ohio State University

Notable Honors MoMA PS1, Young Architects Program, competition winner, 2011; AIA New York Chapter, Urban Design Merit Award, 2012; U.S. Department of Housing and Urban Development and Hurricane Sandy Rebuilding Task Force, Rebuild by Design, selected team, 2013

Website interboropartners.net

01 LentSpace, New York, NY, 2009
02 *Commonplace*, Venice Architecture Biennale, Venice, Italy, 2012
03 *Commonplace*, Venice Architecture Biennale, Venice, Italy, 2012
04 Improve Your Lot!, Detroit, MI, 2006
05 Living with the Bay, Long Island, NY, 2014
06 *Holding Pattern*, MoMA PS1 Young Architects Program, Queens, NY, winning proposal, 2011

Lola Sheppard, Mason White

01

02

Lateral Office, Toronto
(est. 2003)

Education Sheppard: McGill
University, BArch, 1995;
Harvard University, MArch,
2001 \\ White: Virginia
Polytechnic Institute and
State University, BArch,
1996; Harvard University,
MArch, 2001

Teaching Positions Sheppard:
California College of the
Arts; Ohio State University;
University of Toronto;
University of Waterloo \\
White: Cornell University;
Harvard University; Ohio
State University; University
of California, Berkeley;
University of Toronto
Notable Honors S. and A.
Inspiration Foundation,
Arctic Inspiration Prize,
2012; *Architect*, P/A Award,
2013; Venice Architecture
Biennale, Canadian Pavilion,
exhibition organizer and
curator, 2014
Website lateraloffice.com

03

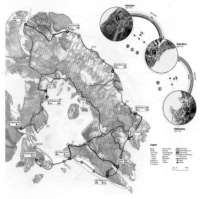

04

05

01 Arctic Food Network, Nunavut,
   Canada, 2011
02 Icelink, Bering Strait, 2009
03 Arctic Food Network, site plan,
   Nunavut, Canada, 2011
04 Water Economies/Ecologies,
   Salton Sea, CA, 2009
05 Klaksvik City Center
   Competition, Klaksvik, Faroe
   Islands, 2012

01

02

03

04

05

06

Roberto de Leon Jr., M. Ross Primmer

de Leon & Primmer Architecture Workshop, Louisville, KY (est. 2003)

Education de Leon: University of California, Berkeley, BArch, 1989; Harvard University, MArch, 1993 \\ Primmer: Kent State University, BS architecture, 1989; Harvard University, MArch, 1993

Teaching Positions de Leon: Boston Architectural College; University of Kentucky; University of North Carolina at Charlotte \\ Primmer: University of North Carolina at Charlotte

Notable Honors *Architectural Record*, Design Vanguard, 2010; Chicago Athenaeum, American Architecture Award, 2012; National AIA, Honor Award, 2013

Website deleon-primmer.com

01 Operations Facility, Mason Lane Farm, Goshen, KY, 2010
02 Visitor Service Building, Riverview Park, Louisville, KY, 2011
03 Gheens Barn and Peyton Samuel Head Trust Pavilion, Yew Dell Botanical Gardens, Crestwood, KY, 2007
04 Visitor Center, Wild Turkey Bourbon, Lawrenceburg, KY, 2013
05 Visitor Center, Yew Dell Botanical Gardens, Crestwood, KY, 2010
06 Filson Historical Society Campus Expansion, Louisville, KY, in progress

Georgina Huljich, Marcelo Spina

P-A-T-T-E-R-N-S, Los Angeles (est. 1999)

Education Huljich: Universidad Nacional de Rosario, architecture, planning, and design, 1994; University of California, Los Angeles, MArch, 2003 \\ Spina: Universidad Nacional de Rosario, architecture, planning, and design, 1994; Columbia University, MArch, MS advanced architectural design, 1997

Teaching Positions Huljich: University of California, Berkeley; University of California, Los Angeles (director, Architecture and Urban Design Summer Program, 2009-present); University of Southern California; Yale University \\ Spina: Harvard University; SCI-Arc (coordinator, Emerging Systems, Technologies & Media, 2011-present); University of Kentucky; Washington University in St. Louis; Yale University

Notable Honors AIA Los Angeles, ARCH IS_ Award, 2011; AIA Los Angeles, Honor Award, 2012; United States Artists, Grigor Fellows, 2013

Website p-a-t-t-e-r-n-s.net

01 Prism Gallery, West Hollywood, CA, 2009. Photo Joshua White

02 Dormitory, Pontificia Universidad Católica de Puerto Rico, Ponce, Puerto Rico, 2011

03 Jujuy Redux, Rosario, Argentina, 2012; in collaboration with Maxi Spina Architects. Photo Gustavo Fritegotto

04 *Lucent Saddles*, Venice Architecture Biennale, Austrian Pavilion, Venice, Italy, 2011

05 FYF Residence, Rosario, Argentina, 2009. Photo Gustavo Fritegotto

01

02

03

04

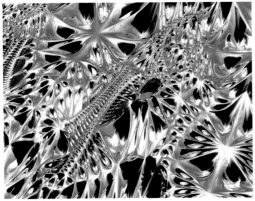

01

02

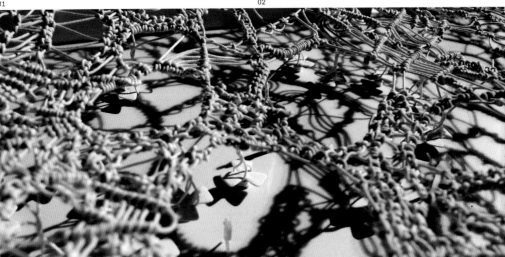

03

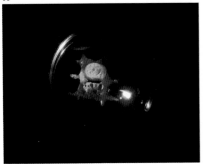

04

05

06

Karel Klein,
David Ruy

Ruy Klein, New York City
(est. 2000)

Education Klein: University
of Illinois at Urbana-
Champaign, BA architecture,
BS civil engineering, 1993 \\
Ruy: St. John's College, BA
philosophy and mathematics,
1991; Columbia University,
MArch, 1996

Teaching Positions Klein:
Columbia University \\ Ruy:
Pratt Institute
Notable Honors Iakov
Chernikhov International
Prize for Young Architects,
finalist, 2006; MoMA PS1,
Young Architects Program,
competition finalist, 2007;
Surface, Avant Guardian
Award, 2009
Website ruyklein.com

01 *Klex*, New York, NY, 2008
02 Tool-Hide, New York, NY, 2006
03 *Knot Garden*, MoMA PS1 Young
Architects Program, Queens, NY,
competition proposal, 2007
04 Output from Bioprinter, 2013
05 Bioprinter, prototype, 2013
06 Stained Glass Bridge, Venice,
Italy, 2006

01

02

03

04

05

06

B. Alex Miller, Jeff Taylor

Taylor and Miller Architecture and Design, New York City (est. 2002)

Education Miller: University of Illinois at Urbana-Champaign, BS architectural studies, 1999; Massachusetts Institute of Technology, MArch, 2004 \\ Taylor: Washington University in St. Louis, BS architectural studies, 1994; Massachusetts Institute of Technology, MArch, 2004

Notable Honors *Architectural Record*, Design Vanguard, 2009; Brooklyn Chamber of Commerce, Building Brooklyn Award, 2012; Architizer, A+ Award, 2013
Website taylorandmiller.com

01 Pull House, Great Barrington, MA, 2008. Photo Gregory Cherin Photography
02 Peel House, Pittsfield, MA, 2007. Photo Gregory Cherin Photography
03 Sanctuary Salon, Brooklyn, NY, 2009. Photo Gregory Cherin Photography
04 Bowl Residence, Stockbridge, MA, 2012
05 Environmental Grantmakers Offices, New York, NY, 2011. Photo Emile DuBuisson
06 Environmental Grantmakers Offices, New York, NY, 2011. Photo Emile DuBuisson

01

02

03

04

05

**Layng Pew,
Claire Weisz,
Mark Yoes**

**WXY Architecture + Urban
Design**, New York City
(est. 1998)

Education Pew: Yale
University, BA architecture,
1984; Yale University, MArch,
1989 \\ Weisz: University of
Toronto, BArch, 1984; Yale
University, MArch, 1989 \\
Yoes: Rice University, BArch,
1986; Yale University, MArch,
1990

Practice Update Adam
Lubinsky, Layng Pew, Claire
Weisz, Mark Yoes (principals)
Teaching Positions Weisz:
Cornell University; New York
University \\ Yoes: Parsons
The New School for Design
Notable Honors Chrysler
Group, Chrysler Design Award,
2006; Waterfront Center,
Excellence on the Waterfront
Awards, Top Honor, 2006;
National AIA, Honor Award for
Regional and Urban Design,
2014
Website wxystudio.com

01 Bronx Charter School for the
Arts, Bronx, NY, 2004. Photo
Albert Večerka/Esto
02 SeaGlass Carousel, New York,
NY, in progress
03 EMS 27, New York, NY, 2011.
Photo Paul Warchol
04 Reconstruction of Astor Place
and Cooper Square, New York,
NY, in progress
05 NYC Information Center,
New York, NY, 2010. Photo
Albert Večerka/Esto

01

02

03

04

Johanna Hurme, Sasa Radulovic

5468796 Architecture, Winnipeg, Canada (est. 2007)

Education Hurme: University of Manitoba, BEnvD, 1999; University of Manitoba, MArch, 2002 \\ Radulovic: University of Manitoba, BEnvD, 1999; University of Manitoba, MArch, 2003

Practice Update Johanna Hurme, Colin Neufeld, Sasa Radulovic (principals)
Teaching Positions University of Manitoba; University of Toronto
Notable Honors *Architect*, P/A Award, 2012; *Architectural Review*, AR+D Award for Emerging Architecture, 2012; Royal Architectural Institute of Canada, Governor General's Medal in Architecture, 2014
Website 5468796.ca

05

01 62M, Winnipeg, Canada, 2014. Rendering BG Studio
02 OMS Stage, Winnipeg, Canada, 2010. Photo James Brittain Photography
03 Bloc_10 Condominiums, Winnipeg, Canada, 2011. Photo James Brittain Photography
04 The Avenue on Portage, Winnipeg, Canada, 2012. Photo James Brittain Photography
05 Centre Village, Winnipeg, Canada, 2010. Photo James Brittain Photography

01

Jose Castillo, Saidee Springall

arquitectura911sc, Mexico City (est. 2002)

Education Castillo: Universidad Iberoamericana, BArch, 1992; Harvard University, MArch, 1995; Harvard University, PhD design, 2000 \\ Springall: Universidad Iberoamericana, BArch, 1993; Harvard University, MArch, 1996

Teaching Positions Castillo: Harvard University; Tulane University; Universidad Iberoamericana; University of Pennsylvania
Notable Honors Holcim Foundation, International Holcim Award for Sustainable Construction, Bronze Medal, 2011; *Interior Design*, Best of Year, 2013; *Travel + Leisure*, T+L Design Award, 2014
Website arq911.com

02

03

04

05

01 Churubusco Film Labs and Producers Building, Mexico City, Mexico, 2011
02 Jamie Garcia Terre's Library, Mexico City, Mexico, 2011. Photo Jaime Navarro
03 Elena Garro Cultural Center, Mexico City, Mexico, 2012. Photo Jaime Navarro
04 Centro Cultural del Bosque, Mexico City, Mexico, 2012. Photo Pim Schalkwijk, courtesy The National Institute of Fine Arts
05 Design Center, CEDIM, Monterrey, Mexico, 2009. Photo Dante Busquets

01

02

03

04

Manon Asselin, Katsuhiro Yamazaki

Atelier TAG, Montréal
(est. 1997)

Education Asselin: McGill University, BSc architecture, 1990, BArch, 1992, post-professional degree in history and theory of architecture, 2001 \\ Yamazaki: McGill University, BSc architecture, 1994, BArch, 1996

Teaching Positions Asselin: McGill University; Université de Montréal \\ Yamazaki: McGill University
Notable Honors Canada Council for the Arts, Prix de Rome, 2007; *Canadian Architect*, Award of Excellence, 2013; Royal Architectural Institute of Canada, Governor General's Medal in Architecture, 2013
Website ateliertag.com

05

01 Montréal Museum of Fine Arts, Fifth Pavilion, Québec, Canada, 2013. Rendering TAG and Doug & Wolf
02 Théâtre du Vieux-Terrebonne, Terrebonne, Canada, 2005. Photo Marc Cramer
03 Théâtre du Vieux-Terrebonne, Terrebonne, Canada, 2005. Photo Marc Cramer
04 Montréal Museum of Fine Arts, Fifth Pavilion, Québec, Canada, 2013. Rendering Doug & Wolf
05 Bibliothèque Raymond-Lévesque, Québec, Canada, 2011. Photo Marc Cramer

Jeffrey Inaba

INABA, Los Angeles, New York City (est. 2005)

Education University of California, Berkeley, BArch, 1985; Harvard University, MDes, 1989, MArch, 1990, MA architectural history and theory, 2010

Teaching Position Columbia University (director, C-Lab, Graduate School of Architecture, Planning and Preservation, 2005-present)
Notable Honors Graham Foundation for Advanced Studies in the Fine Arts, grant recipient, 2012; AIA New York Chapter, Design Award for Interior Design, 2013; Architizer, A+ Award, 2013
Website inaba.us

01 Kiosk, Festival of Ideas for the New City, New York, NY, 2011. © Greg Irikura
02 *Soft Opening*, Whitney Museum of American Art, New York, NY, 2010. © Greg Irikura
03 Red Bull Music Studios, New York, NY, 2013; in collaboration with SLAB Architecture. © Greg Irikura
04 Skylight, Stavanger, Norway, 2012. Photo Ivan Brodey
05 Migratory Anagram, Los Angeles, CA, 2011
06 Migratory Anagram, Los Angeles, CA, 2011

01

02

03

04

Dwayne Oyler, Jenny Wu

Oyler Wu Collaborative, Los Angeles (est. 2004)

Education Oyler: Kansas State University, BArch, 1996; Harvard University, MArch, 2001 \\ Wu: Columbia University, BA architecture, specialization in art history, 1997; Harvard University, MArch, 2001

Teaching Positions Oyler: Cooper Union; Research Institute for Experimental Architecture; SCI-Arc; Syracuse University \\ Wu: Rensselaer Polytechnic Institute; SCI-Arc; Syracuse University

Notable Honors AIA Los Angeles, Presidential Honoree for Emerging Practice, 2012; AIA California, Monterey Design Conference, Emerging Talent Award, 2013; *Architectural Record*, Design Vanguard, 2013

Website oylerwu.com

05

01 *reALIze*, Los Angeles, CA, 2011; in collaboration with Michael Kalish. Photo Scott Mayoral
02 *The Cube*, Beijing, China 2013. Photo Jason Wheeler
03 *Live Wire*, Los Angeles, CA, 2007
04 Lo Res High Rise, Taipei, Taiwan, in progress
05 *Netscape*, SCI-Arc Graduation Pavilion, Los Angeles, CA, 2011

01

02

03

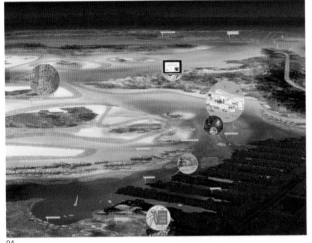
04

05

06

Elena Brescia, Kate Orff

SCAPE / LANDSCAPE ARCHITECTURE, New York City (est. 2007)

Education Brescia: Fordham University, BA art history, 1985; University of Pennsylvania, MLA, 1993 \\ Orff: University of Virginia, BA political and social thought, 1993; Harvard University, MLA, 1997

Teaching Position Orff: Columbia University
Notable Honors ASLA New York Chapter, Design Award, 2012; ASLA New York Chapter, Collaborative Design Award, 2014 \\ Orff: United States Artists, USA Francie Bishop Good and David Horvitz Fellow, 2012; National ASLA, Professional Award Communications Category, cowinner with Richard Misrach, 2013; The National Academy, National Academician, 2013
Website scapestudio.com

01 Oyster-tecture, *Rising Currents: Projects for New York's Waterfront*, Museum of Modern Art, New York, NY, 2010
02 Gardening the Bay: Jamaica Bay, HUD Rebuild by Design, selected team, Long Island, NY, and New York, NY, 2013
03 Mussel Pilot, Gowanus Bay, Brooklyn, NY, 2011
04 Gardening the Bay: Jamaica Bay, HUD Rebuild by Design, selected team, Long Island, NY, and New York, NY, 2013
05 Battery Park Community Center, New York, NY, 2012
06 103rd Street Community Garden, New York, NY, 2011

01

02

04

05   06

John Hong,
Jinhee Park

SsD, New York City
(est. 2003)

Education Hong: University of
Virginia, BS architecture,
1991; Harvard University,
MArch, 1996 \\ Park: Seoul
National University, BFA
industrial design, 1995;
Harvard University, MArch,
2002

Practice Update Cambridge,
MA, New York City, and Seoul
Teaching Positions Hong:
Harvard University;
Northeastern University \\
Park: Harvard University;
Illinois Institute of
Technology; University of
Houston
Notable Honors AIA
Massachusetts and Boston
Society of Architects, Honor
Award, 2012; *Architectural
Record*, Design Vanguard,
2012; Mayor's Office of the
City of Paju, Korea, Most
Beautiful Building Award,
2013
Website ssdarchitecture.com

01 White Block Gallery, Heyri
   Art Valley, South Korea,
   2011. Photo Chang Kyun Kim
   Photography
02 Island of Water, Incheon, South
   Korea, in progress
03 8 Towers, Ordos 100, Ordos,
   China, 2010
04 *Cloud*, Heyri Art Valley, South
   Korea, 2012
05 Songpa Micro-Housing, Seoul,
   South Korea, 2014
06 Braver House, Newton, MA, 2011

01

02

04

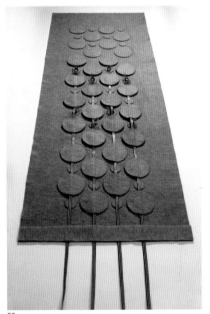

03

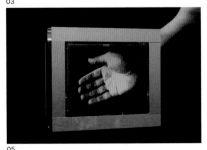

05

Christos Marcopoulos, Carol Moukheiber

Studio (n-1), Toronto
(est. 2001)

Education Marcopoulos:
Cooper Union, BArch, 1993
\\ Moukheiber: Parsons The
New School for Design, BA
environmental design, 1988;
Cooper Union, BArch, 1993

Teaching Positions
Marcopoulos: Architectural
Association; California
College of the Arts;
University of California,
Berkeley; University of
Toronto; University of
Waterloo \\ Moukheiber:
American University of
Beirut; California College
of the Arts; University
of California, Berkeley;
University of Toronto
(director, Master of Urban
Design Program, John
H. Daniels Faculty of
Architecture, Landscape,
and Design, 2010-2013;
codirector, Responsive
Architecture at Daniels,
2011-present)
Notable Honors San Francisco
Museum of Modern Art,
SFMOMA Experimental Design
Award, finalist, 2001; San
Francisco Museum of Modern
Art, permanent collection,
2002; Canada Foundation for
Innovation, grant recipient,
2011
Website nminusone.com

01 Janus House, Toronto, Canada,
2011
02 *IM BLANKY*, Toronto, Canada,
2011; in collaboration with
Rodolphe el-Khoury
03 *IM BLANKY #2*, Toronto, Canada,
2013
04 *Drop Moss*, Toronto, Canada,
2013; in collaboration with
Rodolphe el-Khoury
05 *Digital Window*, Toronto,
Canada, 2008

01

02

03

04

Andy Cao, Xavier Perrot

cao|perrot, Los Angeles, Paris (est. 2006)

Education Cao: California State Polytechnic University, Pomona, BS landscape architecture, 1994 \\ Perrot: Saint-Ilan Horticulture School, 2000; Conservatoire International des Parcs de Jardins et du Paysage, 2001

Teaching Position Cao: California State Polytechnic University, Pomona
Notable Honors Cao: American Academy in Rome, Rome Prize, 2002; Harvard University, Loeb Fellowship, 2011
\\ cao|perrot: Material ConneXion, MEDIUM Award for Material of the Year, 2007
\\ Perrot: French Ministry of Culture, Emerging Young Architects and Landscape Architects Award, 2008
Website caoperrotstudio.com

01 Cloud Terrace, Dumbarton Oaks, Washington DC, 2012. Photo Stephen Jerrome
02 Lullaby Garden, Cornerstone Sonoma, Sonoma, CA, 2004. Photo Stephen Jerrome
03 Jardin des Hespérides, Les Jardins de Métis, Grand-Métis, Canada, 2005. Photo Louise Tanguay
04 Aerial Garden for Champagne Laurent-Perrier, Paris, France, 2009. Photo Stephen Jerrome

01

03

04

02

05

06

Jules Dingle, Jeff Goldstein, Mark Sanderson, Jamie Unkefer

DIGSAU, Philadelphia (est. 2007)

Education Dingle: University of Notre Dame, BArch, 1995; University of California, Berkeley, MArch, 2000 \\ Goldstein: University of Pennsylvania, BA biology and environmental studies, 1998; Yale University, MArch, 2001 \\ Sanderson: University of Notre Dame, BArch, 1993; University of Pennsylvania, MArch, 1998 \\ Unkefer: Earlham College, BA literature, 1987; Yale University, MArch, 1995

Teaching Positions Dingle: Temple University; University of Pennsylvania \\ Goldstein: Temple University \\ Sanderson: Temple University \\ Unkefer: University of Pennsylvania
Notable Honors AIA Philadelphia, Philadelphia Emerging Architecture Prize, 2010; The International Garden Festival, Les Jardins de Métis, participant with Studio Bryan Hanes, 2010; AIA Pennsylvania, Honor Award, 2013
Website digsau.com

01 Iroko Pharmaceuticals Headquarters Building, Philadelphia, PA, 2013. Photo Todd Mason/Halkin Photography
02 Rural Loft, Middletown, DE, 2011. Photo Todd Mason/Halkin Photography
03 Veil Garden, Les Jardins de Métis, Grand-Métis, Canada, 2010-2013; in collaboration with Studio Bryan Hanes
04 Construction Training and Education Center, Wilmington, DE, 2014
05 Sister Cities Park and Pavilion, Philadelphia, PA, 2011. Photo Todd Mason/Halkin Photography
06 Dogfish Head Brewery, Milton, DE, 2013. Photo Todd Mason/Halkin Photography

01

Susannah Churchill Drake

Dlandstudio architecture and landscape architecture, Brooklyn (est. 2005)

Education Dartmouth College, BA art history and fine arts, 1987; Harvard University, MArch, MLA, 1995

Teaching Positions Cooper Union; Florida International University; Harvard University; Syracuse University
Notable Honors ASLA, Fellow, 2013; National AIA, Young Architects Award, 2013; AIA New York Chapter, New Practice New York Award, 2014
Website dlandstudio.com

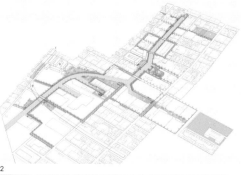

02

03

04

05

01 BQ GREEN, Brooklyn, NY, 2010
02 Gowanus Canal Sponge Park, Brooklyn, NY, 2009-2014
03 Sidney Residence, Brooklyn, NY, 2010
04 Highway Outfall Landscape Detention (HOLD) System, Bronx, NY, 2014
05 Marshes, Staten Island, NY, 2014

01

02

03

04

05

Jorge Gracia

graciastudio, Tijuana
(est. 2004)

Education Universidad
Iberoamericana, BArch, 1997;
Universidad Iberoamericana,
MBA, 2000

Teaching Position Escuela
Libre de Arquitectura
(founder; dean, 2013-present)
Notable Honors *Architectural
Record*, Design Vanguard,
2012; Red Dot, Design
Award, 2012; Universidad
Nacional Autónoma de México,
21 Jóvenes Arquitectos
Mexicanos, 2013
Websites
escuelalibredearquitectura
.com \\ graciastudio.com

01 Vinícola Encuentro Guadalupe,
   Valle de Guadalupe, Mexico,
   2012. Photo Edgar Lima
02 Culinary Art School, Tijuana,
   Mexico, 2011. Photo Luis Garcia
03 Plaza Internacional, Ensenada,
   Mexico, 2013. Photo Luis Garcia
04 Casa Valle de Guadalupe,
   Ensenada, Mexico, 2012. Photo
   Edgar Lima
05 Casa Todos Santos, Todos
   Santos, Mexico, 2006. Photo
   Sandra Munoz

01

04

02

03

05

06

Sierra Bainbridge, Michael Murphy, Alan Ricks, David Saladik

MASS Design Group, Boston (est. 2010)

Education Bainbridge: Smith College, BA art and art history, 1999; University of Pennsylvania, MArch, MLA, 2004 \\ Murphy: University of Chicago, BA English language and literature, 2002; Harvard University, MArch, 2011 \\ Ricks: Colorado College, BA studio art, journalism, 2005; Harvard University, MArch, 2010 \\ Saladik: Boston University, BA independent study in architectural studies, 2004; Harvard University, MArch, 2010

Practice Update Boston, Kigali, Rwanda, and Port-au-Prince, Haiti
Teaching Positions Bainbridge: Boston Architectural College; Harvard University; Kigali Institute of Science and Technology (head, Department of Architecture, 2009-2011); University of Pennsylvania \\ Murphy: Clark University; Harvard University, School of Public Health; New York School of Interior Design (advisory board, Master of Professional Studies in Sustainable Interior Environments, 2012-present); Program for Appropriate Technologies in Heath; School of Visual Arts (advisory board, MFA Design for Social Innovation, 2012-present) \\ Ricks: Clark University; Harvard University, School of Public Health
Notable Honors See page 296
Website massdesigngroup.org

---

01 Umubano School, Kigali, Rwanda, 2011
02 Doctors' Housing, Butaro, Rwanda, 2012
03 Butaro Ambulatory Cancer Center, Butaro, Rwanda, 2013
04 Umubano School, Kigali, Rwanda, 2011
05 Butaro Ambulatory Cancer Center, Butaro, Rwanda, 2013
06 Butaro Hospital, Butaro, Rwanda, 2011

All images Iwan Baan.

Luke Ogrydziak, Zoë Prillinger

Ogrydziak Prillinger,
San Francisco (est. 2000)

Education Ogrydziak:
Princeton University, BArch,
1992; Princeton University,
MArch, 1995 \\ Prillinger:
Princeton University, BArch,
1992; Princeton University,
MArch, 1994

Teaching Positions Ogrydziak:
Harvard University;
University of California,
Berkeley \\ Prillinger:
California College of the
Arts; Harvard University;
University of California,
Berkeley
Notable Honors AIA
California, Merit Award,
2010; AIA San Francisco,
Honor Award, 2011; AIA San
Francisco, Unbuilt Design
Honor Award, 2012
Website oparch.net

01

02

03

04

05

06

01 Triskelion, San Francisco, CA,
2010. Photo Tim Griffith
02 Parallax, Lotus, CA, 2012.
Photo Tim Griffith
03 Ourcadia, San Francisco, CA,
2012. Photo Tim Griffith
04 Shapeshifter, Reno, NV, 2013
05 Hyde, San Francisco, CA, 2014.
Photo Tim Griffith
06 Gallery House, San Francisco,
CA, 2009. Photo Tim Griffith

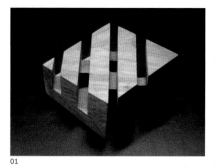

01

02

03

04

05

Carlos Bedoya,
Wonne Ickx,
Victor Jaime,
Abel Perles

PRODUCTORA, Mexico City
(est. 2006)

Education Bedoya: Universidad
Iberoamericana, BArch,
1998; Escola d'Arquitectura
de Barcelona, MArch, 2000
\\ Ickx: University of
Ghent, civil engineering
and architecture, 1998;
University of Guadalajara,
MA urbanism and development,
2001 \\ Jaime: Universidad
Iberoamericana, BArch, 2001
\\ Perles: Universidad de
Buenos Aires, BArch, 1999

Practice Update PRODUCTORA
\\ LIGA, espacio para
arquitectura, Mexico City
(est. 2011); Carlos Bedoya,
Ruth Estévez, Wonne Ickx,
Victor Jaime, Abel Perles
(directors)
Teaching Positions Bedoya:
Instituto Tecnológico de
Monterrey; Universidad
Iberoamericana; Texas A&M
University \\ Ickx: Centre de
Diseño; Texas A&M University;
University of California,
Los Angeles; Universidad
Iberoamericana; Universidad
La Salle \\ Jaime: Centre de
Diseño
Notable Honors The
Architectural League of New
York, Young Architects Forum,
2007; Andean Development
Corporation, Competition
for New Headquarters, first
prize, 2008; Bienal de
Arquitectura de la Ciudad de
México, Honorable Mention,
2013
Websites productora-df.com.mx
\\ liga-df.com

01 Villa, Ordos 100, Ordos, China,
2008
02 A47 Mobile Art Library, Mexico
City, Mexico, 2012. Photo Luis
Gallardo
03 House in Tlayacapan, Morelos,
Mexico, 2011. Photo Luis
Gallardo
04 Bar Celeste, Mexico City,
Mexico, 2011. Photo Rafael Gamo
05 Casa Diaz, Valle de Bravo,
Mexico, 2011. Photo Paul
Czitrom

01

02

03

04

05

Florian Idenburg, Jing Liu

SO - IL, New York City
(est. 2008)

Education Idenburg: Delft
University of Technology, MS
architecture, 1999 \\ Liu:
Tulane University, MArch,
2004

Practice Update Florian
Idenburg, Jing Liu (founding
partners); Ilias Papageorgiou
(principal)
Teaching Positions Idenburg:
Columbia University; Harvard
University; University of
Kentucky \\ Liu: Columbia
University; Parsons The New
School for Design; Syracuse
University
Notable Honors AIA New York
Chapter, New Practices
Award, 2010; MoMA PS1,
Young Architects Program,
competition winner, 2010;
AIA New York Chapter, Design
Award, 2011
Website so-il.org

01 Kukje Art Gallery, Seoul, South
   Korea, 2012. Photo Iwan Baan
02 *Tri-Colonnade*, Shenzhen, China,
   2011. Photo Iwan Baan
03 Frieze Art Fair, New York, NY,
   2012. Photo Iwan Baan
04 *tiNY*, New York, NY, 2012
05 *Spiky*, Beijing, China, 2013

Karen Stein

RESONANCE:
BEST IN SHOW

Most great architects are late bloomers, or so it seems. Unlike star athletes or virtuoso musicians or even mathematical prodigies, architects rarely experience major career breakthroughs before middle age. While Ludwig Mies van der Rohe designed the Barcelona Pavilion in his early forties, he conceived the Farnsworth House, arguably his masterpiece, at age sixty and the Seagram Building even later in life. Louis Kahn was in his fifties before he received significant commissions, in his sixties when he designed the Salk Institute for Biological Studies, and in his seventies when the Kimbell Art Museum was completed. And with the opening of the Guggenheim Museum in Bilbao, Spain, in 1997, Frank Gehry, at sixty-eight, became an overnight sensation, some four decades in the making.

For all of them, of course, there were earlier portents of greatness, but one had to be looking. And this is what The Architectural League's Emerging Voices program is all about—looking for those early signs. Identifying emerging talent in any field is a parlor game played by experts and enthusiasts alike. Ranking systems by academies or professional associations is a long-standing practice, as is the related custom of bestowing medals or prizes for outstanding achievement, at virtually any stage of a career. Each artistic discipline has its own subculture of awards, be it for a specific piece of work or career achievement—some are restricted to a particular medium, age group, gender, geographic profile, or other defining characteristic.

The program has sought to identify distinctive talents in North American architecture and landscape architecture at a relatively early stage in their careers. Though the distinction doesn't come with a medal or significant cash prize, it does provide maturing architects with a platform—literally, in the form of a lecture and related publicity. For some, this is a public debut of sorts that can lead to more lecture invitations, more press coverage, and additional accolades, setting award recipients on a path that is not always predictable and certainly not linear, but one that New York architect Victoria Meyers of hanrahan Meyers architects (EV93) describes as a critical early step on the road to success. Whether a clear step, as Meyers argues, or some invisible threshold, winning the award encourages a growing momentum of exposure and recognition. And while any attempt to assess the foresight or acuity of the award must account for the fact that, at the very least, a tiny piece of the prophecy can be self-fulfilling, it is worth noting that a significant number of the early Emerging Voices have gone on to become leading practitioners in the field.

But what is the consequence of rating those who are in professions that seem to defy statistics, such as the arts? And are the risks magnified in a field such as architecture, in which it takes a relatively long time to assemble a substantial body of work for reasons of both opportunity and requisite experience? As James F. English argues in *The Economy of Prestige: Prizes, Awards, and the Circulation of Cultural Value*, the proliferation of cultural prizes in the past one hundred

Rosalie Genevro

AFTERWORD

Although it was created one hundred years into the life of The Architectural League, the Emerging Voices program is a remarkably pure expression of the organization's original DNA. It has all the markers: youth, creative ambition, expertise, community, and influence. From the beginning, in 1881, the League has been strongly associated with emerging architects. As the young draftsmen who founded the League wrote in a letter to the arts journal the *Critic* in January of that year, "The popular feeling among the body of architectural workmen, especially the younger members of the profession, has recently been inclining strongly toward the opinion that an opportunity to reach a high standard of work is necessary," so they formed an association "having in view the attainment of this end."[1] Two years later, in March 1883, the *Century* reported that members of the League "all deem it essential to convert the public from its predilection for evil ways of building, and as a necessary preliminary to clear up their own ideas about the better way. This is the cause that the Architectural League has at heart."[2] The method for finding that better way was mutual education: aspiring designers would encourage each other, with occasional critique and advice from a more established figure. The young architects who founded the League wanted to develop themselves as creative and influential figures able to engage and affect their milieu.

The League's aspiration to influence architectural quality and taste found a vehicle in 1886 when it launched an annual exhibition, a tradition that continued uninterrupted into the 1930s. Architects from around the country submitted work for the shows, which in most years drew both large crowds and reviews in the *New York Times* and other periodicals. If the organization devoted less energy to encouraging the young during this era, as it increasingly became identified as the architectural establishment, it did substantially increase its national influence as an arbiter of architectural significance.

In 1941 emerging architects had their say again at the League, coming together to mount an exhibition called *40 Under 40*. In the introduction to the show they wrote,

> We are the generation that did not build the New York skyline, the Gothic dormitories, the colleges or the triangle in Washington....We weren't sure what kind of work we wanted to do, but we agreed on one thing: Roman baths were no place for railroad trains, nor medieval nunneries for undergraduates....Our big job has been to break down the prejudices of an outworn eclecticism and to replace them with something more positive and vital.[3]

By the mid-1960s the modernism that the young architects of the early 1940s had seen as more positive and vital had become stale and compromised in the eyes of a new generation. A second (and better known) *40 Under 40* exhibition, presented in 1966, was organized by Robert A.M. Stern, who had recently become the first J. Clawson Mills fellow at the League upon graduation from the Yale

School of Architecture. Referring to the 1941 show,
Stern wrote that "though the 'prejudices of an outworn
eclecticism' seem at last to have been broken down,
still the reaction of sons against fathers, so to speak,
continues in architecture: form and professional attitudes, not so much evolving as changing in a pattern that
has not yet revealed itself." Stern's show anointed a new
generation, whose pursuits he described as "an architecture responsible to program, yet one that casts aside the
shibboleths of functional and structural determinism in
favor of a frank recognition of the primacy of form; an
architecture which seeks to accommodate the often
conflicting demands of urbanistic responsibility and
specific program and not gloss over one or the other."[4]

By the early 1980s the Young Turks of Stern's show had
themselves become the establishment. When the Emerging
Voices program was launched in 1982, the dynamic of youth
eager to displace age was in evidence again. Architect,
curator, and critic Richard Oliver (EV83) wrote in
Skyline in April 1982,

> Curiosity about new talent is a common enough state
> of mind in any field of endeavor, and so there need
> be little justification for a series like "Emerging
> Voices."...Today American architecture is dominated by
> a group of practitioners who were born between 1925 and
> 1940; many, if not all of these were included in the
> Architectural League's 1966 exhibition 40 Under 40....
> The buildings that this older group of architects are
> beginning to build are so distinctive that it is rea-
> sonable to ask if there are any "emerging voices" wait-
> ing in the wings, and, if so, what are they saying?[5]

In the thirty years since the program was created, the
Emerging Voices have had a great deal to say. They have
experimented with materials, form, process, and program.
They have taught at and led design schools. And,
particularly in recent years, they have sought a more
public terrain for their practices and a more public
voice for their ideas.

The annual cycle of the Emerging Voices program, along
with other factors that include the extraordinary
proliferation of digital media during the three decades
of the lecture series, has radically shortened the gen-
erational time frame of earlier confrontations between
those perceived as established and their challengers.
New ideas and forms are produced and consumed much
more quickly; the discipline of architecture is more
dynamic and more pluralist than in earlier eras, and it
is often difficult to identify any dominant thread.

The contributors to this book have invoked several
metaphors to get at the essence of the Emerging Voices
program. I offer one more. The series is a barometer,
in that it takes the measure of the field and suggests
what is to come. But by validating a limited number
of individuals and approaches out of a large number of
contenders, the program, like the League itself, also

helps make the weather. The risk of simply reproduc-
ing the biases and momentum of the status quo is always
present; that is a risk we work hard to minimize. We
seek independent thinkers from unexpected quarters,
and we set our sights on work that shows marks of
the audacity, tenacity, and intensity that meaningful investigation involves. We aim to recognize and
encourage practitioners eager to "clear up their own
ideas about the better way," as the founders of the
League sought to do more than one hundred years ago.

The searching, testing, and honing that emerging
architects and designers carry out is in many ways the
League's work too. With the Emerging Voices program, as
with the League Prize for Young Architects + Designers,
Norden Fund travel grants, design studies, competitions,
and all League initiatives directed toward talented
up-and-coming practitioners, we are constantly working
to become more adept at identifying ideas that are original, useful, challenging, and fertile. We do so not
just to stimulate the community of architects, and
strengthen the discipline of architecture, but also
because we believe architecture of ambition and quality
is an essential part of a vital culture. The Emerging
Voices' probing work provides definitive evidence
that this is a project worth pursuing.

Notes

Introduction
Anne Rieselbach

1 In 1987, after five years of the program, the League held a one-time international Emerging Voices series featuring Australians Norman Day of Melbourne and Espie Dods of Sydney; Austrians Adolf Krischanitz (Missing Link) and Wolfgang Prix (Coop Himmelb(l)au), both based in Vienna; British architect Robert Adam (Winchester Design Group) of Winchester, England; and Czech-born architect Eva Jiricna (Jiricna Kerr Associates) of London. Their work is not included in this collection. The program was suspended for one cycle in 1991.

2 Successor firms, family members, and League staff compiled the work of deceased Emerging Voices. All efforts were made to ensure the accuracy of the information provided by firms and others.

Idea: Claiming Territories
Ashley Schafer

1 The description of the award has changed over the years to be more inclusive. For many years it required "built work," but the current phrase "significant bodies of realized work" allows for practices that are more art- or installation-based to be considered as equally valid modes of operation. However, the expectation remains that there is a relation between thought and intention and action or actualization.

2 For a complete discussion of affects, see Sylvia Lavin, *Kissing Architecture* (Princeton, NJ: Princeton University Press, 2011); she first posed the notion of

affects almost a decade earlier in the essay "What You Surface Is What You Get," *Log* 1 (Fall 2003): 103-6.

3 Specifically, the New York (and East Coast) architectural scene was dominated by a group of architects, the majority of whom had been included in the League's *40 Under 40* exhibition in 1966. Namely, this list included Peter Eisenman, Michael Graves, Charles Gwathmey, Hugh Hardy, Hugh Newell Jacobsen, Richard Meier, Charles Moore, William Pedersen, James Polshek, Jaquelin T. Robertson, Robert A.M. Stern, Stanley Tigerman, William Turnbull, and Robert Venturi.

4 Storefront for Art and Architecture was founded in 1982 in New York City as an exhibition and public meeting space to promote the dissemination and discussion of architecture and design; Coop Himmelb(l)au was selected as an Emerging Voice in 1987, the only year designers outside North America were eligible for the program; *Oppositions 25* was the last issue published with the participation of founding editors Peter Eisenman, Kenneth Frampton, and Mario Gandelsonas. The last issue, *Oppositions 26*, published in 1984, reenvisioned the journal with editors Diana Agrest, Mario Gandelsonas, and Anthony Vidler, and managing editor Kevin Lippert, but when the Institute for Architecture and Urban Studies in New York collapsed a year later, so did *Oppositions*.

5 The text of the debate titled "Contrasting Concepts of Harmony in Architecture" was originally published in *Lotus International* 40 (1983): 60-68, and was reprinted in *Studio Works* 7 (Cambridge, MA: Harvard University Graduate School of Design, 2000), 48-57.

6 Williams and Tsien began collaborating in 1977 and founded their firm in 1986.

7 K. Michael Hays, "Critical Architecture: Between Culture and Form," in *Perspecta* 21 (1984): 14-29. In 1986 he founded *Assemblage: A Critical Journal of Architecture and Design Culture*, which was the primary venue for debates of critical theory in the mid-1980s and throughout the 1990s.

8 See K. Michael Hays, introduction to *Architecture Theory Since 1968* (Cambridge, MA: MIT Press, 1998), 10.

9 Kenneth Frampton, "Rappel à l'ordre: The Case for the Tectonic," in *Architectural Design* 60 (1990): 21.

10 See especially *Assemblage 27, The Tulane Papers: The Politics of Contemporary Architectural Discourse* (1995) and *Assemblage 30* (1996).

11 Having won the Pritzker Architecture Prize in 1981, James Stirling was a controversial figure in the field. At the time of his death, he was renowned as a significant and original modernist whose practice evolved in the 1970s and 1980s to embrace "historical allusion and contextual consideration" (Philip Johnson, from the Pritzker Prize announcement). Although recent studies of Stirling question the notion of his midcareer turn, what remains in both readings is that his design process was staunchly based in composition—that is, a carefully orchestrated relationship of forms. The interest in 1992 in the digital design process was precisely its potential as an alternative means to design without composition and a questioning of the notion of authorship.

12 First published in Stan Allen, "From Object to Field," *Architectural Design* 67, no. 5/6 (1997): 24-31.

13 Ibid., 29, 24.

14 Jorge Silvetti referred to the tendency as "programism" in a lecture, "The Muses Are Not Amused: Pandemonium in the House of Architecture," given at Harvard University in 2002 at the end of his seven-year tenure as the head of architecture. However, he attributed the coining of the term to Preston Scott Cohen during the Harvard University Graduate School of Design's 2000 thesis reviews, at which this author was present. In his lecture, Silvetti defined four "trends": "Thematization, Blobs, Literalism, and Programism." Because of his formal orientation, he defined Blobs as what I refer to as digital experimentalization, but my meaning is more broadly cast.

15 Robert Somol and Sarah Whiting, "Notes Around the Doppler Effect and Other Moods of Modernism," *Perspecta* 33 (2002): 72-77.

16 Somol and Whiting play off the multiple meanings of *plan*—an operational strategy and an architectural drawing.

17 Benjamin Ball stated that his firm is interested in the design of production, rather than the production of design. See Benjamin Ball, "Fast, Cheap & in Control," Vimeo video, 31:51, from a lecture recorded by The Architectural League of New York, March 30, 2011, posted by The Architectural League, http://archleague.org/2011/05/benjamin-ball/.

18 Architizer's A+ Awards program, which has been sponsored by the *Wall Street Journal*, claims that winners will be posted on billboards and bus stations. See Marc Kushner, "Architecture On Billboards! PVBLIC Foundation Joins As Media Partner of A+ Awards," accessed July 9, 2014,

com/blog/architecture-
on-billboards-pvblic-
foundation-joins-as-media-
partner-of-a-awards/;
Architizer boasts
an archive of 54,434
projects, see "About,"
accessed July 9, 2014,
http://architizer.com/
about/.

Commentary 1982–1986
Suzanne Stephens

1 At the time of his
Emerging Voices award
in 1984, Henry Smith-
Miller led Henry Smith-
Miller, Architect. Later
that year he established
Smith-Miller + Hawkinson
Architects with Laurie
Hawkinson. Laurinda Spear
was a principal, with
Bernardo Fort-Brescia,
of Arquitectonica when
she was named an Emerging
Voice in 1982. They had
cofounded the firm in
1977, in partnership with
Elizabeth Plater-Zyberk,
Andres Duany, and Hervin
Romney, who eventually
opened their own offices.

2 In the 1970s a group
of architects—Peter
Eisenman, Michael Graves,
Charles Gwathmey, John
Hejduk, and Richard
Meier—became known as the
"Whites," owing to the
color and abstract purity
of their architecture.
While their various
approaches differed, the
book they published, *Five
Architects* (Wittenborn
& Company, 1972),
demonstrated the influence
of Le Corbusier on their
formal explorations.
When the book appeared,
architect Robert A.M.
Stern (then president of
the League) organized a
group of architects to
review it. The "Grays,"
as they were called, owed
a debt to the "inclusive"
and historicist position
of Robert Venturi,
whose *Complexity and
Contradiction in
Architecture* (Museum
of Modern Art, 1966)
questioned the hegemony
of modernist design.
Romaldo Giurgola, Allan
Greenberg, Charles Moore,
Jaquelin T. Robertson,
and Stern each wrote
a critical essay on
Five Architects for

Architectural Forum's
May 1973 issue,
collectively titled "Five
on Five"—one of the
rare occasions in which
architects criticized
architects in an
architectural magazine.
(As a *Forum* staffer, I
edited those articles.)
The rubrics "White" and
"Gray" stuck, and the
Grays (later joined
by Michael Graves and
others) were to lead the
charge for postmodernist
architecture.

3 In 1983 the Emerging
Voices jury selected
Elizabeth Plater-Zyberk
and her partner, Andres
Duany. Duany Plater-
Zyberk & Company was
founded in 1980.

4 At the time of Richard
Oliver's article, I
was *Skyline*'s editor
and a member of The
Architectural League's
Board of Directors.

Afterword
Rosalie Genevro

1 "A Society of Junior
Architects," the
Critic, no. 2 (January
29, 1881): 8.

2 Roger Riordan, "The
Architectural League of
New York," *The Century*
25, no. 5 (March 1883):
699.

3 *The Architectural
League of New York 125
Years* (New York: The
Architectural League of
New York, 2006), 46.

4 Robert A.M. Stern, *40
Under 40: An Exhibition
of Young Talent in
Architecture* (New York:
The Architectural League
of New York, 1966),
unpaginated.

5 Richard Oliver, "Taft
and Friday at The
Architectural League,"
Skyline (April 1982): 16.

Profiles
Continued

**William McDonough,
J. Woodson Rainey Jr.**
1985 \\ *From page 074*

Notable Honors McDonough:
President's Council on
Sustainable Development,
Presidential Award, 1996;
Cooper-Hewitt, National
Design Museum, National
Design Award, 2004; United
States Environmental
Protection Agency,
Presidential Green Chemistry
Challenge Award, 2004
\\ Rainey: Institute of
Business Designers, Interior
Design Competition, winner,
1992; National AIA Honors
Award, chair of interiors
jury, 1996; Illuminating
Engineering Society, Lumen
Award, cowinner with Jerry
Kugler, 2003

**Ross Anderson,
Frederic Schwartz**
1988 \\ *From page 088*

Notable Honors Anderson:
American Academy in
Rome, Rome Prize, 1989;
Architectural Record and
Businessweek, Good Design
Is Good Business Lifetime
Achievement Award, 2002; AIA
New Jersey, Merit Award, 2009
\\ Schwartz: AIA, Fellow;
American Academy in Rome,
Rome Prize, 1985; *Faith
& Forum*, Sacred Landscape
Award, 2012

Wes Jones, Peter Pfau
1990 \\ *From page 102*

Notable Honors Holt Hinshaw
Pfau Jones: *Progressive
Architecture*, P/A Award,
1989, 1990; *Metropolitan
Home*, "Architecture for
the 90's," 1990 \\ Peter
Pfau: *Contract Magazine*,
Designer of the Year,
2003; AIA, Fellow, 2010 \\
Pfau Architecture: AIA San
Francisco, Design Excellence
Merit Award, 2004

**Clifton Balch,
Mojdeh Baratloo**
1996 \\ *From page 142*

Notable Honors Baratloo-
Balch Architects: National
Endowment for the Arts,
design arts and visual
arts collaboration grant,
1989; AIA New York Chapter,
Interior Architecture Award,
1990; New York Foundation for
the Arts, Fellows, 2002

**Charles Rose,
Maryann Thompson**
1997 \\ *From page 152*

Notable Honors Rose: National
AIA, Honor Award, 2002;
Chicago Athenaeum, American
Architecture Award, 2007 \\
Thompson: Boston Society
of Architects, Women in
Design Award of Excellence,
2005; Boston Society of
Architects, Honor Award for
Design Excellence, 2008; AIA
New England, Honor Award,
2010 \\ Thompson and Rose
Architects: National AIA,
Young Architects Award, 1998;
National AIA, Design Award,
2002

**Jonathan Marvel,
Robert Rogers**
2001 \\ *From page 184*

Notable Honors Marvel: AIA,
Fellow, 2011 \\ Rogers:
U.S. General Services
Administration, Design
Excellence National Peer,
2002-present; AIA, Fellow,
2007; Open House New York,
board of directors, 2010-
present \\ Rogers Marvel
Architects: National AIA,
Honor Award, 2001; AIA New
York State, Firm of the Year
Award, 2011; National AIA,
Honor Award for Regional and
Urban Design, 2011

**Kimberly Holden,
Gregg Pasquarelli,
Christopher Sharples,
Coren Sharples,
William Sharples**
2001 \\ *From page 186*

Teaching Positions
Pasquarelli: Columbia
University; Syracuse
University; University of
Florida; University of
Virginia; Yale University
\\ Christopher Sharples:
Columbia University; Cornell
University; Parsons The New
School for Design; University
of Virginia; Yale University
\\ Coren Sharples: Parsons
The New School for Design \\
William Sharples: Parsons The
New School for Design; Yale
University

**David Lewis, Paul Lewis,
Marc Tsurumaki**
2002 \\ *From page 190*

Notable Honors Venice
Architecture Biennale, U.S.
Pavilion, exhibitor, 2004;
Cooper-Hewitt, National
Design Museum, National
Design Award, 2007; Museum of
Modern Art (New York City),
permanent collection, 2013

**Alan Koch, Lyn Rice,
Galia Solomonoff,
Linda Taalman**
2002 \\ *From page 192*

Teaching Positions Koch:
Art Center College of
Design; Cornell University;
University of California,
Los Angeles \\ Rice: Barnard
College and Columbia
University; Cooper Union;
Princeton University;
Syracuse University \\
Solomonoff: Columbia
University \\ Taalman: Art
Center College of Design;
SCI-Arc; University of
Southern California; Woodbury
University
Notable Honors OpenOffice:
Architectural Record, Design
Vanguard, 2003; *Surface*, "The
New New Yorkers: Emerging
New York Architectural
Firms," 2004; AIA New York
Chapter, Merit Award, 2006
\\ RICE+LIPKA ARCHITECTS:
Municipal Art Society of New
York, MASterworks Award,
2008; National AIA, Honor
Award, 2009; *Architectural
Review* and MIPIM, Future
Projects Award, 2013

**Monica Ponce de Leon,
Nader Tehrani**
2003 \\ *From page 199*

Notable Honors Office dA:
American Academy of Arts and
Letters, Arts and Letters
Award in Architecture, 2002;
Cooper-Hewitt, National
Design Museum, National
Design Award, 2007; United
States Artists, USA Target
Fellow, 2007 \\ NADAAA:
Architect, Top 50 in
Design, Top Firm, 2013;
Chicago Athenaeum, American
Architecture Award, 2013;
Architect, P/A Award, 2014

**Andrew Bernheimer,
Jared Della Valle**
2007 \\ *From page 231*

Notable Honors Bernheimer
Architecture: Design Trust
for Public Space, Fellow,
2012; AIA New York Chapter,
Design Award, 2012, 2013 \\
Della Valle Bernheimer: San
Francisco Prize, first place,
1996; AIA New York Chapter,
Design Award, 2007; Syracuse
University, From the Ground
Up Competition, winning
entry, 2009

**Sierra Bainbridge,
Michael Murphy, Alan Ricks,
David Saladik**
2013 \\ *From page 282*

Notable Honors Curry Stone
Design Prize, 2012; Aga Kahn
Development Network, Aga
Kahn Award for Architecture,
finalist, 2013; MoMA PS1,
Young Architects Program,
competition finalist, 2013

Contributors

Alan G. Brake, executive editor of the *Architect's Newspaper*, has written about architecture, design, and urbanism for *Architecture*, *Architectural Record*, *Azure*, *Interior Design*, *Landscape Architecture*, *Metropolis*, and the *New York Times*. He studied architectural history and urbanism at Vassar College and earned a master of environmental design at Yale University. He is the recipient of a research grant from the Graham Foundation for Advanced Studies in the Fine Arts.

Henry N. Cobb is a founding principal of Pei Cobb Freed & Partners. Throughout his sixty-five-year career he has coupled his professional practice with teaching. He has lectured widely, held visiting professorships at several universities, and served a five-year term as chairman of the Department of Architecture at Harvard University Graduate School of Design. His honors include the AAAL Gold Medal for Architecture and the AIA/ACSA Topaz Medallion for Excellence in Architectural Education. He has served several times as a juror for the Emerging Voices program.

Rosalie Genevro, executive director of The Architectural League since 1985, has articulated and firmly established the League's commitment to design excellence through annual series spotlighting creative accomplishment as well as through consistently innovative events, exhibitions, and publications. She has guided and intensified the League's design advocacy in the public interest; spurred the League's investigations of new areas of interest and concern through ambitious initiatives including Architecture and Situated Technologies and The Five Thousand Pound Life; and originated the League's online projects Worldview Cities and Urban Omnibus.

Reed Kroloff, former director of Cranbrook Academy of Art and Art Museum, is managing principal of jones/kroloff, a design consultancy based in Washington DC. Previously, he served as dean of architecture at Tulane University, where he led the school through the aftermath of Hurricane Katrina and cofounded URBANbuild, the subject of the award-winning television series *Architecture School*. Kroloff cochaired the urban design committee of the Bring New Orleans Back commission. A Rome Prize recipient, Kroloff is former editor in chief of *Architecture*.

Alexandra Lange, an architecture and design critic, is author of *Writing about Architecture: Mastering the Language of Buildings and Cities* (Princeton Architectural Press, 2012). Her work has appeared in the *Architect's Newspaper*, *Architectural Record*, *Dezeen*, *Dwell*, *Metropolis*, *Print*, *New York* magazine, and the *New York Times*. She is coauthor, with Jane Thompson, of *Design Research: The Store That Brought Modern Living to American Homes*. In 2013-2014, she was a Loeb Fellow at Harvard University Graduate School of Design.

Paul Makovsky is editorial director of *Metropolis*. He is a former managing editor of *2wice*, and he held a Smithsonian Fellowship at Cooper-Hewitt, National Design Museum, where he worked on the exhibition and catalog *Mixing Messages: Graphic Design in Contemporary Culture*. Currently at work on a biography of Florence Knoll, he served as a co-curator of the exhibition *Knoll Textiles: 1945-2010* at Bard Graduate Center and contributed to the accompanying catalog.

Thomas de Monchaux, an architect and writer, teaches design at Columbia University's Graduate School of Architecture, Planning and Preservation. His writing has appeared in the *New York Times*, the *New Yorker* "Culture Desk," *N+1*, and *Perspecta*. He received the inaugural Winterhouse Award for Design Writing and Criticism and delivered the 2011 Myriam Bellazoug Memorial Lecture at the Yale School of Architecture on "Seven Architectural Embarrassments." A contributing editor at *Architect*, de Monchaux is at work on *Dream House* (forthcoming from Metropolitan/Holt), a book about cultural and personal histories of American houses and homes.

Anne Rieselbach, program director of The Architectural League, has directed the Emerging Voices program since 1986; that year she edited *Emerging Voices: A New Generation of Architects in America* on the program's first five years. She directs many of the League's lecture series, competitions, exhibitions, and special projects, including the Current Work lectures, Architectural League Prize for Young Architects + Designers, First Fridays curated open studios, Little Free Libraries/NYC (with PEN World Voices Festival), Moleskine Grand Central Terminal Sketchbook (with New York Transit Museum), and FOLLY competition (with Socrates Sculpture Park). Exhibitions on Paul Rudolph, Daniel Urban Kiley, and the history of school design in New York City are among her earlier projects. She serves on the Open House New York board of directors and the *Architect's Newspaper* editorial board.

Ashley Schafer is a writer, designer, educator, and registered architect whose work investigates the intersection of contemporary architecture, urbanism, landscape, history, technology, and practice. She is cofounder and co-editor of *PRAXIS*, cocurator of the U.S. Pavilion at the 14th International Venice Architecture Biennale, and associate professor of architecture at The Ohio State University, where she was head of architecture from 2005 to 2009. Previously, Schafer was associate professor at Harvard University Graduate School of Design and taught at Massachusetts Institute of Technology and Tulane University. She received her undergraduate degree in architecture from the University of Virginia and her MArch from Columbia University.

Karen Stein is an architectural advisor, a faculty member of the design criticism program at the School of Visual Arts, and executive director of the George Nelson Foundation. Previous posts include editorial director of Phaidon Press, senior managing editor of *Architectural Record*, and member of the Pritzker Architecture Prize jury. She is author of *Aldo Rossi Architecture 1981-1991* (Princeton Architectural Press, 1991), and her writing has been published in *WSJ. Magazine*, *Architectural Digest*, *New York* magazine, and *a+u*. She is a board member of The Architectural League.

Suzanne Stephens, a writer and critic, is a deputy editor of *Architectural Record*. She holds a PhD in architectural history from Cornell University and teaches the history of architectural criticism at Barnard College and Columbia University. Stephens is architectural advisor to Checkerboard Film Foundation, producer of *Landmarks in 21st Century American Architecture*, and lead author of *Imagining Ground Zero: Official and Unofficial Proposals for the World Trade Center Site* (*Architectural Record* and Rizzoli International, 2004). She is a board member of the Sir John Soane Museum Foundation and a life trustee of The Architectural League.

Acknowledgments

The Architectural League of New York is grateful to many members and friends for their contributions to this publication. For her insights into the early years of the program, we thank Suzanne Stephens. For helping to galvanize participation among fellow Emerging Voices on the West Coast, we thank Thom Mayne. This book would not be possible without the additional contributions of photographers, and we are particularly appreciative of the generosity of Tom Bonner, Scott Frances, Tim Hursley, and Paul Warchol, as well as Erica Stoller of Esto. And we offer our heartfelt thanks to those who brought the work of deceased Emerging Voices to these pages: Clifton Balch for Mojdeh Baratloo; PKSB for Wayne Berg; the Avery Drawings & Archives Collection at Columbia University and the Van Alen Institute for Roger C. Ferri; Chris Garofalo for Douglas Garofalo; Annie Chu for Franklin D. Israel; Lisa D. Fischetti and Sigmund Lerner for Ralph Lerner; Jackie Mockbee for Samuel Mockbee; Frances Halsband and Matilda McQuaid, as well as her colleagues at the Cooper-Hewitt, National Design Museum, for Richard Oliver; Taft Architects for Robert H. Timme; Peter Rowe for Lauretta Vinciarelli; Sandra Levesque for George Yu; Kenneth Henwood, Robert Kirkbride, Claudia Zambonini, and the Giuseppe Zambonini Archive at The New School's Kellen Design Archives for Giuseppe Zambonini.

Particular thanks are due to Ian Veidenheimer, associate editor, for his intrepid research, gracious communication with contributors, and thorough coordination of the production of this book. We are also grateful to Abby Bussel, consulting editor, whose editorial skills shaped and refined each individual text and whose guidance helped immeasurably to visualize and realize this book in its entirety.

—Anne Rieselbach, editor

Index of Names

Marwan Al-Sayed \\ Stan Allen \\ Anthony Ames \\ Julio Amezcua \\ Mark
\\ Tobias Armborst \\ Manon Asselin \\ Sierra Bainbridge \\ Clifton
Kelly Bauer \\ Karen Bausman \\ Carlos Bedoya \\ Michael Bell \\ Hagy
Andrew D. Berman \\ Andrew Bernheimer \\ Stella Betts \\ Tatiana Bilba
Peter de Bretteville \\ David Brininstool \\ Turner Brooks \\ Eric B
Casbarian \\ Heather Willson Cass \\ Stephen Cassell \\ Jose Castill
Raveevarn Choksombatchai \\ Taryn Christoff \\ W.G. Clark \\ Brad Cloe
Robert James Coote \\ Claude Cormier \\ James Corner \\ Lise Anne Coutu
Dallman \\ Kevin Daly \\ Yolande Daniels \\ Jamie Darnell \\ Peggy D
\\ Jules Dingle \\ Dan D'Oca \\ Evan Douglis \\ David Dowell \\ Susan
Eizenberg \\ Merrill Elam \\ Rand Elliott \\ Ammar Eloueini \\ Frank
\\ Richard Fernau \\ Roger C. Ferri \\ Martin Finio \\ Frederick Fis
Friedman \\ Michael Gabellini \\ Jeanne Gang \\ Douglas Garofalo \\ Ch
\\ Mario Gooden \\ Mark Goulthorpe \\ Jorge Gracia \\ Sarah Graham \\
Han \\ Thomas Hanrahan \\ Gisue Hariri \\ Mojgan Hariri \\ Frank Harmor
Healy \\ David Heymann \\ Gary Hilderbrand \\ Scott Himmel \\ Mimi Ho
Höweler \\ Ray Huff \\ Georgina Huljich \\ Robert Hull \\ Johanna Hur
Franklin D. Israel \\ Lisa Iwamoto \\ Victor Jaime \\ Ziad Jamaleddine
Ralph Johnson \\ Sharon Johnston \\ David T. Jones \\ Wes Jones \\ Ric
Sheila Kennedy \\ Susie Kim \\ Alice Kimm \\ Laszlo Kiss \\ Karel Klei
\\ Ronald Adrian Krueck \\ Tom Kundig \\ Byron Kuth \\ Grace La \\ Da
\\ Mark Lee \\ Thomas Leeser \\ Roberto de Leon Jr. \\ Ralph Lerner \
\\ Linda Lindroth \\ An Te Liu \\ Jing Liu \\ Paul Lubowicki \\ Adria
\\ Mark Mack \\ Brian MacKay-Lyons \\ Dan Maginn \\ Michael Maltzan \\
\\ Jonathan Marvel \\ Audrey Matlock \\ Tom Maul \\ Thom Mayne \\ Mar
McDonough \\ Zack McKown \\ François de Menil \\ Michael Meredith \\
Mockbee \\ Granger Moorhead \\ Robert Moorhead \\ Toshiko Mori \\ Eri
Nelson \\ Anders Nereim \\ Craig Newick \\ Gaston Nogues \\ Enrique N
Alan Organschi \\ Dwayne Oyler \\ Zoltan Pali \\ Peter C. Papademetriou
Abel Perles \\ Xavier Perrot \\ André Perrotte \\ Darren Petrucci \\ L
\\ Elizabeth Plater-Zyberk \\ Monica Ponce de Leon \\ Hadrian Predock
\\ Sasa Radulovic \\ J. Woodson Rainey Jr. \\ Mark Rakatansky \\ Geo
L. Rawn \\ Chris Reed \\ Douglas Reed \\ Jesse Reiser \\ Wellington
Riley \\ Robert Rogers \\ Michel Rojkind \\ John Ronan \\ Charles Rose
Saitowitz \\ David Saladik \\ Franklin Salasky \\ Hilary Sample \\ Dann
Saucier \\ Lawrence Scarpa \\ Sebastian Schmaling \\ Jon Michael Schw
\\ Paul Segal \\ Christopher Sharples \\ Coren Sharples \\ William S.
\\ Robert Silver \\ Mark Simon \\ Hayes Slade \\ James Slade \\ David
Galia Solomonoff \\ Laurinda Spear \\ Scott Specht \\ Lawrence W. Spec
Douglas Stockman \\ Howard Sutcliffe \\ Linda Taalman \\ James L. Tar
Theodore \\ Pierre Thibault \\ Maryann Thompson \\ Russell N. Thomsen
\\ Calvin Tsao \\ Marc Tsurumaki \\ Nanako Umemoto \\ Jamie Unkefer \\
\\ Marion Weiss \\ Claire Weisz \\ Mason White \\ Tod Williams \\ Pe
Adam Yarinsky \\ Mehrdad Yazdani \\ Mark Yoes \\ Mer